S0-FBA-092

50687011608497 2018-09-25 8:12 AM

Ryan, Erica
When the world broke in two
: the roaring twenties and
the dawn of America's
culture wars

ABINGTON COMMUNITY LIBRARY
1200 WEST GROVE STREET
CLARKS SUMMIT, PA 18411
(570) 587-3440
www.lclshome.org

When the World Broke in Two

The Roaring Twenties and the Dawn of America's Culture Wars

Erica J. Ryan

PRAEGER™

An Imprint of ABC-CLIO, LLC
Santa Barbara, California • Denver, Colorado

Copyright © 2018 by Erica J. Ryan

All rights reserved. No part of this publication may be reproduced, stored in a retrieval system, or transmitted, in any form or by any means, electronic, mechanical, photocopying, recording, or otherwise, except for the inclusion of brief quotations in a review, without prior permission in writing from the publisher.

Library of Congress Cataloging-in-Publication Data

Names: Ryan, Erica J., 1976– author.
Title: When the world broke in two : the roaring twenties and the dawn of America's culture wars / Erica J. Ryan.
Other titles: Roaring twenties and the dawn of America's culture wars
Description: Santa Barbara, California : Praeger, An Imprint of ABC-CLIO, LLC, [2018] | Includes bibliographical references and index.
Identifiers: LCCN 2018022565 (print) | LCCN 2018033862 (ebook) | ISBN 9781440842252 (eBook) | ISBN 9781440842245 (alk. paper)
Subjects: LCSH: United States—Civilization—1918–1945. | United States—Politics and government—1923–1929. | United States—Social life and customs—1918–1945. | Nativism. | Nineteen twenties.
Classification: LCC E169.1 (ebook) | LCC E169.1 .R946 2018 (print) | DDC 909.2/2—dc23
LC record available at https://lccn.loc.gov/2018022565

ISBN: 978-1-4408-4224-5 (print)
      978-1-4408-4225-2 (ebook)

22 21 20 19 18   1 2 3 4 5

This book is also available as an eBook.

Praeger
An Imprint of ABC-CLIO, LLC

ABC-CLIO, LLC
130 Cremona Drive, P.O. Box 1911
Santa Barbara, California 93116-1911
www.abc-clio.com

This book is printed on acid-free paper ∞

Manufactured in the United States of America

To Alice, for dancing through life and taking me with you

Contents

Acknowledgments ix

Introduction xi

Chapter 1 The City Challenges Main Street: Reshaping American Culture 1

Chapter 2 Who Belongs in the Nativist 1920s? Immigration, the First Red Scare, and the Revival of the Ku Klux Klan 35

Chapter 3 Prohibition: "A State of Civil War" 69

Chapter 4 Searching for a "Full Life": The Modern Woman in 1920s America 95

Chapter 5 The Dark Shadow of Darwin: Religion Battles Modernism 121

Epilogue 153

Notes 165

Bibliography 183

Index 189

Acknowledgments

Writing a book takes years, and I have depended on the support and generosity of so many. I want to thank my editor at Praeger, James Ciment, for approaching me to write this book to begin with. In many ways it flowed naturally from my previous work, and as the culture wars sharpened following the election of 2016 the subject became more and more relevant. I hope this narrative proves useful to readers as we continue to navigate deep cultural and political divisions. I am thankful to the editorial and production teams at Praeger. And I also wish to acknowledge the Summer Fellowship I received from Rider University, which made the completion of this project possible.

I count myself lucky to be a part of several generous and engaged communities. I am grateful to the friends, fellow historians, and colleagues who read chapter drafts along the way. This includes the Women's and Gender History Writing Group, Brooke Hunter, Anne Osborne, Tanya Moakler, and Sarah Graizbord. I must thank the many funny and kind academics in the #GraftonLine writing group, who helped keep me accountable on a daily basis. Colleagues in the History Department and the Gender and Sexuality Studies Program at Rider offer much-appreciated camaraderie and encouragement day in and day out. And I am also so thankful for my students, who continually remind me that history is important, that it matters, and that it brings great meaning to our lives, especially in times of uncertainty.

I spent many hours writing and editing at the dining room table, but my family and friends made sure that was not all I did. The women I grew up with and will grow old with, my dear college roommate, and my wise and funny friends here in my new hometown provided levity and reassurance whenever I needed it. I have laughed, a lot, and I am loved. I am thankful for them.

My family never fails to hold me up and remind me that I can see the work through. My thanks go to Frank and Sheila for always caring about how my writing is coming along, and to my brother and my aunts for their boundless enthusiasm. I am grateful to my father and Catherine for their steady support, and for encouraging me, always, to keep going. My mother is my solace, and she has been there for me in every way despite her own significant challenges in the time I have spent writing this book. I will never forget that. My husband Matthew is the truest partner and my best friend. In so many ways, he sustains me in doing what I love. And finally, there is my daughter, Alice, who quiets the noise of the culture wars with her enormous heart and her happy feet. She makes the world brighter just by being in it. For all of this, I am so grateful.

Introduction

"A traveler arriving from Mars today would, on all sides, gather that he had timed his visit badly," opined writer Mary Fisher Torrance in the *New York Times*. She continued, "Whereas in other days he would have found us a simple folk, of brave men and virtuous women, whose pleasures centered about hearth and home, we have fallen far." Something was different, and furthermore, "the young people, especially, aren't what they used to be."[1] Torrance joined a loud and dissonant chorus in 1921, lamenting the state of American society and culture in the "modern" era, for Americans in the 1920s lived in an era of culture war. To many like Torrance, life seemed utterly changed in the years after the Great War, as though some chasm opened up to separate the 1920s from a nostalgic, idealized past. When exactly this change occurred, no one could quite tell. Many pointed to the war as the dividing line. Famously, novelist Willa Cather marked the moment as slightly later, writing, "the world broke in two in 1922 or thereabouts."[2] Robert and Helen Lynd, sociologists surveying a typical small American city in the 1920s, acknowledged what felt like monumental transformation in their study titled *Middletown*. They wrote, "We are coming to realize . . . that we today are probably living in one of the eras of greatest rapidity of change in the history of human institutions." They described this change as "frequent and strong culture waves [that] sweep over us from without, drenching us."[3]

In this cultural moment, then, Americans felt deluged by the impact of urbanization, immigration, changing sex and gender norms, Prohibition, and the rise of religious fundamentalism. Massive transformations sweeping the country came together and made people question their place in an increasingly modern world. Amid this great change, many embraced a growing cultural pluralism, a hopeful internationalism, blossoming consumer culture, and a penchant for individual liberty. However, just as many resistors pushed back, creating "narratives of loss and restoration" that focused on reestablishing a nostalgic version of America in a time before this cultural chaos. They rooted their resistance in claims to morality and righteousness, linked their struggles outright to the well-being of the national body politic, assigned great gravity to their cause, and used the martial language that marks a culture war.[4] And remarkably, the battles Americans waged over cultural change in the 1920s are in many ways the very same ones we struggle with today.

Many of these cultural debates, from Prohibition to changing notions of womanhood, manifested in the growing tension between the nation's cities and small towns in the 1920s. At this moment America was officially more urban than ever before, which fostered a feeling of "us" versus "them" in both the countryside and the city center. Many sources of change came from the nation's cities, it seemed, and some anxious observers built up an association between city life and immorality, danger, and disorder. The reality of increasing urbanization, the rise of mass consumer culture, modernizing sex norms, and the "Great Migration" of hundreds of thousands of African Americans from the rural South to the nation's cities provided the backdrop for these emotional responses. And for many these feelings came imbued with great urgency. For example, a chorus of civic leaders, ministers, and parents indicted the excesses of urban nightlife for its impact on young women. Flappers' lives, they argued, were "wrecked by the jazz fire that is consuming the minds and morals of at least part of this generation."[5] An enduring narrative of urban danger and country virtue, a narrative of city versus town, took shape in the 1920s.

Another prominent battle waged by Americans in this culture war grew from the pervasive forces of nativism and antiradicalism after World War I. After decades of unchecked immigration from places unfamiliar to most old stock Americans, countries like Greece, Italy, Poland, and Russia, the experience of world war reinforced calls to close the nation's gates. Swelling patriotism coupled with fears of postwar disorder bolstered nativism, a movement privileging those born in America at the expense of immigrants. Antiradicalism stemmed from similar sources, but it took more concrete and more threatening forms at the decade's start. A cultural, economic, and political push for conformity spread throughout the country in the 1920s as a host of different groups gathered under the mantle of Americanism, a loosely held together conservative ideology supportive of American exceptionalism, white supremacy, patriarchy, free enterprise, evangelical Protestantism, and moral purity. This environment, along with fears of growing internationalism and the Russian Revolution, spawned the first American Red Scare in 1919. Adherents of

Introduction

Americanism claimed the very fate of the nation was at stake as they sponsored government repression, battles with workers, deportations, and years of efforts to produce cultural conformity among African Americans, immigrants, workers, and women.

The resurgent Ku Klux Klan provides one of the most visible examples of this nativism and antiradicalism. After lying dormant for several decades the white supremacist organization exploded in the 1920s, drawing in millions of members in support of the effort to strengthen white, Protestant, Anglo Saxon society. Interestingly, African Americans were no longer the Klan's only targets. While Klansmen still worked to subordinate black men and women, they cared just as much about suppressing the influence of Jews, Catholics, immigrants, and the impact of an increasingly diverse and modern American culture. Flappers, drinkers, adulterers, and other moral outlaws angered them just as much. The era of culture war meant that the KKK also provided association at the same time that it encouraged scapegoating of anyone who was different. Klan activity sprang up throughout the country, and it became, in many places, an organic part of the fabric of the community. This was not a group hiding in shame. A Klan newspaper in Indiana noted in a 1922 editorial, "The public, daily becomes more and more in sympathy with and views with ever increasing admiration and approval the acts and influence for good in our civic and social life, by the Knights of the Ku Klux Klan."[6] The Klan serves as a sort of archetype of the 1920s culture wars, in many ways. It was part of mainstream America, and the group leaves a relevant legacy of struggle over who defines America in times of social and cultural stress.

Perhaps the greatest attempt to enforce cultural unity in a wildly diverse nation can be found in the war on alcohol. Nearly a century of efforts to minimize alcohol, or eliminate its use altogether, culminated in the Prohibition amendment, which went into effect in January 1920. A decade plus–long experiment followed, one that ultimately failed, but this effort has much to tell us about America in the 1920s. The sentiments propelling Prohibition forward, including nativism, religion, and morality, were all contested. Prohibition was a product of the decade's culture wars just as much as it was an effort to curb the nation's drinking habits.

The law and its enforcement changed the relationship between Americans and the federal government, as political leaders intervened in the daily habits of the nation's citizens. Some bitterly opposed this interference, while others welcomed it. A doctor and professor at Johns Hopkins University claimed, in support of the law in 1925, "We insist with every energy at our command that the state has the inalienable right to restrict any action whatever—whether it concerns our eating or drinking or other personal habits—in order to promote the public welfare."[7] Furthermore, the law transformed the criminal justice system in America, and it shaped American attitudes toward drugs and alcohol in lasting and meaningful ways.

The 1920s marked a momentous and controversial shift in the history of American women too, when the nation's state legislatures ratified the Nineteenth Amendment granting women the right to vote in August 1920. The suffrage victory came after decades of activism on behalf of women, and it came just a few short years after the broader notion of feminism gained wide parlance. Birth control agitation coupled with the impact of consumer culture and psychology stretched the very image of womanhood in America into new shapes by the early 1920s. This process thrilled feminists, but it horrified conservative Americans who wanted to hold on to the gender and sex norms of the Victorian Era. Patriarchy undergirded the status quo in many intuitive and apparent ways, and so changes in women's roles and expectations really shook the foundation of American society. The family is most frequently a flashpoint in our current culture wars, and it was no different in the 1920s.

In fact, this period saw the nation's first truly modern women, who, like later 20th-century feminists, imagined that maybe they could have it all—a political voice, a job, and a fulfilling family life. But this prospect proved difficult. Most women found themselves frustrated by the decade's end, as economic and political freedoms garnered little in the way of real, tangible benefits for too many. But the struggles of these modern, emancipated women persisted, just as the battles of conservatives did in their ongoing efforts to uphold the traditional patriarchal family.

As these many forms and permutations of change swept through the country, some Americans embraced an effort by Protestant religious leaders to flatly reject the incursion of modernism in American culture. Protestant fundamentalism, as it was called, originally focused on strictly religious matters, as its adherents opposed modifications and recent interpretations of religious doctrine. But within a few years this argument for holding on tightly to tradition moved from meetings between theologians out to American Protestant laymen and women. High on their list of priorities was antievolution activism, as scientific developments like Darwinism stood as one of many challenges to their worldview. By the midst of the 1920s, antievolution activism was about well more than just Darwin in the classroom. It was about stemming the tide of cultural change more broadly.

Fundamentalism absorbed many flashpoints of the culture war as its proponents mobilized against change. Perhaps most clearly, fundamentalism privileged village values in an attempt to hold the line against the values of the city. Fundamentalist leaders railed against divorce, the use of alcohol, and a host of other "sins" in the modern 1920s. But fundamentalism's moment in the sun came with the prosecution of John Scopes in Dayton, Tennessee, in 1925. Scopes was charged with teaching evolution in violation of state law. Often referred to as the "trial of the century," the Scopes trial pitched the liberal giant, attorney Clarence Darrow, against the fundamentalist hero William Jennings Bryan. Darrow, defending Scopes, lost the trial, but the meaning of that verdict was far from clear. Darrow himself saw it as a culture war victory, when, after the verdict was read, he said, "I think this case will be remembered because it is the first case of this sort since we stopped trying people in America for witchcraft, because here we have done our best to turn back the tide that has sought to force itself upon this modern world, of testing every fact in science by a religious dictum."[8] The trial worked as a powerful symbol of the nation's culture wars, offering Americans a neatly drawn—if oversimplified—narrative of the conflict between the two sides in this struggle. And it magnified a rising and powerful religious right, one that would explode onto the political and cultural scene once again in the late 20th century version of American culture war.

The culture wars raging in the 1920s were not always clearly drawn, and we cannot link them directly to just one or two triggers. But Americans could not deny the arrival of a new, modern culture, one that both excited and frightened. Each of these specific issues, whether it was urbanization, racial conflict, modern views of sex, changing religious values, Prohibition, radicalism, or immigration, they all seemed like they might be connected in one overwhelming, churning tide of change, one that might subsume the country people thought they knew. The Lynds interviewed a man who only recently returned to Middletown from a nearby city, a man who questioned the anxiety he felt among his neighbors, and lamented their narrow-mindedness. With an outsider's view of the culture war in motion, he asked, "These people are all afraid of something. What is it?"[9]

Elizabeth Benson, a young woman writing for the forward-looking *Vanity Fair* late in the decade, answered his question, announcing the sheer enormity of the cultural onslaught by saying, "Nature, and war, and prohibition, and feminism, and psychoanalysis and new fashions in dress; a tottering religion, imitation of our elders, automobiles, radios and free money, the industrial era, indulgent parents and a new physical education—these forces have had their hand in baking the pie out of which, like the four and twenty blackbirds, has sprung the younger generation of today."[10] There was just so much. And for many Americans, it was too much. This is the story of the 1920s culture war.

CHAPTER ONE

The City Challenges Main Street: Reshaping American Culture

Sunrise: A Song of Two Humans graced the silver screen in 1927 with a tale of "The Man" and "The Wife." Their story is set in "every place and no place," a timeless story of love threatened and renewed.[1] But as the words on the screen indicated, this particular telling pitted "the open sky on the farm" directly against "the city's turmoil." In this mostly silent production by Fox Films, German director F. W. Murnau's first character to appear onscreen is called "Woman of the City." She brushes her fashionable bob with a cigarette dangling from her lips, dressed in black satin to appear every bit the vampy seductress. She stands outside the simple farmhouse of "The Man" and beckons him. As he goes to meet her, viewers see his drawn-looking country wife, with long hair and bulky, roughly hewn clothing. The Woman of the City shares a passionate kiss with The Man on screen, and the camera flashes to the tearful Wife comforting a baby.

The palpable strain between the city and the country appears when the Woman of the City repeatedly begs the farmer to leave his life and "come to the city!" The words repeat several times for viewers to see—"Come to the city!" The vamp constructs a murder plot to kill The Wife, and then smothers The Man in kisses to quiet any protest. As the couple lays on the ground, visions of the city flash above them onscreen, featuring dazzling lights, boisterous bands, and couples dancing wildly. The Woman of the City stands up to celebrate their pact, shimmying her body in an unrestrained and sensual dance. The Man is clearly won over, embracing her as he is consumed by desire. He will come to the city.

This fundamental tension in *Sunrise* between the small town and the city would have been immediately familiar to American viewers. The sensationalism of the storyline, with a murder plot that ultimately fails and a love rekindled between husband and wife, reflected Americans' love for scandal in the 1920s, when true confession magazines surged in popularity. Much of the impropriety causing people in the country to raise their eyebrows, or clutch their throats in horror, came from the nation's cities. And more of the population actually lived in cities than ever before, a fact confirmed by the 1920 census. This news worried people. For some, Thomas Jefferson's republican agrarian ideal seemed preferable, still, to the surge of urbanization. Others embraced a changing nation, themselves rushing to "come to the city." Many felt stuck between progress and nostalgia, which manifested in a number of ways. But one of the most apparent locations for this struggle between progress and nostalgia, the struggle animating the culture wars, was in the national conversation pitting the city against the town.

In the background, a broader trend toward the nationalization of American culture helped trigger this conflict. Small towns in 19th-century America were "island communities," as historian Robert Wiebe called them, rural enclaves where people respected and shared ethical and moral codes. These communities first faced challenges from the impact of the Civil War, which spawned a national industrial economy and a larger federal government. Industrialization, immigration, and urbanization continued to stretch the fabric of those communities over time. And, despite efforts to rationalize a growing urban, industrial capitalist nation with the reforms of the Progressive Era in the early 20th century, the seeming threat to the integrity of rural, small-town America only grew larger in the 1920s thanks to a thriving consumer culture.[2]

This process unfolded in one place after another, and the Lynds captured the way it manifested in Muncie, Indiana. In their study of the city they called "Middletown," they found that in the 1890s the social fabric of Muncie kept its inhabitants close to one another. One woman remembered that neighbors used to crowd one another's front porches and lawns after work and on weekends, singing and chatting. Young couples joined in too, and while they might drift away momentarily, their evening centered around these community gatherings of all ages. By the 1920s the arrival of consumer culture disrupted that practice. Parents all over the nation fretted over the newfound independence afforded to the young by the automobile, and they worried over the arrival of dance halls and movie theaters. Couples in Muncie in the 1920s had a "night out," not an evening on their neighbor's porch. In another striking example from Muncie, a Fourth of July celebration in 1925 found the downtown area deserted. In the 1890s, Helen and Robert Lynd reported that the holiday featured bands, community dancing, and shared food. By the 1920s the small city's inhabitants took to their cars and went on adventures of their own individual choosing, in couples or in family groups. The sense of community woven together in the 1890s frayed at the edges in the early 20th century, and in many ways it seemed to be coming apart by the 1920s.[3] This place felt the transformations wrought by the arrival of consumer culture, transformations associated with the rise of the city.

This tension between city and town even framed national politics in the 1920s. The issue captured the 1928 presidential election, as Democratic candidate Al Smith and Republican Herbert Hoover duked it out for the highest office in the land. Opinions on Smith nationwide revealed his association with the city. Born in a New York City tenement, Smith represented an urban version of the American dream, starting out as a newsboy and ending up a three-time governor of New York State. Smith's connection to the city oozed out of him in his style and mannerisms, and his much-discussed Irish Catholicism linked him to the "new" immigrant population. Commentators warned that Smith appealed to those who felt hatred for the old, Anglo-Saxon, Protestant America, implying that his supporters were immigrants, Jews, African Americans, and Catholics, and that they were dangerous. The city and its imagined inhabitants defined Al Smith in the late 1920s political culture of reaction. When Herbert Hoover declared victory over Smith in a landslide defeat, the *St. Paul Pioneer Press* of Minnesota rejoiced over the fact that America was "not yet dominated by its great cities. Control of its destiny still remains in the small communities and rural regions, with their traditional conservatism and solid virtues." "Main Street," they opined, "is still the principal thoroughfare of the nation."[4]

But challenges to the supremacy of that fabled Main Street were everywhere. *Sunrise: A Song of Two Humans* reveals several of them in its tale of the city against the small town. The scenes of the city heavily feature the spectacle of mass culture, a world of popular amusements spreading through America by the 1920s that would change the very way people lived their lives. The vivid scenes of The Man and the Wife enjoying electrified lights, games, and dancing fleshed out this picture of the city for those who had not seen it for themselves. This consumer culture was heavily associated with the city, for better or worse, and it is still.

In addition, the plot of *Sunrise* centers on a salacious love triangle, where the city tries to lure the town to moral ruin with heavy makeup and sensual dancing. Sex and sexuality became public in a new way by the 1920s, in no small part because of that consumer culture. Americans obsessed over changing sex and gender norms that they believed emanated from the nation's cities.

Lastly, the scenes depicting popular amusements in *Sunrise* include no African Americans. In reality hundreds of thousands of them were then streaming into the nation's cities. But public amusements, and the leisure time necessary to enjoy them, emerged at the very same time that Jim Crow laws codified the segregation of such spaces in the South. In the North, the absence of Jim Crow laws did not open the gates of public amusements to African Americans. Robust discrimination developed there too, enforced either by custom or by threat of violence. While a sign on a swimming pool in the South might read "Whites Only," in the North it would read "Members Only," and the result was one and the same.[5]

Racism and segregation shaped the existence of urban popular amusements in the 1920s, and the urban experience overall. Struggles over space, housing, aspirations, and labor plagued the Great Migration of African Americans to urban areas in the 1920s, establishing a long-standing and still troubling association between blackness and cities. Black Americans were coming to the city, and here was the conflict between city and town shot through with racial prejudice.

THE CULTURE OF THE METROPOLIS VERSUS THE COUNTRYSIDE

Americans struggled over the meaning and significance of mass culture, sex, and race in the city at an important moment in the nation's history. The 1920 census announced the crossing of a significant threshold, when for the first time a majority of Americans lived in areas with more than 2,500 people, areas thus considered urban. The number may seem paltry now, but at the time it proved that the nation was no longer made up mostly of rural, agrarian communities scattered through the countryside. In fact, the increasing migration of people from farms and small towns to both larger towns and cities garnered a lot of attention in the popular press, and among intellectuals.

Prominent writers acknowledged the antagonism developing between city and town. Famous philosopher John Dewey commented on William Jennings Bryan's crusade for the supremacy of religious faith over science in the pages of the *New Republic*, pointing to a frontier that now existed between small towns and cities. In Dewey's view, fear and suspicion ruled in one region, while diversity and transformation ruled in the other. The "attachment to stability and homogeneity of thought and belief" that existed in small towns served to buffer the "heterogeneity, rush, and unsettlement" in the cities.[6] Writer and scholar of the city Lewis Mumford went further, arguing in 1922 that those on the nation's farms envied city dwellers, identifying a "breach . . . between the metropolis and the countryside."[7]

For them, the contrast between the growing cities and small towns seemed like a contrast between a shimmering, expanding modernity and the old racial, gender, and class hierarchy, the status quo. They cheered what they saw as the coming triumph of city values over those of the village. On the other hand, rural and small town Americans struggled to hold the line, to maintain their influence, to protect their own values and norms through efforts like support for prohibition and antievolution activism.

Southern intellectuals in a so-called Agrarian movement voiced widespread concern in the 1920s over the threat presented by a modernizing, urbanizing culture. Industrialism threatened what they nostalgically called the "agrarian tradition." The rise of mass culture seemed an assault on southern culture, and movement writers called on southern farmers to "'[t]hrow out the radio' and '[f]orsake the movies' for such preindustrial pleasures as square dances."[8] Advertising firms, publishing houses, and movie studios, those producing and framing a national mass culture, were located in New York and, increasingly, in Los Angeles. Not in the South. For some white southerners, then, these alien messages, borne of industrialism, centered in city life, were better left ignored. And the stakes were high. Southern culture, in part a product of reconciliation between the North and South at the expense of African Americans' civil rights, relied on resisting calls for change. Change in the South would create real unrest.

Famous social critic Walter Lippmann actually attributed the divisiveness of the 1920s overall to this growing distance between city and town. The political rifts of the decade rose "out of the great migration of the last 50 years, out of the growth of cities, and out of the spread of that rationalism and of the deepening of that breach with tradition which invariably accompany the development of metropolitan culture," he wrote.[9] Hot-button topics of the era, such as prohibition, antiradicalism, and fundamentalism, were simply articulations of the worldview of the "older American village civilization making its last stand" against the tide of modernity.[10]

Lippmann's position was a popular one, whether Americans recognized the connections between their own deep-seated anxieties and his commentary or not.

Urbanization and Its Discontents

In reality the transformations wrought by consumer culture, industrialization, migration, and immigration changed people's values and practices all over the country, but Americans who were uneasy over those changes associated them with urban life. In the 1920s, cities were seen as places flooded with immigrants, tainted by communism, subject to moral relativism, and brimming with cultural pluralism. Some of this was true, some of the time. But the visage of life in the city in all of its enormity shook some white, Protestant, Anglo-Saxon Americans' sense of themselves and the country they thought they knew. And by the end of the decade all had to concede that urban values entered the mainstream. Urban values became, by and large, American values.[11]

But this narrative is not as neatly drawn as it might seem. Even as those who raged against modernism condemned the sins of the cities, not everyone who actually moved to the city found life there entirely liberating. And not all of those who remained in the nation's countryside and small towns suffered repression under the blanket of the status quo. But the expansion of cities, the growth of mass culture, changing sex and gender norms, and the demographic shifts of the Great Migration undeniably changed city life. And in the long run this changed American life, too.

Now, urbanization was not a new phenomenon in the 1920s. While 95 percent of the nation's population lived in the countryside in the late 1700s, the development of urban areas had already begun. But the most expansive urban growth came in the late 19th century, when industrialization and the placement of factories near urban spaces fostered it. By 1900, New York had 3.5 million people, Chicago had 1.7 million, and Philadelphia had 1.2 million. At that point almost 40 percent of the nation's population lived in an urban area. And then in the 1920s the scales tilted further, with 51 percent living in an area classified as urban. The number would never slip below the halfway mark again, and at the last census taken in 2010 more than 80 percent of Americans lived in cities.

New York City was the nation's largest city in the 1920s, with 5.6 million inhabitants, followed by Chicago, Philadelphia, and Detroit. At this point the city rose from the earth with many of its familiar features intact or in progress: massive skyscrapers, awe-inspiring bridges, tunnels, and parkways.[12] New York in the 1920s would look strikingly familiar to our modern eyes, and it was the nation's cultural mecca. As hundreds of thousands of black migrants created a black metropolis in Harlem, the city became the epicenter of black enterprise, talent, and expression.[13] Art and entertainment flowered there, borne of diversity and passion and longing. But the whole city actively cultivated and refined this art and entertainment in what was "the first age of the media."[14] Literary greats like F. Scott Fitzgerald and Zora Neale Hurston flocked to New York. Fitzgerald himself noted that in the 1920s "the tempo of the city had changed sharply," as he found "the parties were bigger and the buildings were higher, the morals were looser and the liquor was cheaper."[15] Writer Louise Brooks disembarked from her train in Grand Central Station and just like that "fell in love with New York forever."[16] Publishing innovations like the Book-of-the-Month Club, an array of publishing houses, and widely popular tabloids and newspapers resided in New York. Radio network NBC and music publisher T.B. Harms helped center the nation's recording industry in New York as well. Jazz composers, players, and singers like Duke Ellington converged there in the 1920s, buoyed by the vivid nightlife making their music much in demand.[17]

On October 23, 1929, in New York a crane plucked the steel needle from the top of the Chrysler Building and pulled it up to its final height, making the structure the tallest ever built. The building was one of several impressive high-rises constructed at the time, though the art deco design of automobile titan Walter Chrysler's midtown building makes it a favorite among architects even today. The materials used on the outside surface of the building shone brightly in the sun, as did the imposing metal eagles perched up on the 31st floor. An enormous lobby with red Moroccan marble featured 32 of the worlds' fastest elevators. The lobby also featured a digital clock and a stunning ceiling mural, one that depicted the engineering marvels of the machine age. Famed Swiss-French architect Le Corbusier called the Chrysler Building "hot jazz in stone and steel."[18] Here was modernity on the pages, carried in the sounds, and reflected in the very architecture of 1920s New York.

The iconic city of Los Angeles also became the place we know it to be today in the 1920s. While other cities like Chicago, Detroit, and Pittsburgh hosted big industry, drawing many migrants to jobs in meatpacking and manufacturing, Los Angeles was rising in the west. Its sprawling boundaries, the glitz and prominence of Hollywood, and other defining features of the city developed in this decade, making it a 1920s "modern metropolis." The city boomed after World War I, doubling its population from just over 500,000 to almost 1.25 million people thanks to migration as well as annexation. A predominantly Anglo-Saxon Protestant community diversified, taking in a growing number of Mexican immigrants, African American migrants, Japanese immigrants, and a jumble of other ethnic groups.[19] By the end of the decade Los Angeles was the most populous city in California.

This influx changed the culture of the city. Mexicans transported their cultural institutions to Los Angeles through sports and religion, while African Americans set up a prominent branch of the NAACP in Los Angeles, hosting the national convention there in 1928.[20] By the end of the 1920s Los Angeles was second only to Baltimore among major cities in its percentage of nonwhite residents.[21] The forces of reaction sprang up simultaneously. The Ku Klux Klan thrived in Southern California in its 1920s resurgence, while groups like the Better America Federation espoused nativism and antiradicalism in their efforts to maintain a white, Anglo-Saxon, Protestant society.

As the city took in more people in the 1920s, it began to take up more space on the map. Los Angeles swallowed 45 nearby communities up and down the coast, and opened development into the hillsides. The recognizable sprawl of Los Angeles became entirely visible by the decade's end. An important consequence of this fact was that the city's borders exceeded the scope of the substantial streetcar system. Increasingly, navigating Los Angeles required an automobile.[22]

A multifaceted industrial boom fueled the growth of the city in the 1920s, though the profits of this boom were not evenly distributed. Elites and entrepreneurs carefully constructed a robust factory district, with a quarter of the city's workforce toiling in manufacturing jobs at companies like Goodyear Tire. At the same time, as the city became one of the aviation centers of the nation, the discovery of oil south of the city allowed for the start of significant petroleum production. Large corporations led these business prospects, outpacing the growth of smaller businesses in Los Angeles.[23] Elites in the city promoted a rabidly anti-union, open shop mantra, a repressive regime for many workers.[24] Despite Hollywood's stultifying glamour, the often-overlooked working-class community suffered low wages and poor conditions.

This trend toward corporatization and conservatism marked the bustling movie industry too. A mecca for the stars already by the early postwar period, Hollywood stood as a beacon for the movie business, bringing the sparkle of fame and fortune to the growing city and to a nation awash in celebrity culture. Dozens of companies housed there produced 80 percent of the nation's films, which reflected a wide variety of subjects and political persuasions. By the late 1920s this was more tightly controlled, as a collection of companies known as the "Big Eight" created 90 percent of the nation's major movies, overseeing production, distribution, and often the very theaters themselves.[25] They crushed the strikes of studio workers and scrubbed from mass-market movies any significant reference to class conflict or political radicalism. While many in the nation's heartland believed Hollywood promoted debauchery and sin, by the late 1920s the industry itself was actually quite conservative. But it was also changing the culture of America.

Mass Culture and the Spread of Modernity

With all their promise and heartache, their glamour and their grittiness, cities like Los Angeles and New York moved into modernity in the 1920s. They did so in their size, their height, their inequality, their arts, and their bustling, diverse populations. But just as importantly, they did so as production centers for mass culture. Mass culture refers to the shared values and ideas that emerged through exposure to the same cultural forms and practices produced in the early 20th century. And this mass culture pervaded city streets by the 1920s along with the lanes and roads of the nation's larger and smaller towns. Yet it was cities that Americans associated with both the benefits of mass culture and the drawbacks.

A national mass culture had the potential to bring Americans together in the 1920s, to blur the lines between classes, races, and ethnicities and between the city and the town. This possibility came about with the advent of standardized products on chain store shelves, prominent big-ticket items like the ubiquitous Tin Lizzie, so many mass-market movies in small town theaters and urban movie palaces alike, and the burgeoning medium of radio beaming into living rooms across the nation. Mass culture was in large part produced in the cities in the 1920s, making this development a largely urban phenomenon. Electrification was an urban phenomenon too, making this development possible. But wherever Americans could, they consumed this mass culture in its many forms. In some ways that act of consumption did bridge racial, ethnic, class, and regional divides. When people all over the country read the same newspaper headlines, or purchased the same canned Del Monte goods in an A&P, it had the potential to foster a national unity forged through consumption.

Yet, mass culture played a real role in framing the chasm between the modern city and the traditional farm town. Advertisements, magazines, and movies broadcast the hedonistic delights available in cities like New York, Chicago, and Los Angeles to the rest of the country. And mass culture produced many of those hedonistic delights. It was the amusement park, lit up at night, the dance halls, and the movie palaces, and the ideas about what went on there, that drew the line of demarcation between the village and the city.

The commercialization of leisure and the place of leisure in the lives of Americans were solidified in this decade. Laborers increasingly turned to leisure pursuits in order to counteract the loss of autonomy and power they felt in a changing working world. Increasing corporatization and expanding bureaucracy left many feeling lost, adrift, or powerless. Many no longer found satisfaction in their jobs, and consciously or unconsciously they sought it in advertising copy, in celebrity culture, or in movie theaters.[26] Consumer culture also profoundly shaped the middle class. White-collar men and women moved from a focus on character and self-sacrifice to an obsession with personality and self-realization. This self-realization would be actualized, all the subtle messages told people, through consumption of progress and engagement with leisure activities.[27]

The advertising industry came of age in the 1920s, cementing this modern, therapeutic ethos in the American consciousness. Through the growth of radio and the staggering rise in popularity of mass-market magazines, the advertising industry's volume skyrocketed from $682 million to $2,987 million between 1914 and 1929.[28] Jingles and color layouts promised Americans happiness, love, beauty or adventure, gains to be won with a simple purchase. Advertisers, a group historian Roland Marchand termed "apostles of modernism," purposefully sought to entice their audience to leap into the modern era. They associated the goods they marketed with progress, with change, with adjustment. And in doing so they played up that audience's anxiety about fitting into the modern world. Advertising copy for cereal and medicinal tonics promised to give people energy, charm, or vigor. Products like mouthwash and perfumes had little popularity at the turn of the century, but they were big money by the 1920s thanks in large part to well-developed advertising campaigns. Personal appeals from celebrities or spokespersons served to put a human face on big corporations and fostered a sense of connection between the purchaser and the product. Advertisers empowered consumers to feel as though they were making the right choice, the smart choice. People believed they had some control over their lives even in an increasingly corporate, industrial, urban society.[29]

Radio entered the lives of Americans in the 1920s like an explosion as the first mass medium. Broadcasting began in 1920 when Pittsburgh station KDKA carried the Harding-Cox election results to the country, spellbinding a nation. By 1923 America hosted more than 550 stations, in cities and in small towns. Roughly 400,000 homes enjoyed personal use of a radio set, a vast leap from just 60,000 one year prior. People bought their sets from catalogs like Sears Roebuck Company, and for just over $20 they could get their hands on a radio with a 500-mile range.[30]

While local stations provided radio content early in the decade, national stations emerged by the late 1920s helping to standardize Americans' experience and taste. All sorts of players stepped up to the microphone to begin broadcasting, with programs created by groups like the Palmer School of Chiropractics in Davenport, Iowa, the John Fink Jewelry Company of Fort Smith, Arkansas, and the Detroit Police Department, just to offer a few examples. Stations often created diverse schedules for each day, including music, sporting events, lectures, and plays and stories. But in 1926 the industry giant Radio Corporation of America (RCA) created the first national radio network, the National Broadcasting Company (NBC). When Charles Lindbergh returned to America from his cross-Atlantic flight to Paris in 1927, arriving on the U.S. Navy ship *Memphis*, NBC covered his every move on 50 stations in 24 states, the largest broadcast to date.[31] It is estimated that some 30 million people listened in.

This kind of range on a national broadcast united Americans in a new and meaningful way. Whether you lived in a metropolis or in a rural farm town of 1,000, whether you were middle or working class, whether you were black or white, if you could afford a radio—or if you even knew someone who could afford a radio—you could now experience the same news, the same political speeches, the same baseball games, or the same religious sermons as millions of other Americans in far-flung places around the nation. And you could experience all of these things at the very same time, at the very moment it happened.[32]

Movies also became an American pastime, as more than 20,000 moving picture theaters studded the United States by the middle of the 1920s. Many of the deluxe theaters in operation by then were built and run by production companies who crafted palaces to showcase their own films. The practice of "premiering" a movie took hold in that decade, as filmmakers banked on the wider publicity such an event in a finely adorned theater with thousands of seats would bring. And orchestras accompanied many of the films, both grand orchestras with sheet music and more ragtag groups of musicians who simply improvised.

Movie palaces in city centers coexisted with theaters that catered to various ethnic and racial communities. These theaters often reflected the identity of the neighborhoods that housed them, allowing different racial and ethnic groups to mediate the impact of a standardized American culture by receiving it among those they identified as their own. In Polish neighborhoods moviegoers would likely see a play in their native language before the film reel began. In the Italian section of the city, Italian music would play, along with the film. Ethnic entertainment might even fill the gaps between film reels. Black city dwellers could see the latest Hollywood had on offer in the same venues they might see blues artists play, simultaneously enmeshing them in a national culture while allowing for a reaffirmation of the ties many of them had to the South. But as studios rolled out films with sound in the late 1920s, such small neighborhood theaters often could no longer compete because they could not afford the upgrades required.[33] Larger movie houses helped to solidify a standardized American culture.

Money drove mass culture, then, and as popular amusements cropped up around the country developers realized that fun for the whole family could be very lucrative. Coney Island was a holiday spot for beachgoers in New York City when developers set their sights on it for something far more grandiose. At the turn of the 20th century, entrepreneurs built several magnificent seaside parks on the strip of land in Brooklyn, filled with mechanized horse races, carousels, roller coasters, and fun houses. These sat alongside rows of clam bars, dance halls, and freak shows, making the site a circus for the senses. Luna Park opened in 1903 and featured over 250,000 electrified lights, a sight still unfamiliar for many. The bulbs illuminated a tall tower, promenades for walking, and other structures, dazzling parkgoers with the beauty of the glow in the dark of night. This was what modernity looked like.

Leisure seekers of all kinds flocked to Coney Island as the time they had for leisure expanded. They came in hours stolen after work, or on Sundays, or on holidays in the spring and summer months. A trolley car to Coney from Manhattan cost a nickel in 1895, and eventually in 1920 the subway made the trip even easier. Families talked about going to Coney Island as a great adventure, sometimes saving up for just one trip each season. Boosters for the parks claimed Coney drew 200,000 patrons in one day, and Luna Park logged several million visitors over one whole season.[34] Coney Island drew an incredibly diverse array of visitors of all social classes and ethnic backgrounds, including men, women, families, and young people. This medley led some to herald these sites of public amusement as incubators for democracy in an increasingly diverse nation. There is something to be said for this, especially when considering the inclusion of young immigrants and the children of immigrants, who were eager to assimilate into American culture through consumption.[35]

But at the same time some 1920s observers shuddered at the masses of immigrants in places like Coney, lamenting the loss of "American manners" in the cultural transformation they brought in their wake.[36] And, Coney upheld hardened racial lines in the early 20th century, just like similar parks around the country, including Lakewood Park in Atlanta and Bob-Lo Island near Detroit.[37] Coney Island in New York operated segregated bathhouses and beaches, while the Coney Island of the West in Cincinnati was closed to African Americans entirely.

It was the very potential of these thrilling sites like Coney Island, with their exotic smells and their diverse crowds and their strained rules of propriety, that engendered the policing of their racial boundaries. Historian Victoria Walcott argues that the very whiteness of these spaces marked them as safe and orderly, despite other clear challenges to that safety and order. With so many in the thrall of new pleasure palaces and public spaces of leisure, full participation in these activities signaled a kind of racial equality. And as newer simmering racial tensions built on the sturdy bedrock of older racist ideals, many whites refused to allow for that equality.[38]

Still, marginalized groups found avenues to the enjoyment of consumer culture in this era. Boisterous rent parties drew black revelers in for community support, drink, and dancing. Fraternal orders bolstered ethnic ties in saloons, the celebration of ethnic culture, and networks of financial and social support. Radio stations in the early 1920s largely catered to local audiences. In Chicago, fraternal orders, unions, and churches played a central role in programming, consciously weaving the bonds of class, religion, and ethnicity. "Race" records reinforced a distinct black identity, as African Americans hit record stores in droves to purchase music by Ida Cox and Bessie Smith. Southern whites had "hillbilly," their own musical genre, as did Mexican Americans, Irish Americans, and so on.[39] Mass culture cut both ways, then, fostering distinct racial and ethnic identities, but more and more people felt the power of a standardized national culture coalesce around them. And this had consequences.

SEX IN THE CITY

In the 1910s it struck "sex o'clock in America" according to editor William Marion Reedy, who announced a public obsession with sex, particularly in the nation's cities. Working-class youths mingled with members of the opposite sex in ever-proliferating urban amusements. Wealthy patrons visited houses of ill repute. Sex education reformers lifted the veil of silence surrounding sex and engaged in social investigations in dance halls and on city streets.[40] And then the war brought overt social hygiene programming, intended to combat venereal disease, into the mainstream. Government-funded pamphlets, posters, and speakers infiltrated factories, campuses, and training camps with very frank discussions about sex. Bohemian communities who outright challenged conventions like marriage and monogamy sprung up visibly in San Francisco, Chicago, and New York. Sex radicals like the inimitable Emma Goldman broadcast their modern values in innumerable plays, speeches, books, and magazine articles throughout the 1910s and well into the next decade.

By the 1920s sex saturated American culture, and the story of this so-called sexual revolution is in many ways a story about the city. Observers keenly recognized the crumbling of Victorian sexual norms in the flicker of movie screens and the dim speakeasy lighting. The unique nightlife fostered in cities in the 1920s, the prevalence of leisure opportunities amid a ballooning mass culture, and the room created for the development of outsized symbols like the flapper, all carried the sexual revolution along. The association of the city with sex and sin arose well before the early 20th century, and it lasts today in easy axioms about red states and blue states, in the juxtaposition between San Francisco and Laramie. But in the 1920s popular conservative message makers pitted the old values of the nation's farms and towns against the "decadent" city, enforcing the notion—frightful to some—that city norms could soon dominate the nation.

The Sexual Revolution

Shifting leisure and work patterns caused a sea change by the 1920s in the way Americans determined their values and their sense of self. A job or one's position within the family no longer defined American men and women so completely. And so, as people made decisions about where to spend their time away from work, where to find their sense of self, they pivoted away from the confines of the private home and increasingly toward public spaces. Places like dance halls, movie theaters, and amusement parks represented a public consumer culture, a mass consumer culture, one that replaced the producer-oriented culture of the 19th century. These two different kinds of societies—one producer based and one consumer based—fostered different moral systems, different ways of seeing the world.[41] Historian Kevin Mumford accentuates that shift from a production- to a consumption-based economy, noting that it "had the profound effect of blurring the boundaries between the so-called private and public spheres, reshaping not only how urbanites spent their hours off the job but how they organized and perceived the most intimate aspects of their lives."[42]

Ultimately, then, as America moved from a rural nation to an urban one there were economic consequences as well as more intimate ones. Older communal value systems gave way to more "modern anonymous social relations," which revamped American understandings of sexuality.[43] The revolution in manners and morals of the 1920s reflected real shifts in understandings of gender norms, marriage ideals, and thinking on sex. And the city offered endless opportunities for any American to transgress the moral boundaries of the old Victorian order.[44] At Coney Island, that perennial example, men could gaze on women's bare skin, couples exhilarated in the thrills of the dance floor, and people used the tight spaces of carnival rides to press against one another.[45] Expressions of sex modernism—shifting notions of manhood, womanhood, and sexuality—typically emerged first in black and working-class ethnic neighborhoods, and then moved to other marginalized groups in gay and middle-class bohemian communities. But by the early 1920s in America these ideas seeped all the way through into mainstream middle-class culture, indeed bringing city values to the nation at large.[46]

Yet, despite this chapter's focus on the culture war raging between village values and those of the city, we must also appreciate that the sexual revolution did not move in just one direction, fanning out from cities to small towns and rural hinterlands. It was more prominent and more visible in cities, yes, but both the city and the village underwent a process where certain values and sexual practices became normalized by the late 1920s. In rural areas progressive sex reforms spread through county fair exhibits, and zealous YMCA workers, rather than through consumer culture.[47] Some argue that many in the rural population no longer lived by those middle-class Victorian codes to begin with in the 1920s.[48] And so, even without the immersion in mass culture, some in the nation's villages underwent a process of modernization in ways of thinking about and having sex. But nonetheless, many Americans still associated sex with the city.

It was undeniably true that cities like New York enjoyed a thriving nightclub scene in the 1920s, with thousands of spaces available to challenge the old order. Depending on what you liked, the nightclubs ran the gamut as far as the "scene" on offer. Upscale clubs like Barney's contrasted with "loud and nasty" Club Abbey. Drag queens stalked the rooms at The Club Pansy, while the Trocadero featured the sibling dance team Fred and Adele Astaire. Some clubs featured dancing waiters or burlesque dancers, while others hosted a full orchestra. Prices to enter were often high, and drinks once inside were not cheap either. Most, if not all, served up a space for social dancing to a thrill-seeking crowd.[49]

The very fact of Prohibition promoted an environment of daring and defiance in urban nightlife. Young people embraced social drinking in an act of rebellion against their parents' generation. Middle-class women joined men eagerly in these spaces, drinking and smoking all the while wearing shorter, more form-fitting dresses. Working-class women took part too, in dance halls, and they jumped at the chance to work in the city's nightclubs. High wages and the promise of adventure made it an easy sell. Outside the purview of parents, and the authorities, young women and men pushed the boundaries of propriety in these well-lubricated spaces. The rules, it seemed, no longer applied and as a consequence, risqué or marginalized entertainment forms found a comfortable space in the spotlight.[50]

In this moment gay men and women embraced an urban nightlife particularly open to them. In the 1920s events like drag balls drew crowds in the thousands. Premier event spaces like Madison Square Garden and Webster Hall hosted men in heels and feather boas and women in tuxedoes and top hats. Organized crime syndicates often put up the funds for these extravagant balls. Participants were frequently working-class, but the audience filled with people from all socioeconomic backgrounds, including famous family names like Astor and Vanderbilt. City newspapers, and even those in smaller towns, featured these events in their pages with frequency, and without a sense of alarm. Gay, lesbian, bisexual, and trans people enjoyed visibility and the ability to network both at drag balls and in smaller settings, like speakeasies and apartment parties.[51] Queer urban nightlife found a comfortable niche in dominant culture in the 1920s, as many in America purposefully shoved aside notions of social purity and respectability.[52] It was a niche that would disappear by the 1930s.

But not everyone let go of their moral superiority in the 1920s, as a storm of protest rose against social dancing. A dance craze born in the 1910s was still in full swing, and widespread condemnation of the influence of jazz music came from parents, doctors, religious leaders, and writers. For two months in 1922 the widely circulated *Atlanta Constitution* ran a series of articles on the dangers of jazz music. One of these pieces quoted a doctor, who claimed, "If jazz is not stopped we will have no more clean-minded children. Even our babies are being sullied and enervated by the jazz music, the shimmying and the general looseness of actions they see about them." The complaints these "protectors" of America's youth had about the impact of jazz music, nightlife, and dancing focused in on overstimulation, both sexually and mentally. Martha Lee wrote in the first of these anti-jazz articles, which appeared on the Sunday magazine's front page, "The passion to be always on the go, the desire to be always in a high-keyed excitement, to be keenly alive even though falsely stimulated, and to live much, even though indiscriminately, is the mental world in which many are now living." This, she argued, would not do.[53]

A new era of religious fundamentalism found prominent Protestant religious figures taking a different tack, as they worked to situate the nation's rapidly modernizing culture in a context of sin and immorality. These individuals made names for themselves by vigorously protesting the evils of urban nightlife. To them dancing seemed fraught with peril, from the disorderly behavior it might encourage to the largely unfounded fears of dance halls as funnels for white slavery.

Barnstorming evangelist preacher Billy Sunday exemplified this type of religious leader, as he fanatically opposed dancing and the cultural shifts it represented to him. Sunday appealed to millions of American men and women, stirring those with antimodern, village, and anti-intellectual values. His vitriol centered on the evils of modernity, which were, it seemed in 1920, located in the city.[54] He not only opposed dancing, but smoking, gambling, and drinking too. He famously asked his followers, "Is New York going to heaven?" Sunday exhorted them to pray, to remain sober, to remain chaste, declaring that yes, New York could go to heaven. But as the center of social trespass against the old morality, many Americans were sure the answer was no.[55] New York would be going to hell.

At least Rev. John Roach Straton believed it would. Straton was a famous moral crusader and antievolutionist in the 1920s who believed New York City to be a modern Babylon. He railed against social dancing and drinking, condemning the "jazz wild and dance crazy" youth of New York. Straton warned kids that the "very fires of Hell" were "raging right at them in dance palaces."[56] When fellow members of Calvary Baptist Church questioned his sensationalist attacks on nightlife, he sneered, "surely real preaching is needed in New York. This is no time for pulpit pussyfooting." His high-profile lectures and publications like *The Dance of Death: Should Christians Indulge?* helped to elevate his message beyond the city to the nation at large.[57] Of course, Straton was not alone in his exhortations against social dancing. Other book titles circulating in the 1920s included *From the Ball Room to Hell*, *Dangers of the Dance*, and *The Devil's Ball*.

Dating: An Urban Institution

Undeniably, as these frightening sermons about hellfire attest, changing sex and gender norms existed by the 1920s. Small midwestern Muncie felt its impact too. The Lynds noted a sharp rise in divorces in

"Middletown," with an increase of 622 percent between the 1890s and the mid-1920s.[58] Those who remained married developed decidedly more modern approaches to family life. Almost all of the "business class" women queried reported actively limiting reproduction, though less than half of working-class women did so. Still, these numbers reflect national trends as more and more women embraced the limited options for birth control when they could, having sex for pleasure and not just for reproduction.

The public world of organized activity and leisure drew young Muncie men and women outside the orbit of their families and homes for ever-increasing hours, just as it did for youth in big cities. The Lynds noted that the YWCA, the YMCA, movies, dances in hotels, church events, and automobile rides were, among others, keeping young people away from home on numerous nights during the week, activities their parents hardly appreciated. Fifty-five percent of boys and 44 percent of girls were home for fewer than four evenings in a typical week, and young people reported this as one of the most serious sources of friction between themselves and their parents.

By the 1920s parents in Muncie felt these pressures most acutely in relation to their children's engagement with members of the opposite sex. Where young people had fewer opportunities to be alone in the dark before the turn of the century, by the 1920s movies and automobiles offered them the physical space, while evolving ideas about women and sex offered them the cultural space. More than three quarters of young men and women self-reported their involvement in petting parties, demonstrating the lack of taboo in their own social circles. The Lynds referred to this trend as the "early sophistication" of young people in Muncie, noting a marked difference between generations.[59] These trends appeared even in small cities, then, as the decade wore on.

The features of urban life at this moment ultimately transformed the social norms of courtship altogether, giving rise to the modern system of dating by the middle of the 1920s. The social system of calling reigned in cities and in towns before the 1900s, organizing relations between men and women. This highly scripted set of rules and rituals allowed a man to express romantic interest in a woman he desired, but ultimately this was a woman's world. Calling took place in a woman's home on certain days and in certain time frames. A young man in "well-bred" society would present his calling card and either be admitted or be declined, thus making his status in the social hierarchy clear to him. If admitted, his visit would typically be supervised by the woman's mother, at least at first, and a host of rules governed his stay, from whether refreshments

The City Challenges Main Street

would be served to who walked him to the door when he left. Women held a degree of power in this system, for they set the rules and enforced them.[60]

Increasingly even those outside high society sought to emulate the calling system in a bid for respectability, and by the early 20th century calling pervaded America. Countless women's magazines that prescribed women's fashions and behaviors with rigid standards consistently made the "dos and don'ts" of calling well known to their readers. Men received these cultural messages too, for they often wrote in to magazine advisors in titles like the *Ladies Home Journal* seeking advice on how to properly navigate the world of calling. As late as 1907 *Harper's Bazaar* ran an article titled "Etiquette for Men" detailing the rules for those still in dark.

But by then the popular etiquette was almost out of touch, as increasing urbanization and commercialization of leisure changed the game. While calling met the needs of upper-class society, it made little sense to many working-class youths by the 1910s and 1920s. Girls in tenements often shared two rooms with their entire families and surely did not have a parlor to invite male suitors to visit in. And so, by necessity, for those who could break away from the supervision of their families their dating rituals evolved in public rather than in private.

On stoops, on city streets, in dance halls, and in other sites of commercial amusement working-class youth engaged in the practice of courtship far removed from the rules of calling, which changed the power dynamics involved. Dating, as this would become widely known, involved much less structure and far fewer rules. It also cost money. Going out into public spaces most often required paid entrance, and working-class girls who could not afford amusements on their own sometimes allowed men to "treat" them in exchange for romantic attention and sexual favors.[61] Women often needed men to engage in this world of courtship because they lacked financial security. These women were also only able to enter into the world of public amusements without supervision because of their liminal position. A respectable woman would not be seen in a dance hall on a man's arm. But then again working-class girls did not enjoy the status of respectability in the early 1900s.[62]

Nevertheless, upper-class men and women sought the freedom that seemed to come with dating, and they pushed the bounds of respectability in their own efforts to find it. Some mimicked the habits of working-class youth in restaurants and dance halls, engaging with members of the opposite sex in public, away from their parents and the formality of calling. Women were also seeking more access to public spaces overall in the

1910s and 1920s, making room for more traditionally "respectable" women to gain entry to such places. College girls found ways to date men outside their protective campus gates. And in areas more far flung from the cities, in suburbs and country towns, the tremendous popularity of the automobile provided the means for young people to get in on this exciting trend. Throughout the 1920s, then, the practice entered the mainstream. By the 1930s dating became a "universal custom," an "American institution" no longer associated with one particular subset of the population.[63]

Ultimately then, affirming many of the fears Americans held in the 1920s, the culture of the city largely trumped that of the village. The values and the leisurely pursuits of those living in the nation's urban areas dominated American culture by the end of this decade, thanks to the influx of people into the city and the unstoppable growth of mass consumer culture. As a result of these two developments, the sexual revolution hit the mainstream, carried forward by this large-scale shift from an agrarian, producer culture to an urban, consumer culture. The only group consistently left outside this mainstream consumer culture were African American women and men. Their experience of life in the city in the 1920s is one of the most important and consequential stories of this time.

THE GREAT MIGRATION: AFRICAN AMERICANS IN THE CITY

A horrifying race riot gripped the city of Chicago at the end of July in 1919, and newspapers around the country ran front-page headlines detailing chaos, terror, and bloodshed. Tales of a "race war" figured white assailants angry over losing ground, and black assailants bitter over their poor treatment. The *Chicago Defender*, a black newspaper, portrayed white rioters as bloodthirsty, claiming, "the presence of a black face in their vicinity was the signal for a carnival of death."[64] The *Chicago Whip*, another black newspaper, avowed peace in ordinary circumstances but found these particular circumstances to be extraordinary. "The bombers will be bombed," they cried.[65] Individuals and groups fought one another using guns, knives, and razors. Crowds dragged white and black city dwellers alike from cars and lunch counters, pummeling them in the city streets. A week after the conflict began, with thousands of state militia men on the streets, the riot came to an end. White and black mobs killed 23 African Americans and 15 whites, and they injured over 500 people.

In just the hot summer of 1919, a season NAACP head James Weldon Johnson christened the "Red Summer," race riots rocked 22 cities and towns. Many of these conflicts occurred in the South, as white southerners lashed out in anger and fear at the newfound determination and resolve of African Americans. When whites attacked, which they did in Arkansas, South Carolina, Texas, Tennessee, and Washington, D.C., to name but a few places, African Americans fought back. But this happened in the North, too, in New York, Pennsylvania, and Connecticut, as well as in Illinois. Yet it was the Chicago riot that got the most attention.

The migration of southern blacks to northern cities like Chicago triggered a host of antagonisms, ones that built upon preexisting notions of white supremacy, but racial tension over the use of public amusement sites helped create a powder keg. And the death of a 14-year-old child lit the fuse. For although several factors were at play in Chicago, this was also what historian Victoria Wolcott calls a "recreation riot."[66] The proliferation of mass culture and public amusements in urban areas created conflict between competing groups. As more and more African Americans left rural farmland and moved to urban areas, millions of people now shared semi-public spaces where the mixing of races became an ever more contested issue. These recreation spaces were central to the construction of what historian Elizabeth Grace Hale calls a "culture of segregation," codified in law in the South and by custom in the North. Whites erected this culture, and African Americans increasingly resisted it.[67]

The riot in Chicago began with a conflict over the use of a city beach. Eugene Williams, a young black teenager in a raft, drifted too far over an imaginary line in the water denoting that particular spot for white bathers. There were no posted signs to this effect—it was custom in Chicago that Twenty-Ninth Street beach was for white swimmers, while the beach two blocks down was for black swimmers. As Williams drifted north and over this "line," whites on Twenty-Ninth Street beach threw rocks at him until he slipped into the water and drowned. An angry confrontation on the beach followed, and when police refused to arrest the white rock throwers, instead arresting a black man for the scuffle, the riot was set in motion.[68]

The riots speak to the opening of an era of yearning and strife for a generation of new black city dwellers. The thousands of black migrants streaming into northern cities like Chicago pitted a growing black working population against white workers in competition for jobs. Significant housing pressures divided white and black as each group tried to gain ground in limited housing stock. And even more so, as black aspirations rose in the wake of the war, white communities actively sought ways to tamp them down, to reaffirm the social order as it once was, producing a cultural divide. Ultimately, as black Americans became urban dwellers en masse, for the first time, the Great Migration, the emergence of the architecture of the black ghetto, and the flowering of the Harlem Renaissance framed city life and its deepening tensions in the 1920s.

"Come Out of the South"

Nearly 90 percent of all black Americans lived in rural villages, towns, and cities below the Mason Dixon line before World War I, in a social hierarchy framed by white supremacy. Racist state governments run entirely by whites set up Jim Crow laws that prevented black men, and then black women after 1920, from exercising the right to vote. Poll taxes, grandfather clauses, literacy tests, and white primaries facilitated this effort. The same laws required segregation in all aspects of life, including transportation, school houses, bathrooms, and cemeteries. Black children had access only to second-class schools and often did not enroll beyond the eighth grade.[69]

Most southern whites expected deference and submission from their black neighbors. Whites demanded that African Americans make way for them when they walked down the street. They insisted African Americans call them mister or ma'am regardless of their age or social status. Humiliations both large and small threaded through daily life. Life in the South was also inherently dangerous. Lynchings pervaded the region in the years after Reconstruction, and they happened in the North too. These killings, perpetrated by whites in response to a range of perceived infractions, almost always went unpunished as local police turned a blind eye. White vigilantes often raised the specter of the black male rapist to justify murder, claiming their victims made sexual advances on white women. But in actuality most lynching victims committed different "crimes" against white supremacy, by speaking out against Jim Crow or achieving economic success. According to the NAACP, just 20 percent of lynchings actually arose from accusations of sexual assault.[70]

In reality, any real physical or psychological threat to the white social hierarchy could end with a publicly sanctioned murder. While the number of lynchings fell in the early 20th century, in the first year after the war the total shot up to 76. The NAACP responded by calling for a federal antilynching bill, but an unsympathetic president Woodrow Wilson ignored them.[71] The Republicans who replaced him in the 1920s temporarily supported an antilynching bill, but ultimately it was withdrawn after southern senators mounted a Democratic filibuster.

Halting and sporadic efforts to reform race relations in the South developed after the war, but little changed, and poor economic conditions made life in farming towns extremely difficult. Sharecropping, a system developed after slavery's demise, kept most African Americans in wretched poverty. Black farmers and their families seeking autonomy essentially rented land owned by whites, working the land in hopes of making enough to support themselves after paying the landholder with a portion of the year's crops. But by the start of the 20th century, with cotton prices declining, many of these men, women, and children were in a vicious cycle of debt. They rarely made enough to pay what they owed for land and the use of tools, and each year the amount of their debt grew. Substandard housing and living conditions left rural southern blacks vulnerable to high rates of disease. And to top it all off, the boll weevil made its way across the continent by 1921, destroying existing cotton crops in its wake.[72]

But African Americans in the 1920s bore the joys and the burdens of high expectations, thanks to their experiences with the war. During World War I black soldiers marched off to fight, over 350,000 of them. They endured continued discrimination at home in spite of, or at times because of, the uniform they wore. Many noted bitterly the lack of racial discrimination in France when they arrived there. Collectively, they expected better things to come from a war for democracy.

At this moment, in an effort to escape the squalor and hopelessness of life in rural villages and towns, many African Americans moved to southern cities in search of better horizons. But conditions were not much better. Segregated in the worst housing, they often lived without running water and electricity. Southern white city dwellers threw up intense competition for jobs, leaving black workers stuck in only a few menial professions. Men worked in textile and tobacco factories, as janitors and porters, and as hospital orderlies. Women took up work in the professions open to them, including wash work, cooking, and domestic service. While some preferred this southern city life to one on the farm, in the 1920s, as never before, the cities of the North beckoned.[73]

Jobs were a major draw for many of these migrants. The war effort opened new positions to African Americans, as men mobilized and marched off to fight. White women moved into many of the higher-status jobs, and then for the first time a wave of employers decided to offer their lower-status jobs to black workers. Dreams of the "promised land" carried along by a network of kin and connections led 500,000 north by the end of World War I, with another 700,000 making the journey in the 1920s. Changing labor practices that expected workers to work fewer hours, along with immigration restriction, kept jobs available throughout the decade. Upon arrival in northern and western cities, most black women found themselves confined to domestic service jobs, while men, who also took domestic service jobs, found industrial work too.[74]

But these industrial workers faced difficult challenges in the racialized urban landscape. Employers often brought black workers in as scabs during strikes, and had done so for decades. White workers, threatened by this, both condemned black workers and urged them to join unions. Black union workers on the picket line could not be scabs. And white employers did everything in their power to further sow the seeds of distrust between black and white workers, quashing organized labor's efforts at interracial cooperation when they could. Ultimately black workers resisted unionization over the long term, seeing their opportunities and their roadblocks in terms of their racial position rather than as members of a broader working class.[75]

Still, hundreds of thousands of African Americans found life in northern cities, however imperfectly framed by systemic racism, preferable to life in southern cities and towns. They had more economic opportunity, and more of a chance to forge a rich cultural life in public spaces.[76] Migrants already in northern cities called to those still in the South to cross the Mason Dixon Line, because many felt as Richard Wright did when he asked, "What kind of life was possible under that hate?"[77] The *Chicago Defender* had a "Come Out of the South" department and played a significant role in networking between would-be migrants and those already settled outside the South.[78]

When migrants arrived in cities throughout the country, they entered urban areas changed dramatically by industrialization. This process of industrialization shaped the geography of cities in profound ways, spurring the development of tenements near factories, giving birth to a largely white managerial class, fueling the meteoric rise of the retail industry, and altogether increasing the degree of social segregation by class. Into this landscape arrived several hundred thousand black migrants, and this migration changed city life considerably. A massive shift was now under way. In 1870, 80 percent of the nation's African Americans lived in the rural South, but by 1970 the reverse was true: 80 percent of African Americans lived in northern or southern cities. And as this shift took place, something curious happened. Generally, city dwellers did not live in racially segregated areas in the late 1800s and early 1900s. Some evidence of urban segregation exists before the 1910s, but more often than not urban spaces were integrated, and different racial groups encountered one another frequently on a day-to-day basis.[79]

Only with the start of the "Great Migration" in the mid-1910s do we see widespread evidence of rigid segregation in the North.[80] Most African

Americans in larger cities by the 1920s lived in neighborhoods that were very much segregated.[81] And at that time people began referring to these urban spaces as ghettos, a reference to walled sections of Italian cities where Jews were forced to reside.[82] When these ghettos emerged in American cities, they did not do so by happenstance. Rather, a series of deliberate decisions by individuals, communities, and government policy makers created the ghetto and maintained it going forward.

These migrants, pulled by the lure of jobs and pushed by the poor crops and the brutality of Jim Crow, streamed into cities where white Americans received them with a great deal of trepidation. Economic competition, housing pressures, heightened racism, and the propensity for second- and third-generation immigrants to cement their own whiteness by lording over different groups of racial "others" fueled white people's anger and their efforts to discriminate. Racial conflict stalked the spread of black migrants. White neighborhood associations fought to keep African Americans from moving into their neighborhoods for fear of plummeting property values and an increase in crime and disorder. Discrimination efforts rankled black newcomers and mobilized white, upwardly mobile workers and their families to try to hold the line against changing demographics. By the 1920s and into the 1930s, neighborhoods where it was acceptable for black migrants to settle, regardless of whether they were middle or working class, became more "narrowly circumscribed." And unlike immigrant groups, who typically assimilated and moved out of clustered urban enclaves, African Americans were trapped. As two historians phrased it, "The era of the ghetto had begun."[83]

While most black migrants had little choice but to settle in black neighborhoods like Harlem in New York and Black Bottom in Detroit, those who moved up the socioeconomic ladder were continuously thwarted in their efforts to move out of the city into surrounding white areas. The loyalty of one white neighbor to another helped enforce this roadblock to black home ownership, as individuals upheld a sometimes-tacit but sometimes-quite open promise not to sell to black families. Neighborhood associations often reinforced the fabric of these individual refusals to integrate. Meetings were called and attended by dues-paying members, many of whom hoped to prevent the economic misfortunes they felt might come with the arrival of black neighbors. Home ownership or "improvement" associations helped maintain the color line in cities around the nation through zoning restrictions and the use of restrictive covenants, which contractually prohibited a homeowner from selling his home to a black person. These began to see widespread use in the 1910s with the support of realtors. The Supreme Court upheld the constitutionality of such covenants in 1926, and their legal, acceptable use continued until the Court finally struck them down in 1948. Discriminatory real estate practices undergirded the association between black Americans and the city's ghetto.[84]

White city residents used extralegal methods to contain the growing black population, too. Many deployed violence with gusto. The spate of race riots reflected one kind of violence, but other more personal efforts abounded. As upwardly mobile black families crossed over into white neighborhoods, a pattern of harassment followed, from threatening letters to offers to purchase the property. If these failed, cross burnings and rock throwing typically followed, punctuated most often in the 1920s by physical attacks and fire bombings. Between 1917 and 1921, 58 black homes were firebombed in Chicago alone. This kind of racial violence not only drove vulnerable black homeowners back to those developing black ghettos, but it also built up an ever-increasingly impermeable wall between these racially divided neighborhoods.[85]

Tragic stories of violence and intimidation plagued would-be black homebuyers in the 1920s. The case of Dr. Ossian Sweet in Detroit, Michigan, offers one example. Dr. Sweet, a successful physician, along with his wife and a newborn child, purchased a home on an all-white street, Garland Avenue, in the summer of 1924. Sweet migrated north from a segregated town in Florida where he witnessed, at age five, a black man being lynched. The white mob burned the victim alive. Sweet went on to attend an all-black college, and then medical school at Howard University where he lived through a race riot in Washington, D.C., in the "Red Summer" of 1919. As devastating rampages tore through black communities in the years after World War I, Dr. Sweet knew well the fear of the white mob. It haunted him.[86]

When he moved into his new home in September, purposefully waiting for the school year to start so he might avoid crowds on the street when unpacking his belongings, Dr. Sweet found a tinderbox of racism and anger on Garland Avenue. A neighborhood association, stiffened by a resurgent Ku Klux Klan in Detroit, riled up the neighborhood in meetings before the Sweet family's arrival, setting the stage for violence. A white mob encircled the house on the Sweets' second night, throwing rocks and breaking windows under the purposefully un-watchful eye of Detroit police officers. Sweet, worried about being overrun and lynched, amassed several friends and an arsenal of guns to protect himself, his family, and his home. As the rocks rained down on the Sweet's house and the mob seethed, Dr. Sweet's brother fired his gun into the crowd. He injured one white man and killed another.[87]

The Sweets' trial caught the eye of James Weldon Johnson, head of the NAACP, who seized on the case as a perfect opportunity to expose—and stop—the powerful rise of segregation in northern cities. The NAACP already had several efforts under way, one of which was a legal challenge to racial covenants in the Supreme Court. The group drew famous lawyer Clarence Darrow—fresh from the Scopes Trial—to the case as the Sweets' defense attorney. And Darrow, always one to see the significance of the big picture, litigated the case in the fall of 1925 as a strike against systemic racism and mob violence. Sweet himself, on the witness stand, explained his actions along similar lines: "When I opened the door, I saw the mob and I realized I was facing the same mob that had hounded my people throughout our entire history." Sweet's defense, and Darrow's framing of the circumstances surrounding his and his family's actions, ultimately worked in their favor. The jury was hung, and in a retrial Ossian's brother Henry was acquitted. Ossian's own charges were then dismissed. Sweet never returned to the home on Garland Avenue, but as one 21st-century writer phrased it, Darrow's approach "insisted, in other words, that black lives matter."[88]

Another kind of white violence, perpetrated by police, also terrorized African Americans. In Detroit black residents regularly experienced police brutality in their communities. In fact, police shot more than 50 black men in the city in just the first half of 1925, some of whom were killed execution style.[89] The officers were not charged with a crime. Police used violence against black inhabitants of Harlem, too. While black leaders had once urged people to appeal to authorities to find redress, by the 1920s a new spirit of empowerment and anger changed things. Activists and leaders of the black press now called for African Americans to stand up for themselves, and to confront the problem head-on.[90] This new spirit was evident in 1928, when a black woman chastised several police officers for beating a black man on the street. One of those officers smacked her in the face, and Harlem responded in kind. People threw objects and debris at the police for several hours, and were only quelled by a tremendous show of force from authorities.[91] Police brutality was a persistent feature of black life in the city.

When these formal and informal strategies failed to stop the integration of a community, when whites simply could not hold the color line, they fled. White flight, a phenomenon that would empty whole urban neighborhoods with disastrous effects in the post–World War II era, actually emerged here in the 1920s in response to the Great Migration. It played out in the same way again and again around the country, becoming a kind of self-fulfilling prophecy with real economic consequences.

White fears of declining property values, after even just one black family moved into their neighborhood, were borne out again and again. White families rushed to sell their homes before the prices in that neighborhood went into a free fall, taking their profits to buy somewhere else, somewhere still peopled by whites alone. If they chose to stay, or waited too long to sell, white homeowners in newly integrated neighborhoods often found themselves in foreclosure as their property values dropped, loans became due, and they could not afford to pay them.

Black families endured great economic consequences too, however. Most Americans hold their wealth, their savings, in their homes. It is often a family's largest investment. Starting in the 1920s, and for decades to come, black families were prevented from building a nest egg in the form of a home. They also lost the opportunity to pass this wealth from one generation to the next. It mattered little whether a family could save enough money to pay the inflated prices black buyers encountered. An ugly array of prejudices, policies, and violence often prevented them from making the purchase. Systemic racism tarnished the promise of the city for African Americans in many, many ways.

The "New Negro"

Both the perils and the promise of life after World War I in America helped to birth the "new negro," a man apart from his forefathers, one distinct from the past. The birth of this new black man was widely heralded in the black press, and among black writers. The term encompassed a host of developing identities in the early 20th century, ranging from militant opposition to violence and repression to a more conservative push for black economic self-sufficiency. By the late 1910s the "new negro" represented educated, uncompromising African Americans made savvy by the war effort, keen to enjoy the freedom and democracy the nation claimed to embody. And black resolve to fight surpassed the act of self-defense: blacks mobilized for economic and political rights with a new vigor. After the Chicago race riot an interracial commission solicited residents' opinions on why the violent conflict happened. Black war veteran Stanley Norvell put it simply when he wrote to the commission, explaining, "Today we have with us a new negro. A brand new negro, if you please."[92] White America did not know black people, Norvell argued, and with the arrival of this "new negro," they needed to.

In 1925, black writer and philosopher Alain Locke made a formal introduction in the journal *Survey Graphic*, editing a special edition on life in Harlem called "Harlem: Mecca of the New Negro." Locke's own essay, titled "Enter the New Negro," heralded the arrival of this new black American. His appearance, Locke argued, was in part a product of black movement "city-ward and to the great centers of industry."[93] Significantly here, this meant that the Great Migration changed more than geography, for it made the "Negro problem no longer exclusively or even predominantly Southern."

The impact of the war, migration, and urbanization fundamentally reshaped the terrain of racial conflict in America. In Locke's view, "The mind of the Negro seems suddenly to have slipped from under the tyranny of social intimidation and to be shaking off the psychology of imitation and implied inferiority." This awakening by African Americans in all parts of the nation made room for empowerment, for new opportunities. Locke said, "By shedding the old chrysalis of the Negro problem we are achieving something like a spiritual emancipation."[94]

In his essay Locke highlighted the numerous voices challenging racism in the 1920s, particularly in Harlem. He quoted from James Weldon Johnson's 1920 poem "To America," where he asked, "How would you have us, as we are? Or sinking 'neath the load we bear, our eyes fixed forward on a star, or gazing empty at despair? Rising or falling? Men or things? With dragging pace or footsteps fleet? Strong, willing sinews in your wings, or tightening chains about your feet?"[95] Locke celebrated a group of African Americans who were at a crossroads, thanks in part to their arrival in the city. They called for equality as he urged readers to do the same. Self-expression mattered, it was necessary, and it was happening in Harlem.

The exuberant and defiant "new negro" emerged most vividly in Harlem, then, in the midst of the flowering Harlem Renaissance. Black migrants, attractive to Harlem landlords because they were charged higher rent, moved in to the tree-lined streets and majestic brownstones vacated by German, Irish, and Jewish residents beginning in the 1900s. Black Harlem grew through the 1910s and 1920s, ultimately stretching more than twenty-five blocks north and twenty-five blocks south from 135th Street, sweeping across the city from St. Nicholas Avenue in the west to Lexington Avenue in the east. In the grand rooms of the Harlem Opera House, in vibrant churches, in speakeasies and dance halls shimmering with jazz music, and in apartment rent parties, a new postwar black identity blossomed in Harlem between the Great War and the Great Depression.[96]

The cultural movement known as the Harlem Renaissance was a product of its time and place: it was a modern, urban movement. Race, and its social implications, captured the art, music, and politics that flowed from this group of intellectuals and artists as their modern social identity materialized in the midst of the move to the city. Magazines like W.E.B. Du Bois's

Crisis carried both fiction and poetry in their pages, and unlike writers of the largely white "lost generation," the literature flowing from the pens of the Renaissance writers carried notes of optimism rather than cynicism. Alain Locke published a collection in 1925 titled *The New Negro: An Interpretation*, an anthology of art, fiction, and nonfiction examining the changing racial landscape. The pieces were both joyful and contemplative, and contributors alluded to the fact that such a book would not be conceivable in an environment like the one that still existed in the American South.[97] Here were urban black intellectuals convinced that they had something unique, something important, to contribute to American culture.

Harlem drew white tourists from New York City and well beyond, who ventured into a particular version of Harlem's nightlife as voyeurs and thrill-seekers. Establishments like the Cotton Club in Jungle Alley enticed white visitors with its flamboyant display of exoticism in a "safe" space that featured no real immersion in black culture. Well-dressed and well-lubricated patrons streamed up into Harlem after the midtown clubs closed, late into the night. Cotton Club bouncers refused to admit black patrons, and once inside white celebrants paid premium prices to sit at tables that separated them from the black musicians and the light-skinned black dancers. Duke Ellington and his dance band played the Cotton Club starting in 1927, moving adoring audiences to jump up and do the Turkey Trot and the Shimmy.[98] Jazz music appeared all over Harlem with similar results, as these flashy clubs put blackness on display to be enjoyed by whites. These clubs did not promote the mixing of cultures, or the mixing of black and white people.[99]

Other spaces appealed to white audiences precisely because they did allow black and white patrons to enter. Social fluidity drew many to speakeasies in Harlem, where several hundred people jammed into cramped cellars. These unadorned spaces offered wooden tables, close together, along with poor-quality bootleg liquor. Typically patrons also enjoyed a crowded dance floor and music until well after the sun came up. Black working-class Harlemites sat alongside the more adventurous white patrons who caroused in a world outside the bounds of polite society.

But black New Yorkers also reveled in their own nightlife, which featured wide variety. Rent parties took place every night of the week in apartments throughout the neighborhood. Traditionally black renters paid higher prices for their lodging than did whites, and rent parties helped make ends meet. Party hosts printed and distributed cards advertising their event, and then welcomed revelers for a fee. Once inside partygoers could buy food and liquor, they could dance to live music, or they could gamble. Numerous nightclubs in the neighborhood also catered to gays and lesbians, demonstrating Harlem's remarkably open environment in the 1920s. One artist declared, "Nobody was in the closet. There wasn't any closet."[100] In clubs like the Clam House and the Garden of Joy mixed crowds watched lesbian cabaret singers openly flout gender conventions, sporting tuxedos and men's hats. All of this only heightened the allure of some of Harlem's nightlife, where an older, traditional society's rules seemed not to apply.

Harlem served as an incubator for more than arts and entertainment, as vibrant and passionate leaders vied for black America's political affections in the 1920s. Towering black intellectual W.E.B. Du Bois led the charge in Harlem, railing against passive tolerance of racism in *The Crisis*, reflecting the heightened demand for basic civil rights among many African Americans. A. Philip Randolph galvanized black socialists, arguing for a class analysis of the nation's race problems in his Socialist journal the *Messenger*. But Marcus Garvey wore the populist crown in Harlem in the 1920s. His wildly appealing Universal Negro Improvement Association set forth the powerful possibility of black independence, both economically and politically. Garvey wanted to establish an independent black state in Africa, hoping to spur connections and pride among black people around the world. He held garish parades, urged his followers to rejoice in the beauty of blackness, and inspired many. His radical tactics frightened white observers as well as more traditional leaders like Du Bois, and pressure from these groups spurred a federal investigation for mail fraud that led Garvey to prison time and deportation. His stirring presence in the United States, however short lived, is important in that it reflects a growing militancy in the 1920s.[101]

While the Harlem Renaissance was a movement of the city, writers in this movement sought to give voice to a larger sense of regeneration they felt surging forth from black communities all over the nation. The writers themselves were a select group, better educated than most of the black population. Hailing mostly from the South, but from states all over the nation and abroad, almost all of these writers resided in New York or had close ties to it. They, along with many others, felt a moment of awakening—a rebirth even—in the 1920s.[102] Amid other prominent literary tides of the 1920s, with Sinclair Lewis criticizing the vapid life of the middle class in *Babbit*, and F. Scott Fitzgerald bemoaning the spiritual emptiness of the 1920s lifestyle, the themes of the Harlem Renaissance stood out for their optimism. But the movement did not last beyond this decade. Langston Hughes wrote, "The Negro vogue in Manhattan . . . reached its peak just before the Crash of 1929, the Crash that sent Negroes, white folks, and all rolling down the hill."[103] Many of the Renaissance's members decamped to Paris by the close of the decade, further hastening its end.

But the Harlem Renaissance gave voice to the "new negro" and represented a kind of victory of the city in the lives of hundreds of thousands of African Americans. It was the very tension between the city and the town that drew so many migrants to cities in the first place. They came out of the South in search of something better. The opportunities offered in the urban North, and the persistent violence and discrimination, helped to reframe the problem of race in America for the century to come.

The film *Sunrise* concludes with a sentimental victory for the values of the village, as The Man and The Wife reconcile in their simple rural home while The Woman of the City pouts on a rickety cart loaded up with her luggage. Many in America wanted this to be the way the story ended. But the triumph of America's small towns was not a foregone conclusion in the 1920s. The nation's cities grew in prominence and in influence throughout the decade, a culmination of so many long-term shifts sweeping through the country. Mass consumer culture helped to standardize a national culture, one produced in the nation's cities, where pluralism, tolerance, and moral ambiguity held more sway.

These city values found their way into all the nooks and crannies of the nation through popular films, magazines, radio, and public amusements. And these thrills of consumer culture reorganized the way many Americans lived their lives. Sex became public by the 1920s, a remarkable shift, something no longer encountered only behind closed doors between a husband and wife. The so-called sexual revolution carried tremendous consequences for women, men, families, and the economy. Together these developments marked growing cities as subversive spaces, places that challenged a widely shared sense of moral order rooted in the 19th century. This pitted villages against cities, in both culture and politics, in enduring ways. Today we live in a nation that considers itself divided by Republican or conservative red states and Democratic, or liberal, blue states. It is worth noting that of the nation's five largest cities, four are located in typically blue states.[104]

Contemporary Americans also hold deeply seated assumptions about race and city life that stem from the 1920s. The erasure of African Americans in *Sunrise*'s scenes of public amusement reflected reality to some degree. In the midst of the Great Migration, a population that was once heavily centered in villages and farms became concentrated in cities. Within these cities black migrants lived their lives in heavily segregated areas and experienced segregation within an expanding mass consumer culture. White Americans confined black migrants to specific areas within cities with a range of tactics, including outright violence. And these circumstances helped give rise to the image of an urban ghetto peopled by poor African Americans in American popular and political culture. The city became, in the 1920s, a place of pervasive racial conflict. And in this crucible the "new negro" had room to grow, fostering black culture and building upon a legacy of black resistance to racial oppression. This resistance undoubtedly laid important groundwork for future efforts to secure civil rights. But at the same time, the association between blackness and urban space gave rise to almost one hundred years of persistent racial stereotypes and damaging public policy.

CHAPTER TWO

Who Belongs in the Nativist 1920s? Immigration, the First Red Scare, and the Revival of the Ku Klux Klan

In the 1920s, Americans believed immigrants to be a national menace. Philadelphia's *Public Ledger* carried a front-page story in 1920 with the headline, "Curb Immigration to Halt Crime." The sentiment of the article was commonplace at the time, and the writer quoted a New York City grand jury expressing support for congressional efforts then under way to stop the flow of immigration into the United States. Jurors cited statistics claiming that in the city "all of the homicides and most of the graver, more desperate and heinous crimes were committed by foreigners who palpably have no understanding of the genesis or genius of American institutions." As such, the jurors felt, these immigrants were "unlikely under present conditions ever to be assimilable."[1] The *New York Tribune* covered the same story on the same day, arguing, "Anarchists, Bolsheviki and other Reds from Europe are invading America by the thousands. Their methods of gaining admission are over the Mexican and Canadian borders, as stowaways on liners entering New York, as members of ships' crews who desert on arrival and as immigrants who pass through Ellis Island without revealing their political faiths." The jurors conceived of America as a target for radicals, and if nothing was done, they said, "It will foster disunion instead of promoting union. Instead of continuing as a nation of high ideals, we shall degenerate into a mere medley of races, a hodgepodge of nationalities."[2] Their alarm and their characterization of this immigration problem sound strikingly familiar.

In the 1920s, many white, middle-class, Protestant, native-born Americans radically reshaped the country's relationship with immigrants and other outliers due to their xenophobia and their desire to forestall the loss of their own power in the face of immigration, urbanization, and industrialization. Motivations for this impulse ran the gamut, from white supremacy to economic stress to nativism to fears about radicalism and crime to the disorientation of living in a rapidly changing era. But this anxiety about social and cultural change and loss of status found expression in a vitriolic nativist movement to curb immigration, in a Red Scare targeting radicalism, and in a powerful resurgence of the Ku Klux Klan.

And so, the multifaceted movement to scapegoat immigrants, minorities, and other outsiders as the cause of all the nation's woes was not new in the late 1960s, when Richard Nixon called upon his "Silent Majority" to rebuke the transformations sweeping through America. And it is not new now, in the 21st century, when anger and invective are once again hurled at immigrants, radicals, and challengers to the status quo. Then, as now, concerns about power and social stability dominated political culture, and in the 1920s, Americans grappled with these tensions in the context of a culture war over exactly who and what was American.

AMERICAN NATIVISM AND THE FIRST RED SCARE

Immigration exploded as a political and social issue in the early 20th century in response to massive numbers of foreign-born men and women arriving each year leading up to World War I. As Americans took stock of immigrants already in the country, and debated over whether and how to limit arrivals going forward, much was at stake for them. Many in the nation felt a strong nostalgia in the 1920s for an apparent homogenous past, one suffused with equality and democratic ideals. A shared worldview among native, white, middle-class Protestants encouraged them to position themselves as figureheads of that idyllic, fictional past. They wanted to hold onto, rescue, and revive this past and make it present once again.

The Arrival of "New" Immigrants

Real life in America hardly resembled this nostalgic past. "We are no longer a homogenous people," wrote poet and playwright Langdon Mitchell ruefully in the summer of 1926. "There are some fourteen millions of foreign-born among us, whose ideals are not ours. When we seek to Americanize them, they tell us in their foreign tongues that the country is as much theirs as ours." And furthermore, to add insult to injury, Mitchell complained, "When we protest, these people accuse us of intolerance."[3] Feeling overwhelmed and desperately out of control, many shared a sense that the nation was fractured by immigration in the years after World War I. But nativism had a long history.

Before 1890, most immigrants to America traveled from northwest Europe, Canada, or China, and they met with varying degrees of welcome. German and Irish immigrants came in significant numbers—several million—starting in the 1840s. Americans largely embraced the Germans, many of whom moved to farms or to midwestern cities. The Irish experienced the opposite reaction, facing intense rancor and discrimination from the outset. The potato famine that pushed over 1 million Irish men, women, and children to America's shores only magnified that reaction. Americans disliked the Irish for their Catholicism, which marked them off from the largely Protestant nation. Americans also condemned the intense poverty of the Irish, attributing their numbers to increases in crime and decreases in wages.[4] The Know-Nothing movement of the 1840s and 1850s, which denounced poor and Catholic immigrants, became the nation's first formal expression of nativism.

The Chinese fared even worse, however, when the gold rush in California drew them to the West Coast in hundreds of thousands between 1850 and 1882. Americans rejected these hardworking immigrants, ones who provided backbreaking labor on railroads and in mines, for familiar reasons. They provided economic competition in a labor market where workers felt vulnerable. Charging them with working for "coolie wages," white workers organized against Chinese immigrants. But here they went further, keying in on a potential racial threat. Anxiety over the "yellow peril" spread in the mid-1800s as self-interested workers and policy makers acted on economic interests but through racial means. The Chinese threatened perceptions of America as a white man's country, and self-interested organizations, with the help of the press, portrayed these immigrants as heathens, as inferior to white men. The Chinese Exclusion Act resulted in 1882, with the Chinese becoming the first racial group targeted for exclusion by the United States. This act remained in force until 1942.[5]

The American "nativism" against these two groups shape-shifted as other immigrants filtered into the population in the latter years of the 1800s. Racism against the Chinese ebbed somewhat, given the cessation of their immigration into the country. Discrimination against the Irish abated after the Civil War and continued to diminish as successive waves of Irish immigrants became more and more "typically" American.[6] They mixed in comfortably with a continuing stream of Germans and a host of other British, Dutch, Swedish, and Norwegian immigrants. All of these groups assimilated relatively well, in due time, thanks in no small part to their whiteness.

By the 1890s, a different immigration scene unfolded. A host of "new" immigrants touched down on the nation's shores, new in that they did not hail from the British Isles, from Germany, or from Scandinavia. Instead, they came from southern and eastern Europe. Italians, Slavs, eastern European Jews from Poland, Lithuania, and Russia, Hungarians, Greeks, and Portuguese immigrants arrived in ever-increasing numbers. After 1910, Armenians and Syrians and migrants from West Africa joined the mix. All in all, between 1890 and 1920, some 25 million immigrants entered the United States. Because they desperately sought money to provide for themselves and loved ones either in America or back at home, very few of these immigrants moved south, where wage work was more difficult to come by. They stayed in the North or went west. But in many cases, they stayed in or near their point of arrival. And therefore popular port cities such as Boston, New York, and Philadelphia attracted very large immigrant populations. In other cases, immigrants moved on to cities with high numbers of their fellow countrymen, in cities like Buffalo and Detroit. Within cities some groups mixed in with the crowd, while others segregated themselves in smaller ethnic neighborhoods, like the Polish area of Chicago or the Italian section on the North End of Boston.

By 1910, roughly half of the nation's population consisted of immigrants and their children; native-born Americans became increasingly alarmed.[7] Unlike the "old" immigrants, many of these recent arrivals professed a different faith—they were Catholic or Jewish. Many recent arrivals did not speak English. And many of them were desperately, utterly poor. As discussions about the changing face of the nation spread in the early 1900s, questions arose about whether these new immigrants could be assimilated. Could they become American?

By the 1920s some hoped they could, with the will to change and with help from Americans themselves. The impulse to "Americanize" immigrants governed both policy and popular thought. Even though nativism existed in the mid-1800s, back then most Americans felt satisfied that, left to their own devices, awash in American culture and society, immigrants would indeed become American. The turn of the century marked a shift in thinking, notably in a decade of economic uncertainty.

Perhaps, many argued, immigrants needed to be purposefully and intelligently schooled on the ways one should be an American. Two competing impulses emerged in response. One celebrated cultural diversity in hopes of smoothing the transition to life in America, while the other moved to impose conformity on immigrants through policy and social pressure.

These two varieties of Americanization programming coexisted throughout the Progressive Era. Settlement houses most prominently offered the former, seeking to support immigrants in their efforts to fit in. Settlement workers opened their homes to immigrant women for English classes, to girls for social hours, and to men for union meetings. They encouraged immigrants to celebrate the cultural gifts they brought to America as a way to help ameliorate the difficulties they endured upon arrival.

On the flip side, a number of patriotic societies appeared in America at the turn of the century, and they advanced the more coercive brand of Americanization. Often fueled by suspicion and resentment, this type of Americanization sought to stamp out radicalism and crime through intense efforts to cultivate patriotism, loyalty, and good behavior. Organizations like the Daughters of the American Revolution sponsored patriotic education classes for men at work, women at home, and children in school, teaching citizenship and civics lessons. This type of education privileged Americanness to the exclusion of, or even denigration of, immigrants' native cultures.

This stance on immigration proved popular with many national leaders. Theodore Roosevelt supported it as he traveled the country in the later years of the 1910s, calling for unity and preparedness for war. He sought to cultivate patriotism and a submission to all things American with his oft-repeated motto "America for Americans."[8] He stood firmly against "every form of hyphenated Americanism." One could not be Irish American, or Italian American. To do so would be disloyal and unpatriotic. Rather, one needed to be American and American alone.

Interestingly, for Roosevelt this was not about "creed, birthplace or national descent, but of the soul and of the spirit." He said, an American "has the right stuff in him." If a newly arrived immigrant simply loved America and gave over his allegiance to it, body and soul, he was welcome. And if he did not, "then he is out of place in this country, and the sooner he leaves it the better."[9] This framework of Americanism essentially offered acceptance in return for conformity. By acting like an American, privileging American things and American ideals, one could enjoy the benefits of being an American. There was no room for criticism.

Both strands of Americanization coexisted in the early part of the 20th century and neither garnered a great deal of notice, but this changed at the end of the 1910s. The start of the war and the rise of the Red Scare shifted thinking on immigration in America. Suddenly, Americanization seemed a matter of utmost importance, vital to national strength and integrity. At the outset of American involvement in the war, fear of disloyalty among immigrants pervaded the country. Could recent German or Slavic arrivals truly maintain their loyalty to America, to the Allies? Americans felt deeply uncertain. At the same time, the war machine fueled by the War Information Board whipped up a burning hatred for all things German, making life for German immigrants very difficult even as it gave average Americans an enemy to rally around. And then the war ended, abruptly, when patriotic fervor was at its height. Swiftly, American anger and hatred shifted from the German Hun to a new enemy: the Bolshevik. The Red Scare was about to begin.

The First Red Scare

Americans did not care too much about communism and socialism before 1919. Karl Marx and Friedrich Engels popularized the theory in the mid-1800s in reaction to the brutal working conditions fostered by the Industrial Revolution in England. Marx believed that those conditions would inevitably cause a revolution on the part of the working class, and that they would overthrow capitalism and create a world not focused on individualism, a world without private property. And the conditions of Gilded Age America drew some supporters to the tenets of socialism. Large corporations, unregulated by the federal government, exploited the work and health of men and women who had no legal right to organize unions. Bloody labor conflicts marked the 1890s, including one at the Pullman Palace Car Company outside of Chicago in 1894. Eugene V. Debs of the American Railway Union led the strike, and even though he made every effort to follow the law, he was arrested. Federal troops broke up the strike, killing 10 workers.

This was far from the first time a prominent strike ended in bloodshed, with the government sending in troops, siding with employers, but for Debs it was a transformative moment. Unions, prominent on a national level for several decades by the 1890s, failed to wrest power from the hands of employers. For Debs, the Pullman strike proved to be the final straw. While in jail he became a believer in socialism, firm in the conviction that workers would only have power when they took the reins of government. This process would be political, not violent, and Debs worked to secure this future by helping to found the Socialist Party of America in 1901. The emerging Progressive movement, one focused on reform not revolution, absorbed some of the sentiment driving the party, making some socialist tenets more palatable to average Americans. Socialist candidates ran for local and state elections with some success in the first two decades of the 20th century, with party members serving as mayors and as congressmen. Debs himself ran for president five times on the Socialist Party ticket, garnering nearly 1 million votes in the 1912 election. But after World War I, the national mood soured on socialism rather quickly.

This was due to the Russian Revolution, which stunned the world and reconfigured global politics. A wave of uprisings against an autocratic government, and the nation's involvement in World War I, led the Russian tsar to abdicate the throne in early 1917, after which a provisional government emerged led by Socialist Revolutionary Party member Alexander Kerensky. In November of that year, Vladimir Lenin's Russian Communist Party, or the Bolshevik Party as many called them, overthrew the provisional government, demanding an end to a "capitalist war" and for land to be given to peasants. After a bloody civil war, the Bolsheviks established the Communist International in 1919, calling for a worldwide proletarian revolution.

Discomfort with the potential impact of this revolution spread through the United States. Americans first disavowed the revolution when Russia pulled out of the war in 1918, abandoning the Allies on the eastern front. The war ended soon thereafter, and many frenzied citizens shifted their patriotic fervor from hatred of the German Hun to hatred of the Bolshevik. The menace of communism was on the move, so it seemed, and Western leaders looked on with horror and fear as events unfolded in Russia. Attending the Paris Peace Conference in early 1919, President Woodrow Wilson could not shake his concern over the wave of radicalism he believed was poised to threaten democracy and order around the globe. On tour later to drum up support for the League of Nations among Americans, Wilson declared Bolshevism to be "the negation of everything that is American."[10] He signed off on some rather repressive measures intended to squelch radicalism at home both during and after the war, and eventually he sent 14,000 troops to wage a secret war with the Allies against the Bolsheviks, from 1918 to 1920.

The Russian Revolution forever changed the way America and the world viewed socialism. To those opposed to radicalism, after the revolution the effort to hold it at bay seemed inherently more challenging. The *Saturday Evening Post*'s editors acknowledged in 1922 that the "maddening vision of the Russian proletarian dictatorship" egged on advocates of disorder and revolution, making the struggle to stop them "a hundred times more difficult."[11] Socialism was no longer a thing to be tolerated in America. At the same time some American progressives and radicals cheered the revolution, celebrating the fact that capitalism no longer seemed the only viable economic model. Feminist and radical journalist Louise Bryant noted the profound fear of change in America after the revolution, realizing that in its wake "it threatens to undo our present civilization."[12] Bryant herself had few qualms about that possibility, but many, many other Americans reacted with alarm.

Overall, Americans felt anxious, then, in the war's aftermath. People were jittery as a postwar recession spiked the price of food, clothing, and housing. Soldiers streamed back into cities and towns in search of work and lodging. Disappointment with the Versailles Treaty threw a shadow over the noble intentions of the war for democracy. Surging nativist sentiment bolstered calls for immigration restriction. And the Senate's refusal to join the League of Nations seriously damaged an earnest movement afoot seeking to promote internationalism and tolerance. The environment was ripe for antiradicalism to explode in America.

The first flare-up came from Seattle. The city boasted an active labor community, including many members of the Industrial Workers of the World (IWW), a revolutionary union committed to challenging the capitalist status quo and America's leading conservative unions. Workers planned a general strike there in February 1919 to demand better wages across the city's industries. Two days before the strike began, radical activist and journalist Anna Louise Strong wrote an editorial for the *Union Record*. This was a labor paper where Strong worked as an editor, and her knowledge of the strike came from her place on the General Strike Committee. She wrote, "On Thursday at 10 A.M. there will be many cheering and there will be some who fear. Both of these emotions are useful, but not too much of either. We are undertaking the most tremendous move ever made by LABOR in this country, a move which will lead—NO ONE KNOWS WHERE!"[13] Her unbridled enthusiasm and optimism at the potential of a general strike, the potential of workers acting in concert to gain higher wages, while also working to ensure the city's safety and well-being, this swelled workers' pride even as it chilled the hearts of many vested in the status quo of American capitalism.

When more than 65,000 workers stayed away from their jobs for almost a week, shutting down much of the city's industry, Seattle's Mayor Ole Hanson fashioned himself as having a date with destiny. He would make it his mission to protect that status quo. Hanson effectively linked the strike in his city with the much larger threat of communism, calling on those both in and out of Seattle to stand up with him in defense of Americanism. While the strike accomplished little that was tangible, Hanson declared it an attempted revolutionary coup and warned of the imminent arrival of Russian Bolshevism. The first American Red Scare had begun.

Americans were inclined to believe Hanson's assessment of the situation when on May 1, 1919, a terrorist made an attempt on his life. Hanson received a bomb in the mail. His assistant opened the May Day package and the device failed to detonate, but radical agitators put more than 30 other bombs through the U.S. postal system. The maid of Georgia senator Thomas Hardwick suffered injuries when a bomb delivered to his house exploded. Hardwick cosponsored the Immigration Act of 1918 allowing the government to deport "radical" immigrants. And then a postal employee in New York heard news stories about the bombs and realized he had seen similar packages in the previous few days. The parcels lacked sufficient postage, and he had placed them in a sorting office, so authorities intercepted these, which were addressed to prominent men in American capitalism and government, like J. P. Morgan, John D. Rockefeller, as well as several congressmen. Headlines in papers across America screamed of the threat of radicalism on the next day.

Another set of bombs went off a month later, solidifying the national panic. One exploded on the doorstep of the staunchly antiradical attorney general A. Mitchell Palmer, in downtown D.C. On a hot summer night, as Palmer and his wife moved toward their bedroom, they heard something hit the front door. A few seconds later the blast blew out the front of the building entirely, leaving every room visible from the outside. Both Palmers emerged unscathed, but debris covered the blast zone, as did a confetti spread of anarchist leaflets. The bloody remains of the bomber himself littered the Palmers' walkway, along with surrounding trees and rooftops. News of bombs exploding in several other cities soon spread, and while there was just one casualty, the coordinated attack desperately frightened many.[14] Authorities believed they knew the identity of the dead Washington, D.C., bomber, but no one else was found and charged with a crime. For all of these reasons, Americans plunged into a state of hysteria over the threat presented by foreign and domestic radicalism.

While the media focused attention on the threat of radicals, conservative reactionaries spilled blood on the streets too. At several May Day parades in 1919, members of the veteran's group the American Legion, along with other citizens, pummeled those marching in the name of workers' rights. The marchers were, to super patriots like the Legionnaires, antiradical and un-American. Seattle mayor Ole Hanson gave a May Day speech calling for radicals to be strung from the nearest lamppost.[15] Rather than protecting parade participants, police in cities like Boston and Cleveland helped beat them up. Outrage followed a separate incident later that year, after the brutal murder of an IWW organizer in Centralia, Washington. After a violent attack on an IWW hall during an Armistice Day rally, an angry mob seized Wesley Everest, castrated him, and hung him over the edge of a city bridge before shooting him to death. No one was charged with a crime as Everest's death was declared a suicide.[16]

As the hot summer waned, a spike in labor activism further fanned the embers of unrest. During the war many workers pledged not to strike in return for wage guarantees, but afterward, as a recession deepened and wages remained stagnant, angry workers took action. First, on September 9, over 1,000 Boston policemen, more than two-thirds of the force, walked off the job. The strikers met harsh criticism from the press and from President Wilson, who called their action a "crime against civilization." The strike fell apart two days later after Massachusetts governor Calvin Coolidge called in the National Guard. Every striker lost his job. By late September, though, all attention moved to a new strike, this time a nationwide action by steel workers. Some 365,000 workers seeking higher wages, better pay, and the right to organize left the job for several months. Meanwhile, employers purposefully played upon Red Scare fears and portrayed the strikers as dangerous radicals aiming to undermine American values. Violence and bloodshed between strikers and the National Guard glued Americans' interest to the strike until it collapsed in January 1920. Before that collapse, however, another strike exploded into the nation's consciousness. After anti-Bolshevik activity enflamed smaller, local strikes by miners, more than 350,000 members of the United Mine Workers stayed out of the mines starting on November 1, this coming after the federal government enjoined their union from striking. The *Chicago Daily Tribune* ominously noted that "war between the government and organized labor looms large tonight."[17] Bloody conflicts plagued the strikes, which continued at different mines for years afterward. By the end of 1919, labor's numbers painted a frightening picture for those vested in the status quo: there were more than 3,600 strikes that year, involving over 4 million workers.

Labor flexed its muscles in a critical moment, then, when conservatives and government leaders readily declared any labor activism a harbinger of revolution. Some American labor activists did indeed look to the

Russian Revolution as a hopeful development in world affairs. Of the revolution, writer and progressive activist Lincoln Steffens said, "I have seen the future, and it works." But the truth was that many Americans were tolerant of radicalism before the war. Prominent socialist leaders like Eugene Debs and Kate Richards O'Hare found broad popularity among progressives in the years leading up to the Red Scare. But the war signaled a shift. A swift opposition to radicals developed, and authorities imprisoned those leaders for their opposition to what they called a capitalist war. In this new climate, labor activism stood out to many conservative and fearful Americans as unequivocally Communist inspired. Elizabeth Gurley Flynn called the decade after 1917 a "hideous nightmare" in America.[18]

The Scare dismantled organized radicalism in America in the 1920s. The Socialist Party boasted robust numbers at the end of the war—with some 100,000 members. But in the midst of the Scare, they expelled tens of thousands of people due to their radicalism. These outcasts went on to form not one but two communist parties in the summer of 1919. The Communist Party and the Communist Labor Party both operated underground in their efforts to support the Bolsheviks and act as American revolutionaries. But they faced raids and mounting arrests, and their numbers dwindled.

Understandably shaken by the bomb blasts—with one literally at his doorstep—Attorney General A. Mitchell Palmer took the threat of radicalism very seriously. He felt compelled to believe the theories of a young Justice Department lawyer, J. Edgar Hoover, who argued that the nation's radical immigrants were planning to overthrow the government with the help of international communists. Hoover exhaustively researched individual immigrants and a host of radical organizations, creating an index file with more than 200,000 entries. He employed 40 translators to read through more than 600 radical publications, offering translations and reports on their contents.[19] Palmer nursed presidential ambitions for 1920, and in this perceived crisis he saw himself as a great crusader against radicalism. In public, Palmer claimed that millions of communists and their allies were actively organizing a coup in America, and he set up an appropriate defense.

Some historians argue that the government's response to the Scare did more to publicize radicalism than the radicals themselves. Senators certainly found a convenient tool to combat radicalism in the massive bureaucracy that had been set up during the war. As early as February 1919, there was an expansion of the work of a committee set up to investigate German propaganda, as the U.S. Senate Committee on Bolshevism took on the task of investigating "Bolshevism and all other forms of anti-American radicalism in the United States."[20] A similar body convened in New York State a month later. But the Scare really reached a crescendo in the winter of 1919 when Attorney General Palmer, egged on by Hoover, launched his own investigation into the bombings.

He authorized sweeping raids on the offices of radical organizations and newspapers around the country, coming down hard on suspected radicals as he cast aside concerns about civil liberties. Hoover led the investigation after federal agents and local police damaged property, assaulted people, and arrested anyone in or near a suspected radical meeting hall or office that November. More than 4,000 supposed radicals, most of whom were Slavs and Jews, ended up in jails in 33 cities, with many suffering physical abuse at the hands of the police. Shocked communities of immigrants and radicals protested the raids, but most Americans supported Mitchell's firm hand. In fact, positive public reaction to the raid pleased Palmer so much that he authorized a larger round of raids in January 1920 with similar outcomes.

When more than 450 foreign radicals departed the nation's shores on the USS *Buford* in late December 1919, deported for alleged crimes, those same Americans applauded the measure. More than half of those forced on board had been charged only with membership in the Union of Russian Workers, a social group for Russian émigrés and their allies. Many were given less than a day's notice of their impending deportation, leaving families broken with no chance for goodbyes. Fewer than 40 trunks were stowed, with most of those aboard leaving their belongings as well as more than $45,000 behind them in America. Conditions on the boat horrified passengers, many of whom took ill. Only on the 20th day of the voyage was the final destination revealed: Soviet Russia. The passenger list included famous Lithuanian-born anarchist and women's rights activist Emma Goldman.[21]

The repression fueled by the Scare expanded in these years, beyond the reach of just the federal government. The Bureau of Investigation, still in its infancy, could not effectively watch over the nation's internal enemies on its own, and so it relied on the vigilance of numerous patriotic organizations. Groups such as the National Security League, the American Defense Society, and the Daughters of the American Revolution joined with a host of other voluntary organizations in their efforts to counter subversive activities during and after the war. Boasting elite backers like J. P. Morgan and John D. Rockefeller, these groups publicly attacked individuals they identified as radicals, they published patriotic propaganda, and they actively engaged in Americanization efforts for both immigrants and unruly Americans. These often wealthy, elite Americans battled against radicalism because they were deeply invested in the old order. Fearful of Bolshevism and the spirit of unrest it threatened to unleash around the world, these citizens joined government actors in fighting antiradicalism in the first American Red Scare.

As the decade progressed, the Red Scare eased but did not disappear. It stalked many groups in America for the duration of the 1920s. Another bomb blast on Wall Street in September 1920 killed almost 40 people, yet it failed to provoke the same kind of hysteria, demonstrating a real shift in public mood. At the same time Palmer's celebrated raids failed to turn up more than a few guns, and authorities found no explosives. No arrests were made in the 1919 wave of summer bombings, and officials failed to unearth any evidence of a vast radical conspiracy. The overt government repression animating the Scare in 1919 and 1920 began to peter out by 1921. But radical groups withered in this hostile environment. And a deep and abiding antiradicalism, an aversion to modernism and feminism, and a lasting nativism endured as fundamental elements of the coalescing culture war. But U.S. officials handled the immigrant "problem" more directly.

Immigration Restriction

The sheer number of recent immigrants and the shock of the Scare left many white, Anglo-Saxon, Protestant Americans feeling as though their country was in peril. Rhetoric in the halls of Congress, in the press, and in popular culture associated radicalism with foreignness. Political cartoons depicted immigrants as wild haired and crazy-eyed men holding bombs with lit fuses behind their backs. And antiradicals used immigrants as scapegoats for all of the nation's ills. In this moment, antiradicalism and nativism reframed the national conversation on immigration in America.

Amid the crisis mentality of the Red Scare, coercive efforts to Americanize immigrants garnered a great deal of support. Business interests, government officials, and self-interested civilian organizations articulated their belief that a cohesive Americanism would fight off the threatening spirit of Bolshevism. Initially, this impulse materialized in a wave of federally sponsored legislation aiming to teach immigrants English as well as citizenship skills. Learning the language and acquiring naturalization papers could accelerate assimilation, some believed. When a post–World War I recession took the financial wind out of the sails of these bills, state governments stepped into the void. But these programs, including requiring all teachers to be citizens and requiring all children to be educated in public schools, lost steam too. Once the initial jolt of the Scare passed, politicians and patriotic groups advocating for these repressive measures had trouble financing them.[22] But the interest of average Americans in the "problem" of immigration remained.

The sense of crisis allowed nativists and antiradicals to move the political discourse beyond just Americanization toward outright restriction. Discussion of restricting immigration stretched back 20 years before World War I, but by the 1920s the conversation was different. Undoubtedly, nativism was a persistent feature of American life since the early 1800s. As the nation made the transition from an agrarian society to an industrial one, as the economy cycled from stability to crisis and back again, nativism appeared and disappeared accordingly. American political culture absorbed or rejected immigrants based on this economic and political context. By the 1920s nativism truly exploded, leading to real conversations about restricting the number and type of immigrants to America.[23]

People favoring restriction sounded the alarm when they warned that Europe's war-ravaged poor were about to beat down the nation's gates. With the economy in steep recession in 1920 and 1921, restrictionists argued that those fleeing the destruction of the war had no real purpose in the United States. They were not needed for jobs, the argument went, so why should they be allowed to enter? In a moment of economic instability, the scare tactics proved effective. Congress passed a measure suspending immigration, appropriately calling it the Emergency Immigration Act. The Senate and the House went back and forth over just whom to restrict, and how many. Ultimately, the final decision by a joint committee limited immigration to 3 percent of the number of immigrants of each nationality present in the 1910 census. This measure heavily favored older immigrants, the Irish, British, and German groups. While America would accept over 67,000 immigrants from Germany, only slightly more than 30,000 were allowed from Poland. Of the total 357,000 spots provided by the bill roughly 200,000 were offered to older immigrant groups. Wilson, a Democrat with ties to urban demographics, would not sign the measure, but newly elected president Harding did so in 1921. The bill at first restricted immigration for one year, but both houses of Congress agreed to extend it in 1922 for two more years.[24]

Some imagined this "emergency" measure to be temporary, but circumstances foreclosed that possibility. More and more Americans began rejecting the notion of the melting pot, and instead they saw the United States as a dumping ground for Europe's refuse. Gaining interest in eugenics greatly bolstered this view. Intellectuals like Madison Grant, in his book *The Passing of the Great Race*, and Lothrop Stoddard, in *The Rising Tide of Color against White World-Supremacy*, captured the willing imagination of a wide audience in the 1920s who believed that inherent racial inequalities marked the poor masses streaming in from southern and eastern Europe. As inferior immigrant stock reproduced itself on American shores, eugenicists argued, this fundamentally weaker, less intelligent, criminal class would outnumber native, white, Protestants of the Nordic race. A declining birth rate among white native-born women amplified this fear significantly. Stoddard implored Americans to understand, "If America is not true to her own race-soul, she will inevitably lose it, and the brightest star that has appeared since Hellas [ancient Greece] will fall like a meteor from the human sky, its brilliant radiance fading into the night."[25]

The emotional weight behind nativism by the mid-1920s and the popularity of eugenics matters here because average Americans were becoming less and less tolerant of immigrants. After the arrival of millions and millions of newcomers, here, in this moment of the 1920s, anti-immigrant sentiment tipped the scales in the debate over immigration in America and permanently changed the country's future. Here lay a key part of the foundation of the 20th-century culture wars. In the "us versus them" conjured by this culture war, nativist America was winning.

Truthfully, few in the country worked to block immigration restriction once interest in it swelled. Employers, on the whole, got over their initial resistance to the emergency bill when they came to believe that mechanized labor could replace the working factory hands they would otherwise miss. The American Federation of Labor advocated for restriction, hoping to protect the jobs and wages of native-born workers. Existing anti-Semitism reinforced the impulse to stop immigration. African Americans found themselves competing with immigrants for jobs as they themselves migrated north, and they too supported restriction. An administrator at Howard University urged U.S. Steel chairman Elbert Garry to hire African Americans rather than immigrants, highlighting their native birth, their loyalty, and their lack of association with Bolshevism. Some religious and ethnic groups, like Jews, Armenians, and the Irish, pushed back against anti-immigrant bias. But for mostly self-centered reasons, few people with influence cared or dared to raise their voices against the moving train of immigration restriction by the mid-1920s.[26] Conservative union leaders and old Anglo-Saxon elites who had long called for restriction now, suddenly, found themselves in good company.

Administrative problems with the practical workings of the 1921 emergency bill led congressmen to draft an entirely new bill to replace it, and nativists found a clever way to achieve their desired goal of cutting off the supply of "new" immigrants. Representative Albert Johnson—an admirer of Madison Grant, along with his fellow committee members on the House Immigration Committee, developed a new equation to use in the bill with the help of restrictionist experts. By using the 1910 or 1920 census numbers to determine the quotas available to each nation, experts argued, the bill would be too accommodating to new immigrants, the more recent arrivals. Instead, if they utilized the 1890 census data on the nation's foreign-born population, the bill would favor British, Scandinavian, and German immigrants. This method would cut Italy's allowable annual immigration numbers from 42,057, based on the more recent census, to 3,912. It would only move Germany's number from 67,607 to 51,299. These were numbers restrictionists could feel good about.

The House bill entirely omitted nonwhite immigrants through a citizenship provision, a measure targeting the Japanese in particular. The 1870 immigration law declared only white individuals, as well as those of African descent, suitable for citizenship. The new 1920s bill then moved to exclude all immigrants ineligible for citizenship in the United States. Fervent anti-Japanese sentiment earlier in the century, especially in the West, led to previous agreements between the two nations, limiting the number of Japanese making the journey. But those formulating the new bill went further, relying on U.S. naturalization law that categorized Japanese individuals as nonwhite. Thus, under the immigration law being formulated, if Japanese were unable to apply for citizenship, they—along with Koreans—could now be excluded from entering entirely.[27]

When the bill went before the House, congressmen engaged in little real debate over its passage. They failed to conceal the desire to privilege older immigrant groups and used harsh and ugly language to describe those "mongrelized" immigrants considered unworthy.[28] Political cartoons echoed their sentiments, announcing the nation's refusal to continue as the world's garbage can. Representative Johnson put it more kindly in the *Outlook*, claiming "that the countries of the world shall no longer dump upon the United States their criminals, their feeble, their aged, and their undesirables."[29] Some representatives from more urban districts—more likely to include these undesirables—did condemn the bill in the House, most notably including Representative Fiorello La Guardia from Italian East Harlem in New York City. But their opposition went largely ignored.

Congress made one more significant change to the bill before its seemingly inevitable passage. When the measure moved to the Senate, concerns about just how discriminatory it seemed bubbled to the surface. Most legislators still planned to largely exclude the new immigrants, but they hoped to be slightly less transparent about it. Pennsylvania senator David A. Reed offered a plan to survey the national origins of the population in 1920 and to use those numbers rather than the 1890 census. When the Senate passed the bill it allowed for the 1890 numbers to be used for several years, until the government finished the survey. When implemented in full it would limit immigration to a total of 150,000 per year and would use the 1920s numbers for the white population of the nation. Calvin Coolidge signed the bill into law when it crossed his desk in May 1924.[30]

The buildup to the Johnson Reed Act took many years and the work of countless individuals and organizations, but its passage in the 1920s represents a watershed in America's history. The nation of immigrants, who for many years believed in their ability to digest and assimilate more and more newcomers, faltered in that belief, claiming what one congressman called "acute indigestion." Rather than the lifeblood of the nation, a stream of endless opportunity, now immigrants represented a threat, a danger. The bill passed with surprisingly little fanfare in the media, perhaps because the nativist tenor of the day made the outcome entirely unremarkable. Those immigrants maligned by the law protested but to little avail. And this development reshaped the nation in the coming decades. Here was the concrete manifestation of the culture wars in 1920s America, spelled out in law.

"Healthy" patriotism by the mid-1920s incorporated support for immigration restriction. But, while the Johnson Reed Act seemed to settle the problem of new immigration, an insistent Americanization campaign continued to hound immigrants already in the country, and their children, in the years that followed. And antiradicals in ongoing Red Scare efforts continued to mark immigrants in the country as particularly dangerous. This blend of antiradicalism and nativism sealed the fate of the Red Scare's most famous victims: Sacco and Vanzetti.

Sacco and Vanzetti

"Sacco and Vanzetti are Italian immigrants, labor unionists, 'red' socialists and war slackers," wrote the editors of the *Albuquerque Morning Journal* in 1922, making the prominent facts in the case plain. They continued, however, "The *Journal* disagrees with about every political view which Sacco and Vanzetti entertain. But that hardly constitutes a reason for our desiring to convict them of murder."[31] The swirling anxieties and fears surrounding immigration, crime, and radicalism collided in April 1920 when two men murdered a guard and a payroll clerk at the Slater and Merrill Shoe Company in Braintree, Massachusetts. The men got away with payroll money, some $15,776 in cash. Witnesses claimed the perpetrators shot both men, took the cash, and then pumped more bullets into the suffering bodies of Alessandro Berardelli and Frederick Parmenter. The case that followed tormented many, as people realized for better or worse that the culture war framing American life—what the *Journal* called "our social order"—loomed over the trial of these two Italian immigrants. "Democracy is on trial in this case," the editors warned Americans, "for hundreds of thousands of foreigners, radicals, and political students are watching to see whether democracy can control its prejudices."[32]

The heinous murder came as police were already investigating a different robbery in nearby Bridgewater several days earlier, and investigators quickly determined, without evidence, that the culprits in both crimes were likely Italian anarchists. Soon after the Braintree murder, police picked up two Italian immigrants, Bartolomeo Vanzetti and Nicola Sacco. Both carried a pistol and ammunition when arrested, along with anarchist literature, and both had ties to the anarchist movement in America.[33] Here, police found the perfect suspects. Despite little evidence, and no prior criminal history for either man, despite both men's insistence on their innocence, the lead investigator charged them with the Braintree murder.[34] Vanzetti was shocked to learn that he was also then charged with the Bridgewater robbery, a charge Sacco was spared as he had evidence he was at work on the day the crime was committed.

Probably the most important element in the case was that in addition to being Italian, the most hated immigrant group in 1920, both men belonged to a militant anarchist group headed by Italian anarchist Luigi Galleani. Both men arrived in 1908, and upon their arrival they found all the ugliness and inequality of early 20th-century industrial, urban America. And they were in the process of organizing a protest against Palmer's heavy-handed antiradical tactics. While no one is certain, still, who planned the bombings in the spring and summer of 1919, or the blast on Wall Street in 1920, many historians believe Gallianisti anarchists were the culprits. So these two men did have close ties to violent, radical groups in the nation at the time. But, at the same time, there is no evidence that Sacco or Vanzetti had a direct part in those bombings, and the evidence of their involvement in the robbery and murder was also very unclear.[35]

Recognizing the injustice born of this cultural moment radicals and allies organized in their defense, forming the Sacco-Vanzetti Defense Committee in Boston. With the help of Elizabeth Gurley Flynn, defenders hired a prominent labor journalist to write a pamphlet titled "Are They Doomed?," directly connecting the men's arrest to the nationwide attack on labor and radicalism in 1920. Art Shields, a labor reporter, authored the pamphlet, and he stated the problem outright: "Three factors weigh heavily against Sacco and Vanzetti. 1. They are Italian. 2. They were thinking workers, active in the New England labor movement for years. 3. They opposed the vicious and brutal methods of the Department of Justice against their comrades."[36] Their arrest stemmed from forces well beyond the circumstances of the Braintree murders, and those rallying in their defense provoked fear and outrage in their readers, declaring at the pamphlet's end, "This thing may happen to *you!*"[37] The pamphlet traveled throughout the country, spreading news about the case and spurring an outpouring of fund-raising for the defense.[38]

Unsurprisingly, perhaps, when the case came to trial, the court judged the two men on their nationality and political beliefs, not on the evidence against them. The trial for the South Braintree crime began at the end of May in 1921 and lasted seven weeks. Forty-four individuals claimed to have seen Vanzetti elsewhere on the day of the murders, and defense witnesses testified that Sacco was nowhere near the crime on the day it took place. More than 30 witnesses claimed to have spoken to or purchased fish from Vanzetti on the day of the Bridgewater robbery. And several eyewitnesses gave threadbare testimony identifying Sacco and Vanzetti at the scene of the Braintree murder. Both sides cast doubt on the facts in the case. Many feasible alternative theories and alternative suspects were brought forth in the courtroom, but none were investigated. Most of those testifying in Sacco and Vanzetti's defense were themselves Italians, and therefore their words carried little currency. The defendants' own struggle with English as a second language marked them as slow or stupid in the eyes of native-born Americans. And maybe, most important, the two men bore the weight of Americans' deep resentment against them. The way nativists drew the narrative, here were two men kindly allowed entry into America who turned around once they arrived and engaged in violent rebellion against their new nation.

In truth, many openly felt that as anarchists, as Italians, whether Sacco and Vanzetti committed the crimes was somewhat irrelevant. They were guilty of crimes against America, even if not this particular crime. And they should pay. Webster Thayer, the judge in the case, referred to the men as "anarchist bastards." The press called them worse names. And Sacco and Vanzetti knew this all too well. Italians in America, let alone radical Italians, were accustomed to this kind of reaction. The judge made note of their evasive behavior upon arrest, pointing to that behavior as an indicator of guilt. But here were two Italians, two labor radicals, in nativist Red Scare America, arrested while in possession of a weapon. Even if they knew nothing of the Braintree murders, they had every reason to be evasive, to be afraid that they would be considered guilty of whatever crime they were being arrested for regardless of the truth. And it took the jury just six hours to convict both men of murder on July 21, 1921. Both Sacco and Vanzetti were sentenced to death.[39]

While historians still debate their guilt or innocence, many Americans and people around the world felt a profound injustice at Sacco and Vanzetti's conviction. And they mobilized with greater urgency than before. Literary luminaries like Upton Sinclair and Edna St. Vincent Millay protested in the streets. Hundreds of thousands of people signed petitions. Streets and coffee shops were renamed in their honor throughout the world. Even Felix Frankfurter, noted Harvard law professor and future Supreme Court justice, attacked the case on legal grounds. The uproar spread all over the globe, with rallies and even bomb blasts in cities such as Paris, Rio de Janeiro, and Zurich.[40]

Despite repeated appeals, defense attorneys could not get their case reopened and the two men's fates were sealed. In 1925, an inmate on death row in the same prison confessed that he murdered the men in Braintree. He happened to look very much like Nicola Sacco. But even this failed to persuade the courts.[41] In frustration after this revelation came to light, Frankfurter wrote in the *Atlantic Monthly*, "Every reasonable probability points away from Sacco and Vanzetti," but it made no difference.[42] Ultimately, whether each man was guilty or not, after eight different appeals, including one that made it all the way to the Supreme Court, the death sentences were final.

The two men made eloquent statements attesting to their innocence in court, stating their belief in their own status as scapegoats in nativist and antiradical America. Sacco, who had less of a command of English than Vanzetti, said "I know the sentence will be between two class, the oppressed class and the rich class, and there will always be collision between one and the other. . . . That is why I am here today on this bench, for having been the oppressed class." Vanzetti, a more fluent English speaker, indicted America for being swept up in the Red Scare, and he laid out his circumstances as he saw them quite plainly. He did not commit the crimes he was convicted of, he said, "but I have suffered for things I am guilty of. I am suffering because I am a radical and indeed I am a radical; I have suffered because I was an Italian, and indeed I am an Italian . . . but I am so convinced to be right that if you could execute me two times, and I could be reborn two other times, I would live again to do what I have done already." They knew they were victims of the culture war, the virulent nativism and the hard-line antiradicalism interlaced in the fabric of American society in the 1920s. First Sacco and then Vanzetti died in the electric chair in Charlestown Prison in Massachusetts in August 1927. Nicola Sacco's last statement before being electrocuted included loving words for his wife and children in English, and in Italian, a cry of "Long live anarchy." Bartolomeo Vanzetti's last words were more somber, and generous. He said, "I am an innocent man. I wish to forgive some people for what they are now doing to me."[43]

The case touched so many, and its reverberations have echoed out through time. The two men's bodies were brought through the streets of Boston on the way to the funeral parlor, thronged by crowds of mourners. Vigils took place around the nation. People rioted at American embassies around the world as the word spread. Their case spawned novels and songs and plays. And more than a few histories, as researchers have worked for decades trying to determine the men's guilt or innocence. Determinations on that matter have shifted back and forth over time, but none have disputed that the trial itself was fundamentally unjust. And the trial served as a symbol of the ugliness of American repression and intolerance for generations to come. It marked the decade where America closed its hearts and its gates to the world's huddled masses, the needy, and the oppressed. But there might be one more notorious example of nativism in the 1920s.

THE ARMY OF THE CULTURE WARS

In the midst of a winter night, a glaring red cross, electrically lit, floated above the water on the Delaware River. Wearing long white robes as they rowed their boats, Ku Klux Klan members from Mercer County, New Jersey, and Bucks County, Pennsylvania, reenacted George Washington's historic crossing in celebration of the founding father's birthday. Hundreds of Klansmen lined a nearby bridge and the shoreline of both sides of the river, carrying torches in a dizzying display of light and power.[44] For some in America in 1925, this passed for patriotism as its best. A few months later, more than 50,000 Klansmen donned their robes and proudly walked down the streets of the nation's capitol, hoods removed. With men marching shoulder to shoulder, 18 or 20 abreast, the parade went on for hours with the dome of the nation's capitol towering in the distance.⁴⁵ This second Klan, which emerged in the 1920s, was repressive, violent, and motivated by racial interests, but it was also nostalgic, nativist, antiradical, and antimodern. Here was the army of the culture wars.

The frustration, fear, and hatred among Klan members in the 1920s drew from a much broader base than their original post-Civil War brethren. The Klansmen of the 1860s and 1870s lashed out against what they saw as the tyranny of equal rights for white and black Americans, ultimately inflicting a devastating blow to the effectiveness of the Fifteenth Amendment. While the Democratic Party worked to eradicate Republican power in the South, the Ku Klux Klan and other groups waged a campaign of violence, making politics deadly for white and black Republican leaders and would-be voters. Successful, ultimately, in their efforts, with Democratic victories in states across the South, Klan activity diminished. Legislation outlawing Klan violence, and, more important, the reimposition of white supremacy, led the Klan to fade away. In 1915, however, D. W. Griffith's film *Birth of a Nation*, based on the 1905 book *The Clansmen* by Thomas Dixon, revived interest in the Klan. The film depicted Reconstruction as a travesty of justice, a repressive racial tyranny of black over white imposed on undeserving southerners by savage blacks and colluding northern whites. This misrepresentation of Reconstruction in the South aligned with popular historical memory of the post–Civil War era in the early 20th century. And this provoked admiration for and, ultimately, imitation of the old Klan.

The tensions creating the culture war in America allowed Griffith's film to birth a revived Ku Klux Klan. The group still challenged black economic and political power, but its members cared as much, if not more, about the increasingly pluralistic nature of American society, about the surge in Catholicism in the nation, and about seemingly loosening moral standards.⁴⁶ The Klan called itself a defender of real "Americanism," 100 percent Americanism, in a moment of rapid and unsettling upheaval in American life. More than any other group in the 1920s, then, the resurgent Ku Klux Klan acted as an army dedicated to winning "their" side of the emerging culture wars.

The new Klan obsessed over law and order, a phrase pregnant with meaning at the time. To them the acute need to strengthen law and order stemmed from a bevy of dangers: fears of criminality among unassimilated immigrants, concerns about prostitution, the rise of women's rights, radicalism, illegal alcohol use, and political corruption. Anxieties about these issues reinforced their overriding concern in the 1920s: native, Protestant, Anglo-Saxon American men like themselves seemed to be losing their grip on power and influence at the local and national levels. The social hierarchy they benefited from for generations rocked with uncertainty as the winds of modernism shook its very foundations. The Klan offered these individuals a place, membership in a militant organization, one committed to championing the needs and concerns of a group used to a position at the top.

The Second Ku Klux Klan

The organization first reemerged in 1915 with a gathering of 16 men who lit a cross on fire on Stone Mountain in Georgia. Col. William Simmons organized this fraternal order in the image of the old organization, this time utilizing sophisticated recruiting tactics and elaborate initiation rites in order to maximize profits in dues and fees. He found success. After a series of exposés in the press and in Congress, the Klan only grew larger, benefiting from the broad publicity by the early 1920s. Historians cannot know the true number of men in the second Klan, as membership rosters were kept secret, but estimates are that the group had more than 5 million members at its peak in the mid-1920s, far more than the original Klan.

A sense of moral superiority and a kind of status anxiety drew men to the second Klan in such high numbers. Those enamored with the message and the spectacle of the group reflected Middle America in many ways. To start, these Klansmen were almost always white. They often had a history of supporting efforts to police immorality or lack of religion in others, including a great deal of crossover in membership with the Anti-Saloon League. Klansmen rarely drew members from the upper class, or from the ranks of farmers and industrial workers, though some did join up. Most worked in shops, owned small businesses, practiced as lawyers, preached as ministers. They came from fraternal orders. They felt above immigrants and African Americans, and resented elites. The changing nature of the country, including the changing population, sexual modernism, scientific advances, and the increasing corporatization of the economy, fueled their anger and anxiety.[47]

Geographically, they hailed most frequently from the Midwest, and often lived there or in the southern states. The national headquarters was in Atlanta, and an uneven smattering of Klan centers of activity developed across the country, with the greatest concentration found in overwhelming Protestant areas. Ohio saw a great deal of Klansmen, along with Texas, Oklahoma, Arkansas, Kansas, Colorado, California, Montana, Oregon, and Indiana.[48] In Indiana, the Klan grew larger than any other similar organization in the state.[49] Though historians once believed Klan activity to be limited to rural America, as a protest against urbanization, evidence has proven this to be false. The Klan made significant gains in the nation's largest cities, including Chicago, Los Angeles, and Atlanta. And Klan activity typically flourished in larger towns, despite prominent groups in both rural and urban areas.[50] The group boasted over 24 newspapers by the middle of 1923, and each carried articles featuring local coverage as well as syndicated articles on events of national concern. This tactic allowed the organization as a whole to both curry local favor and provide some sense of unity across vast distances.[51]

While the original Klan focused almost exclusively on suffocating black freedom, even in the most southern states the new Klan rarely focused their anger or their violence specifically on African Americans. Though, this did happen occasionally. More generally, the group targeted prohibition scofflaws, men who beat their wives, purportedly loose women, Catholics, immigrants, and abortion practitioners. This was a morally robust movement for national purity, one that incorporated a host of issues then fueling the nation's culture wars.[52] When the Klan arrived in "Middletown," Robert and Helen Lynd noted the powerful use of both patriotism and religion in that moment, pointing to the flurry of activity that came in the group's wake. Keen observers that they were, in making sense of the town's embrace of the group, the Lynds recognized the feelings of alienation and powerlessness among the residents of Muncie, Indiana. The support for the Klan, they wrote, "afforded an outlet for many of the constant frustrations of life, economic tensions and social insecurity, by providing a wealth of scapegoats against whom wrath might be vented."[53]

The economic troubles and social chaos of the postwar years really boosted the Klan's rise nationwide, which was meteoric after 1920. Willing recruits streamed in after a few years of slow growth. This was also due to a concerted marketing effort by the group's leaders. The mix of patriotism, antiradicalism, nativism, isolationism, and antimodernism proved potent and compelling. Foregrounding the phrase "100% Americanism," the group's efforts bore fruit in Red Scare America. Condemnation of the Klan's activities by the *New York World* sparked a congressional investigation in 1921, but that served mostly to provide free publicity. The movement continued to grow, especially after a change in leadership when power struggles and alleged improprieties led Hiram Wesley Evans to take over the group in 1922. The dentist from Texas made an important move when he purposefully cloaked the group in the politics of respectability. Given their focus on wholesome American values, coupled

Who Belongs in the Nativist 1920s?

with white Protestantism, the push for respectability was a necessary development to the group's success.[54]

The Klan used the power of association and spectacle to reach and recruit members in new areas. Once a group of sympathetic members got together in a city or town, they typically burned a large cross in an open space, allowing word of their presence to spread. Then they would visit local Protestant churches to announce themselves, usually with the blessing of the minister, gathering new recruits along the way. To foster goodwill in a new place, Klansmen donated food, money, and supplies to local charities, schools, and hospitals. They both drew more interest and threw their own weight around by hosting very public parades through town centers, sometimes with music and floats. Crowds thrilled at the break from the monotony of everyday life. And once a large enough group of men appeared eager to join, the Klan put on a dramatic initiation ceremony in the dark of night. Men took an oath in front of their peers, using symbols like the flag and the Bible, affirming their wish to support the self-professed "Protestant American giant."[55] In areas with a lot of Klan activity, members were open about their association, using signs in store windows to encourage the spending of money at Klan-owned shops and boycotting those who went against Klan values.

Each local Klan group framed its efforts in part with its own local needs and prejudices. Whether a certain immigrant group clustered in their area, or city officials engaged in corrupt practices, local recruiters gathered followers by highlighting these issues. One of the most notable things about the 1920s Klan was their deep interest in affecting change through politics, and this was filtered through local lenses too. Klan members ran or backed candidates at the local and state levels and succeeded by winning more than five Senate races and as many gubernatorial races.[56] The organization wielded considerable power in states like Indiana and Colorado. The main thrust of their political efforts centered on education, or the broader issue of law and order. But these victories were short lived. In the end, Klan politicians alienated many and their efforts fell flat, or were deemed unconstitutional.[57]

But regardless of how exactly they wielded power, and regardless of location, all members of the second Ku Klux Klan cared deeply about several things in common. They were staunchly anti-Catholic. Anti-Catholicism appeared in America long before the 1920s, but it resurfaced with a vengeance in the wake of the Klan's rise. They demonized the pope and called the loyalty and patriotism of American Catholics into question. How could these people hold fealty to the American government and at the same time take higher orders from the man in Rome?

That the man in Rome was also an Italian only served to heighten Protestant disgust, given the strength of anti-Italian sentiment in that moment. The Klan harbored deep suspicion for the Knights of Columbus, a fraternal organization of Catholic members named for Italian Christopher Columbus. Klan members spread rumors that the K of C mustered a secret Catholic militia, one that would try to take over the country. They also demonized Catholics for their perceived backwardness, and their propensity to educate their children in Catholic schools. Klansmen believed the threat presented by Catholicism was real and present in the 1920s.[58] And while they also trafficked in anti-Semitism, it took up much less of their attention.

Klan antagonism to Catholics also played into their anger over the breaking of prohibition laws, a crime they deeply detested. With roots as a vigilante organization, the 1920s Klan easily justified using its own muscle to beef up the offense in the war on alcohol. Enforcing the law gave the Klan more robust reasons to attack immigrant groups, both Catholics and Jews, who in many places made up a significant portion of the nation's lower-class scofflaws. Corruption among city officials and police enforcers, a well-known and pervasive problem in the country, only buoyed the Klan's sense of purpose and self-importance. Truthfully, in many cases, their efforts to threaten bootleggers and clean up vice districts found favor with equally frustrated local officials.[59]

Another issue embraced by the Klan was nativism, and this proved particularly potent once Hiram Evans led the national organization in 1922. The Klan stood behind notable beliefs about scientific racism, ideas supported by writers like Lathrop Stoddard, marking immigrants off as undesirable and unfit "others" who would weaken the nation and dilute America's racial stock. Never ones to shy away from stating their true intentions, Klan leader Hiram Evans spelled out his organization's nativist priorities in the *North American Review* in 1926, using the slogan "Native, white, Protestant supremacy." He cloaked this call in the robes of patriotism, claiming the need to maintain "America for Americans." This America needed to remain pure, which meant the "pioneer stock" had to be upheld against the forces of "mongrelization." The mixing of races in the early years of the republic, between the English, German, and Irish, for example, strengthened the nation's stock, he claimed. Other kinds of "interbreeding" between groups not closely related—not Anglo-Saxon—weakened the nation's stock. This racial understanding of humanity and citizenship colored their view of the possibilities inherent in newcomers to America in the postwar years. However loyal a man might be to America, however good his intentions, in Evans's view, without "racial integrity" stemming from links to the Anglo-Saxon world, it was impossible for him to be a good American.[60]

Protestantism was also essential to the fabric of the American nation, according to Evans, and the Klan would defend its position. Klansmen saw the very founding of the nation in the colonial era as an act borne of the need to escape from the control of Catholic Rome. But Protestantism meant more than religion. Evans argued it was "the expression in religion of the same spirit of independence, self-reliance, and freedom which are the highest achievements of the Nordic race."[61] To Klansmen, religion embodied both their patriotism and their racial beliefs, tying the three priorities together.

The group's very prominent call for 100% Americanism was an effort to blunt the social, economic, and political impact of "others," anyone who was not white, native born, Protestant, and Anglo-Saxon. But some Klan chapters used the framework of nativism—playing on ethnic prejudice—to meet other ends. For example, the Klan in Oakland, California, fanned the flames of ethnic division in an effort to stamp out government corruption and pursue better city services. Their desired goals did not necessarily stem from a defensive white nativism, but they used the nativist narrative available to them.[62]

But at heart the revitalized Klan still cared about maintaining white supremacy, and they still targeted black Americans. The "new negro" movement was not lost on them—in fact, it was impossible to miss. White southerners reported a new attitude among their black neighbors, along with increased spending power thanks to higher wages during the war. Fancier clothes and automobiles seemed to many white southerners, who gripped their fragile sense of racial superiority with both hands, like power. Returning black war veterans served as a troubling and undeniable symbol of claims for black freedom. And these advances bled into the political realm.

W.E.B. Du Bois scoffed at the revived Klan in 1919, asserting his own firm belief in the power of the "new Negro." The new Klan, he wrote, "will fail to terrify men who have trained at camp, who have stood sentinel in the French forests, who have met and battled with a magnificently trained and relentless foe. . . . It is a new Negro who inhabits the South today, especially it is a new Negro youth—a youth that will not be cowed by silly superstition or fear."[63] Some African Americans in Atlanta, Georgia, went so far as to circulate a letter condemning the violence they routinely endured, demanding their rights as citizens, including the often-denied right to vote. The number of southern NAACP chapters exploded, from just 6 in 1916 to 155 by 1919. The energy and determination of black

Americans after the war, in both the South and the North, reverberated through communities of concerned white men.[64]

In response, white southerners and those in the West and North feeling the impact of the Great Migration pushed back hard on the rising aspirations of black America, most notably here through membership in the Ku Klux Klan. They helped to uphold Jim Crow laws in the South, threatening and engaging in violence to keep black southerners from the polls, and to enforce segregation.[65] In northern cities, the Klan provided the strategy and the muscle for broader social and political efforts to keep African Americans from buying homes in white neighborhoods and to stifle their growing political power.[66]

The group also engaged in physical violence and intimidation with some frequency. They had not left that part of the legacy of the first Klan behind. In just the early months of 1921, the following incidents reveal both their menace and their mission. In Bay City, Texas, a banker who cheated on his wife suffered a beating and was then tarred and feathered. In Enid, Oklahoma, the operator of a movie theater was whipped and then covered in oil and cotton. And in Dallas, Texas, a black boy who was believed to have associated with white women was whipped and had KKK seared into his forehead with acid. A Klan march in Dallas, Texas, proceeded with no interference from authorities, featuring a burning cross and large banners that read, "White Supremacy," "Pure Womanhood," "Our Little Girls Must Be Protected," "All Native Born," and "The Guilty Must Pay." Their signage and their choice of targets demonstrate the broad nature of their agenda.[67]

That broad agenda included antimodernism, which appeared in efforts to curb the impact of new forms of mass culture. By 1920, they began protesting against a long list of movies, plays, and radio programs for negative portrayals of Protestantism, lampooning Prohibition, featuring interracial mixing, and celebration of loose morals.[68] The Klan homed in on the 1923 film *Bella Donna*, famous "femme fatale" actress Pola Negri's first Hollywood movie. They opposed it for several reasons, one of which was its "low ideals of womanhood" reflected in portrayals of "cigarette-smoking devils." Furthermore, by featuring intimacy between a white actress and an "Egyptian Negro," the film seemed to the Klan paper *Fiery Cross*, "open propaganda for social equality" and "a disgrace to the white race."[69] With criticisms like this, the Klan acted as a real social force, getting films banned locally and forcing cinemas to close on Sundays. The motion picture industry acknowledged their influence as the group shrewdly tapped into larger debates taking place about the dangers of consumer culture. The Klan exerted their sense of superiority and their

Protestantism in the public arena by capturing a shared and growing interest in protecting the nation's morals.

Along the same lines, young people, and young women specifically, also came in for their share of the Ku Klux Klan's wrath. The revolution in manners and morals among the nation's white, middle-class youth deeply troubled these keepers of the flame of the old order, who condemned necking and petting in their towns. Flappers epitomized all that was wrong with America in the 1920s, according to the Klan, as they demonstrated a love for pleasure and a lack of restraint. They disregarded the trappings of voluminous Victorian attire and hitched up their skirts. The popular press's focus on these young women, as well as on the increasingly public nature of sexuality in America, fueled the Klan's outrage. Rising numbers of young women pressed for, and won, entry in more of the nation's colleges and universities. At the University of Georgia, the fact that a mere handful of these coeds smoked in public caused a ruckus.[70] Klansmen spoke out against just this type of behavior, because women who challenged gender and sex norms might not live up to the roles laid out for them as wives and mothers of Anglo-Saxon families.[71] The Klan's focus on "pure womanhood" policed sexual norms at the local level and in the larger culture.

Klan members' unease with the impact of modern culture gave rise to a curious side group of family members, women who wanted in and were given the next best thing to a real initiation. The Women of the Ku Klux Klan (WKKK) emerged in 1923, building on the motives and goals of the Klan in a uniquely gendered way. They mimicked the pomp and circumstance of the male-only Klan, along with their hierarchy and sense of urgency. But the women's group focused their energy on more traditionally "womanly" pursuits, seeking more narrowly to protect family, women and children, and the home from the nefarious influences of modernism, immigration, Catholicism, Jews, and African Americans.[72]

The symbolic "pure womanhood" provided them with a tightly scripted gender norm for women, one that was racially coded. A Klan advertisement written in 1923 called out to other women who cared about not only the "welfare of our Nation" but also "the sanctity of the American Home," "American teachers," and the "UNDERMINING OF THE MORALS OF OUR YOUTH."[73] While they did not mention white supremacy or nativism outright, the use of the word "American" signaled to readers that the WKKK believed their native-born, white families, headed by an "American Mother," were entitled to the benefits of a native-born, white society. This included a morally upright environment for their children, something many in America believed was not possible in the midst of immigrants and African Americans.

For years, white middle-class American women ventured beyond their own parlors to fight for the home and hearth, and this instance may not seem remarkable on that front, except that it was. Ironically, the WKKK's very existence capitalized on the new woman, which is significant here because this was a figure most Klansmen viewed with ambivalence if not outright suspicion. The Klan women entered the political fray in an effort to claim their newly acquired rights as voting citizens. Appeals referred to potential female recruits specifically in their capacity as "enfranchised women."[74] They claimed their right to exist autonomously from the original male Klan, asserting themselves as actors in a political culture. And yet they saw their very reason for acting in the public sphere, given their rather traditional views on family life, as necessary only in order to reassert their position in the social and racial hierarchy of white supremacy.

Opposition to the Klan

The crusading efforts of Klansmen and women met a great deal of opposition, as Americans readily recognized the reactionary forces at work within the group. Notable leaders took issue with the Klan's racial frameworks and their exclusive claims of Americanism. Maine's attorney general wrote in the *Forum* in 1925, "Americanism, of course, is really an ideal and a spirit—a faith in freedom, tolerance, humanity. It cannot discriminate because of color, birthplace, or creed."[75] A beautiful notion, surely, but in reality the idea of Americanism was very much in contest, up for grabs in the 1920s. In the framework of the culture war, Americanism as a worldview was constructed and fleshed out by a disparate group of Americans who were invested in clinging to the status quo in the face of internationalism, Bolshevism, feminism, modernism, immigration, and the "new Negro." So, while many did feel it was "an ideal" or "a spirit," just what constituted that ideal provoked much discussion. The Klan's fervent belief that a certain racial background fostered Americanism, and that it excluded others, proved compelling to many but not to all.

Americans opposed the Klan for different political and social reasons, though Catholics often took the lead. Fed up with anti-Catholicism in general and fearful of Klan efforts to outlaw parochial schools, Catholic men and women organized to blunt the group's impact in their communities and on a national scale. Police chiefs and mayors who were themselves Catholic took the lead in outlawing Klan marches and banning Klan figures from podiums in their cities and towns. Well-known political leaders like New York's Al Smith and Colorado's Judge Ben Lindsey publicly attacked the organization by blocking their ability to engage in public activities and stymying their political advances. Black leaders and newspapers denounced the Klan as well but often noted wryly that no one much minded the hooded order when blacks made up their only victims. Many of these groups came together in an organization set up in Chicago to bring down the Klan in 1922. The American Unity League touted a multicultural vision of America as a direct challenge to the Klan's nativist, racist, and isolationist outlook.[76] They published the names of Chicago Klan members in a newspaper, forcing them to face consequences for their membership. Within a few years their efforts proved successful as the Chicago Klan's numbers dwindled.

In addition, violence employed by those opposed to the Klan weakened the group by 1923. As they sought to spread beyond their largely Protestant enclaves, the Klan faced the reality of the impact of their message. Catholics, Jews, African Americans, bootleggers, immigrants, progressives, and any others who challenged the group's strict framework of morality, law, and order stepped up in their own neighborhoods and towns to block the Klan's advances. Angry groups disrupted Klan meetings and rallies, often beating Klan members who were at the mercy of local law enforcement—who sometimes purposefully took their time. At event after event across the country, Klan members found themselves cowering inside local meeting halls and churches, hiding from organized protestors who were unafraid to use bricks or weapons to get their message across. These crowds were sometimes comprised of local townspeople, industrial workers, or college students. They were rarely spontaneous, but rather demonstrated a spreading willingness among Americans to stand up and put their physical safety on the line in order to weaken the influence of the Klan. And Klansmen rarely dared to fight back or engage in physical violence with this opposition. Many members, as it turned out, were not aggressive purveyors of violence, eager to inflict harm. Instead, they were likely dissatisfied with their lot and found easy scapegoats to make themselves feel better. Or they joined because it seemed patriotic in their neighborhood to do so, or because they felt they needed to succeed in business, or because they thought the world was just changing too fast and they wanted to do anything to hold on to power. In any case, when violence beckoned, many Klansmen were afraid.[77]

Understanding the Klan's Rise and Fall

The expansive nature of the Klan's targets compels us to understand their rise in relation to both racism and xenophobia, a widespread status anxiety, and a sense of powerlessness among citizens reeling from what felt like a whirlwind of upheaval. In Indiana, historians find that Klan members represented a broad swath of the state's population and were not more likely to be from urban or rural areas, or from the working or middle or professional classes. Historian Leonard Moore argues that their only consistent overlap was their Protestantism. Furthermore, he points out that there were relatively few foreigners and African Americans in the state. So, what compelled these Klansmen to join the organization? It was something bigger than race. Indiana Klan members typically paid little attention to minorities in their midst, and racial violence present in other states failed to materialize there.[78] It is quite likely that despite this, immigrants, Jews, Catholics and African Americans in Indiana felt threatened by the strong presence of the Klan in their state, but the group did not primarily focus on controlling them. Instead, their overt clashes came with business elites who struggled to maintain their own claims to power by holding on to the new status quo.

Here, the Klan's anger blossomed in response to the shifting hierarchy of status among white men. Those coming of age in the 1920s entered a world far from the one their fathers mastered, and to put it plainly, this stung a bit. A man could no longer reasonably expect to build a business, to be his own boss. Immigrants and African Americans and even men's own families no longer accepted white men's power, unquestioningly. The ranks of the truly powerful moved beyond local or state networks, putting any real contact with those in control of national affairs well out of the average man's reach.[79] In a country where at that very moment consolidation of a national culture undermined local, more traditional values, where corporations enlarged the scope of industrial capitalism, and where crime and corruption seemed increasingly pervasive, some Klan activity reflected a populist effort. Through their involvement with the Klan, average Americans sought to make their mark on American life, to impact government and society in a meaningful way.[80]

The wide variety of associational activity belies the organization's frequent characterization as a shadowy, white-robed, fringe terrorist group. This version of the Klan surely existed, and some members embraced the group only because of the secrecy afforded to them in their membership. But the very public parades, picnics, and pageants found many Klansmen openly announcing their affiliation. A whole culture of media offerings, including things like Klan newspapers, novels, and pamphlets, fostered a deep sense of connection and community.[81] Some in this hooded army of white supremacists, nativists, and antimodernists were not necessarily outliers on the fringes of the American dream but rather were central to it in the 1920s.

By 1924, the Klan gathered somewhere between 3 million and 5 million members, and at that moment the group entered a steep decline.

The opposition was certainly a part of that. Another issue was the organization's identity crisis. To some they represented a fraternal organization, to others a political pressure group, and others still saw them as menacing moral police force. And in different cases all were truthful representations. There was little real central organization—Evans did not lead the whole group very effectively. Essentially, each local Klan organization set its own agenda. The only thing they did in concert was collect membership dues that enriched Klan leaders. Another reason for the group's rapid decline was the growing publicity around the scandalous behavior of some of those leaders, ranging from theft to rape. An organization calling for a more righteous and pure America could not bear the fallout.

The passage of time in America also served to hasten the Klan's demise. As the war moved further into the distance, and the bright hot glare of the first Red Scare cooled to a still powerful but less conspicuous glow, the urgency of the group's members diminished. The Johnson Reed Act purported to solve the nation's acute immigration problem in 1924. By then it became apparent that women voters would not overturn the political system as Americans knew it, but rather they too would vote for Democrats or Republicans and not as a women's bloc. More and more Americans adapted themselves to the growing disregard for the Prohibition law. And consumer culture softened the edges of the challenges presented by sexual modernism.

The Klan served as a panacea, an oasis for frightened and anxious white, Anglo-Saxon, Protestant Americans who worried over the apparent loss of their own power in an increasingly modern and pluralistic society. As the urgency of that fear dissipated for all of these reasons, the draw of the Klan dissipated too.

White, native, middle-class Protestant Americans recognized the undeniable impact of industrialization, immigration, modernism, and urbanization on their lives. They recognized their own loss of power, privilege, and prestige. Change was coming to America, and these men and women took up one side of the culture war in a desperate attempt to stop it. Scapegoating immigrants amid conversations about pure Americanism, a Red Scare deployed through all areas of American life, and the resurgence of the nation's most notorious white supremacist group were all last ditch efforts to stem the tide of change. And while developments in American culture continued to marginalize these people's power in some ways, their efforts did the work of reshaping the nation's identity with lasting consequences. The nativist 1920s reframed an enduring narrative about who belongs in America.

CHAPTER THREE

Prohibition: "A State of Civil War"

As Prohibition finally became law in January 1920, evangelical leader Billy Sunday declared, "Men will walk upright now, women will smile, and the children will laugh."[1] Many devoted to him, and to the cause, heartily agreed. The fight to ban alcohol in America stands out as one of the nation's most spectacular reform efforts. This movement lasted for over a century, buoyed by a desire among many Americans to dramatically improve their society. It spurred massive organization efforts and passionate arguments. It cut down drinking, significantly, for decades.[2] It reflected utopianism and progressivism. It framed politics. And it invited debate. While some applauded the measure, others bitterly resented it. Commentator and humorist Will Rogers famously said in 1919, "Prohibitionists just seem sore at the world."[3] But what really motivated them? And how did their efforts play into the emerging culture war?

Questions about the role of drinking in American life reflected a deeper question plaguing Americans in the 1920s: "who are we?"[4] And once again the issue of immigration framed the question. The 20th-century movement for Prohibition hoped to save society by eradicating saloons, spaces associated with immigrant culture. Saloons symbolized the evils of the city and many saw them as havens for corruption, prostitution, violence, and un-Americanness. In some ways then, Prohibition represents another side of the nativist, antimodern coin.[5] As Americans experienced the unsettling rifts between city and town and the impact of massive immigration, as the cultural ideals of crumbling island communities broke even further, Prohibition served as one more way for bearers of the old culture to reassert their power and authority. Much as the Red Scare can be cast as a movement to revitalize the power and influence of native-born, Protestant, Anglo Saxon elites, advocates of Prohibition too sought to "impose cultural unity on an increasingly heterogeneous and complex society."[6]

Prohibition, then, represented the sum of many American fears in the early 20th century. And it left a complicated legacy, even though it lasted only in federal law for 13 years. It changed the relationship between the federal government and the states, and it grew the federal government substantially. It revamped the approach to fighting crime, including a transformation of the criminal justice system. And it profoundly impacted American attitudes toward drugs and alcohol through the next century.

THE ROOTS OF NATIONAL PROHIBITION

The call to limit alcohol had a long history. The early 19th-century temperance movement, as it was then called, sprang in part from the evangelical nature of popular religious revivals, but it also worked to assuage middle-class uncertainties about a changing society in the early decades of the 1800s. In the face of increasing mobility, the beginnings of industrialization, and the expansion of the right to vote to the common man, community standards seemed fragile. As alcohol consumption rose, many middle-class Americans saw in the temperance movement a way to maintain order, to impose sobriety, to teach morality, and to promote prosperity.[7]

The emergence of the "progressive movement" for reform in the later years of the 19th century also contributed to the eventual success of the Prohibition amendment. Starting in the 1890s, the movement reflected a deep desire on the part of the middle class to come to terms with the conflicts brought forth by the coalescing corporate industrial order. Progressive reformers were a multifaceted group, working for a wide variety of different ends, but they believed it was their civic duty to work to ameliorate the impact of unchecked industrial capitalism, and most focused on one or more of the following: urban poverty, corruption, fraying social bonds, economic inequality, immorality, and the adjustment of immigrants. Significantly, progressivism drew in many different people because of its flexible and, at times, all-encompassing nature. And it motivated people to organize at the grassroots, state, and federal level to use government as a change agent. These two facts are important.

The very broad appeal of prohibition in this moment fueled its successes and led to the passage of the Eighteenth Amendment. Employers supported it, hoping for a more productive and less troublesome workforce in an era rife with labor unrest. Middle-class Americans acted for Prohibition as a nativist measure as well as for larger reasons relating to the maintenance of the social order. Evangelicals saw it as a move toward a stronger Christian nation. And progressives envisioned it as one more reform measure, informed by expert knowledge and statistical study of social problems. But despite the range of motivations, most supporters of Prohibition came from the same ethnic background, and most anticipated that the measure would help engineer social stability through the idealization of middle-class Protestant values.[8]

Progressivism also encouraged reformers to believe fundamentally in the power of government to work for the greater good, despite a historically deep American attachment to small government. Progressive activists looked expectantly to city, state, and local officials to step in and mediate the power of industrial capitalism over the early years of the 1900s, seeing great benefit in an interventionist state. This flowered, perhaps most fruitfully, under the presidency of progressive Theodore Roosevelt, who envisioned the federal government as a sort of umpire intended to mediate between the common man and business owners, to ensure the best interests of all. Roosevelt's stance, based on the belief that the general welfare of the many outweighed the personal liberties of the individual, marked a departure in American politics up to that point. In the Progressive Era, then, this worldview lent itself to an easier acceptance of the power of the federal government to reach into the lives of individuals to outlaw alcohol.

This decidedly modern sense of what the state could and should do made the movement to limit alcohol more successful by the early 1910s. A focus on the evil nature of alcohol consumption still shaped the movement, and, as in the 19th century, advocates certainly still wished to impose their moral certainties on others. These things were not different. But now, people envisioned this moral policing within the purview of the federal government. And this would prove to be a powerful mix. One historian put it well, saying, "This propitious marriage of state power and moral suasion would yield a dramatic expansion of federal policing and an increase of state and local policing in the quasi-military sphere of crime control."[9]

While there was more than one reason for Prohibition, many supported it as a means to control immigrants. Bogus racial science and many racist jeremiads argued with confidence that the new immigrants from southern and eastern Europe were driven by their base instincts, incapable of self-control. This is largely what temperance reformers feared for the rest of America, that this loss of control seemingly so prevalent among immigrants would overtake those of "better" stock as well. Immigrant culture needed to be boxed in and rehabilitated.

The bearers of native, white, Protestant American culture, represented in this moment quite powerfully by Protestant churches, waged war on what they saw as the intemperate, lustful culture of immigrant newcomers. These largely small-town Americans wielded their attachment to the Prohibition cause like a badge of superiority, separating themselves from and exerting power over the dens of corruptions they perceived American cities to be.[10] Native-born Americans' support for Prohibition as a kind of culture war bears out in the way the movement spread. The South was almost exclusively native born in 1910, and broad Prohibition support began there. Next came the West, where 82 percent of the inhabitants were native born. And then the East came over last, where just three-quarters of the region's population were born in America.[11]

The nightmare vision of saloons as dens of depravity was not entirely correct. Competitive brewers did entice workingmen to drink their cares away in saloons with lower and lower prices, allowing them an escape from brutal conditions in an industrializing nation. But immigrants themselves saw the saloon as a welcome respite in a harsh world. It provided a space to maintain and celebrate ethnic ties with other immigrants and a supply of foreign language newspapers. While liquor undoubtedly created real problems in American life, the apocalyptic visions of Prohibition advocates greatly exaggerated the impact of alcohol on immigrants.[12]

Broad support for Prohibition did not just come from a growing fear of foreigners but was woven into the high tide of racism in the "new south." A revived and reconstructed white supremacy enveloped the South in the post-Reconstruction era, featuring segregation, disenfranchisement, and terrible violence. Often times, the popular myth of the black male rapist legitimized and "justified" these forms of racial tyranny. White men defended their right to commit senseless violence on black communities by saying it was a necessary deterrent to the seemingly inevitable desire of black men to ravish white women. Activists like Ida B. Wells fought to explode this myth with facts, noting that fewer than one-quarter of all lynchings came upon the heels of a rape charge. But the myth remained credible for decades despite the pervasive criminal violence, including rapes, committed by white men against black women.

Tightly linked to this image of the unreconstructed black southern man was his perceived affliction for overindulging in alcohol.[13] This, despite the fact that many, many black men and women actively supported Prohibition at the local and state levels. Political activists relied on black churches—keen to display their respectability—to provide soldiers for the cause. Rallies for Prohibition saw black and white men and women coming together. And in separate, but similar, organizations, members of both races in the south worked to achieve Prohibition. Not all black southerners opposed alcohol, just as not all white southerners did, but enough worked to achieve it that historian Edward Ayers went so far as to say that "blacks enjoyed their greatest political activity and visibility in the entire New South Era in the prohibition movement."[14]

But this did not matter much. Racism and the overwhelming desire to maintain power and control over their black neighbors led white southerners to structure their call for as something vitally necessary to protect them, and their women, from savage black men. Sadly this script played well beyond the south, too.[15] It was not poverty or brutal racism or the grinding industrial capitalist system that encouraged drinking, according to so many white American Protestants, but rather the moral failings of the new immigrant and the southern black man.[16]

Prohibition Organizations

The crafting of the amendment and its passage came about due to the incredible organization work of two distinct voluntary associations, the first of which is the Women's Christian Temperance Union (WCTU). Women active in the temperance cause founded the organization in Cleveland, Ohio, in 1873, with a focus on their perspective as women, on the belief that alcohol distinctly and uniquely affected women. To start, Americans had long positioned women as moral guardians over the home and hearth. And alcohol was framed as a threat to the home. The WCTU used the rallying cry "home protection" to create the country's first mass movement of women because it immediately drew sympathy, and at the same time it justified women's role in this struggle in the public arena.

Women needed to protect their homes from alcohol for many reasons, the WCTU argued. When men drank—and the conversation here centered on working-class, typically immigrant men, of course—they took wages from their wives and children and instead gave them to saloonkeepers. Many joined the WCTU in this argument that drinking men impoverished families living on the margins. In addition, men's drinking threatened women and children in more concrete ways. WCTU members decried the domestic violence they believed to be a result of men's drunkenness. The group's leader Frances Willard painted horrific portraits of life in homes with drunk men, saying in a frequently offered speech, "He goes to the house where he is best beloved. . . . Yet upon that wife that loves him so well and little children clinging about his neck, he inflicts atrocities which imagination cannot picture and no tongue dare describe."[17] Lastly, the use and abuse of alcohol had a sexual component. Immorality, vice, and drunkenness went together, many believed. Some men forced their wives to submit to their sexual desires when drunk, taking away women's control over their own bodies. And others sought out prostitutes when drunk. This related quite directly to home protection in a moment when Americans were obsessed with venereal disease. Men would meet prostitutes at saloons and engage in illicit sex, the thinking went, and then come home and spread disease to their unwitting and underserving wives and future children.[18]

Through these arguments, the WCTU helped capture the interests of the middle classes in favor of Prohibition and worked to carve out a significant role for women in the public sphere. Temperance as an issue became fairly tied to women. While Frances Willard did support suffrage for women, and the activism of WCTU members undoubtedly politicized some women, leadership of the group divided on the issue of women and politics. And, while the organization honed strategies to create effective propaganda and push for prohibition laws at the local and state levels, they did not develop a politically sophisticated plan for a federal amendment. This is where the Anti-Saloon League played an important role.[19]

The Anti-Saloon League brought its considerable organizing skills to bear on the push for temperance at the turn of the century, swelling the movement's momentum. Founded in Ohio in 1893, the group's activities reflected what historian Lynn Dumenil calls an "organizational revolution" in American life. League leaders utilized a corporate approach with polished propaganda strategies that they deployed in the popular media and in churches. The organization formed its own publishing house and put out many anti-alcohol publications every single month.[20] At the same time, they operated from a place deeply rooted in their own moral certainty. All of the nation's problems, in their view, stemmed from the moral depravity created by alcohol.[21]

The ASL presented prohibition as a simple, one-stop answer to a host of complex problems that many were unsure how to handle. They saw prohibition as a way to lower taxes, as fewer social services would be needed in a sober country. It would lower crime rates and poverty rates. Corruption would diminish. Labor troubles would abate without the need for any pesky labor legislation or other concessions to workers. Immigrants would assimilate better and be more efficient workers.[22] To these eager architects of reform, Prohibition promised all of this and more.

Essentially, the ASL operated as a non-partisan lobbying group akin to contemporary lobbying efforts we see today, and they did so with great success. The organization threw its weight behind dry political candidates, regardless of party affiliation, and fought to hobble wet candidates. With the motto "the Saloon Must Go," they effectively worked to secure prohibition legislation at the local and state levels. Where only a handful of states initiated Prohibition laws by 1905, two-thirds of the nation's states passed some form of prohibition legislation by 1917. Some brought in full prohibition of alcohol, while others allowed local governments to make that decision for themselves. When local governments took action, they often had a difficult time insulating their towns from those nearby where liquor still flowed. And states faced a similar problem. According to the Constitution, each state had no legal right to regulate interstate commerce, so anyone in a wet state could ship alcohol to someone in a dry state. Prohibition advocates realized that individual state efforts really needed backing from the federal government.[23]

Together the ASL and the WCTU moved to achieve that federal support, proposing the Webb-Kenyon bill in 1912 to prohibit shipping alcohol from a wet state to a dry one. This measure brought the discussion to a new level, and ASL-style lobbying groups entered the fray on both sides. Ultimately, the act passed in 1913, though President William Howard Taft vetoed it because he felt the measure violated the Constitution. When and if a state voted to make itself dry, it would in effect regulate interstate commerce, he claimed. But Congress went ahead and overrode Taft's veto, stepping in to ensure the sanctity of state authority over alcohol.

Under mounting pressure, representatives in the House debated a federal amendment for national prohibition on the sale of alcohol in 1914. A heated battle ensued, with great passion and bluster. Prohibitionists pointed to the health risks associated with drinking, the crime it spawned, the labor ramifications they believed it created, and the overall disorder it brought to American life. Wets responded by warning of the danger such a move presented to cherished American political and personal ideals. The measure would grow the government substantially. And giving the federal government this blanket control over Americans' personal decisions on alcohol flew in the face of states' rights, they opined, as well as on the sacred rights of the individual. What would happen to personal liberty? Wets also foresaw a different kind of disorder on the horizon if the amendment became law. Flouting of the law, corruption, and possible drug use were all potential by-products of a federal ban on the sale of alcohol. After a robust debate, the House passed the amendment but only by a few votes and not by the two-thirds majority required.[24]

The ASL went after wet politicians with a new vengeance, and after the election of 1916 they felt confident in their ability to win an amendment. In 1917, a bill intended to stop advertising for liquor in dry states was attached to a mail bill, and in an ill-fated effort to squash the measure Senator James Reed from Missouri—a wet—added a rider making it illegal to transport all liquor in dry states. Few states actually banned all alcohol at this point. Most set up restrictions on unsavory saloons but allowed morally upright and economically able individuals to import alcohol or make it on their own. Reed thought this extreme measure would kill the bill. But instead it swept through Congress. The United States entered World War I by this time, and with the great need for the mail to function, Wilson signed off on the measure even though he did not fully support it.[25]

The war is actually a significant part of how Prohibition became federal law. America's entry into the war allowed temperance advocates to frame Prohibition as one more part of the need for collective sacrifice, part of the nation's willingness to put aside unnecessary distractions in favor of the true aim of winning the war. Advocates of the measure framed it as patriotic, as an act taken in the interest of American strength and goodness. Brown University's president put it baldly to his graduating seniors in 1917, saying, "Patriotism spells Prohibition."[26] At the same time, Prohibition propagandists highlighted perceived connections between the German enemy and the brewing industry, a historic tie that was easily exploitable amid high-wartime emotions. When brewers pushed back on Prohibition, the anti-alcohol community could call it treasonous.

As the war raged then, the U.S. Congress passed a national Prohibition measure as a wartime act intended to ensure the capability and productivity of the nation in 1917. The measure was feasible due to the emotional appeal of wartime, the need to conserve grain for food, and due to the income tax. A reform called for by many progressives, the income tax became a reality with the ratification of the Sixteenth Amendment in 1913. This provided the federal government with much needed tax revenue that, for the first time, allowed it to do without the funds gathered from tax on alcohol. This was crucial. Taken together these impulses helped ensure the passage of the War Prohibition Act in 1918, which outlawed the production and sale of intoxicants with an alcohol content higher than 2.75 percent.[27]

There now existed a clear path forward for a constitutional amendment. In fact, the wartime bill gave way to the Eighteenth Amendment far more easily than the naysayers predicted. Even before Wartime Prohibition passed, a constitutional amendment forbidding the manufacture,

Prohibition

sale, transport, import, and export of intoxicating liquor sailed through the Senate with a vote of 65 to 20. It then moved through the House with minor modification, after just a single day's discussion. Within a few days, in late December 1917, the Senate approved of the final bill and sent it out to the states. It then leapt from state legislature to state legislature, meeting the necessary number of state approvals on January 16, 1919, in little more than a year's time. Rhode Island and Connecticut were the only states of the 48 not to ratify the amendment. It would go into effect one year later on January 16, 1920, at the stroke of midnight.

However, the passage of the Eighteenth Amendment did not deal at all with implementation of national Prohibition. This required the passage of another law altogether, in addition to individual state enforcement laws. Much still needed to be done. The Volstead Act, national enforcement legislation, would take care of part of this. Wayne Wheeler, head lawyer for the Anti-Saloon League, largely wrote the bill but House representative Andrew J. Volstead of Minnesota submitted it. The Volstead Act laid out expansive definitions and regulations for enforcement of the amendment, with some 67 different sections. After a summer of debate, the bill made it through the House in July 1919. Wilson vetoed it, as he opposed Prohibition even though he believed in the movement for temperance. But Congress ultimately overrode his veto. The enforcement bill moved into law but not without controversy.

The phrase "intoxicating liquors," cleverly used to pass the amendment, was fully hashed out in a section of the Volstead Act that took many by surprise. While many supporters expected the definition of the phrase would line up with the wartime prohibition measures, allowing light beer and wine up to 2.75 percent alcohol, this was not the case. The Volstead Act instead declared all intoxicating beverages over 0.5 percent illegal. The fact was that the amendment needed the support of two-thirds of each House of Congress and then three-quarters of the states to approve, and so Wayne B. Wheeler purposefully made the wording vague. Those who were uncertain about a total ban on alcohol, or those optimistic, halfhearted drys who thought beer and wine would be exempt, could approve of an amendment prohibiting intoxicating liquors. But the enforcement act needed far fewer votes in Congress to pass and needed no state legislatures at all.

Here, in the Volstead Act, Wheeler made his intentions known. Anything at all that had more than 0.5 percent alcohol would be prohibited. This included even light beer, even weak wine, and technically, even some sauerkrauts.[28] Evidence suggests that many Americans did not understand the details and were surprised when the Volstead Act used such a broad definition of intoxicating liquors. Many hoped or expected that products like wine and beer would be exempt from the law. But they were wrong, and according to the dictates of the new law, America was to be completely dry.[29]

Another debate arose over what the amendment should mean when it came to "possessing" alcohol. The phrase "manufacture, sale or transportation" of intoxicating liquor did not say one could not drink alcohol. And as the Volstead Act went through Congress, wets exploited that lack of specificity. They allowed individuals to possess alcohol in their own private dwelling, provided the liquor was for personal use and not for sale. And they provided that authorities would not be able to execute a search warrant unless property was "being used for the unlawful sale of intoxicating liquor." Ultimately, then, while it was illegal to sell alcohol, you could have it at home. And no one could come looking to see whether you had it or not. This was carefully done. If drinkers and buyers could be prosecuted for their actions, no one would ever be willing to testify against those who furnished them the alcohol to begin with.[30] And anyone who stockpiled enough liquor to last through Prohibition could keep it at home and drink all they liked. Many wealthy Americans did just that.

Prohibition Becomes Law

Prohibition officially began at the stroke of midnight on January 16, 1920. The *New York Times* announced "John Barleycorn Died Peacefully at the Toll of 12" on its front page. The ancient character from a British folksong, a symbol of the cereal crop, and the intoxicating liquors it helped create, loomed large in popular culture as Americans settled in to the long, dry future. The *Christian Advocate* claimed there was "no more aggressive or bitter enemy of John Barleycorn" than evangelical preacher Billy Sunday.[31] And Sunday went big to mark this occasion. He hosted an elaborate funeral service for dear old John in front of more than 10,000 people in Norfolk, Virginia. In a grand spectacle, the "mourners" marched in a procession through the streets, while a man dressed as Satan followed behind in obvious anguish at the potential loss of so many sinners. Once they arrived at the church, Sunday, with a "delighted grin," delivered his funeral sermon. He spoke to the grand vision Prohibition represented to many Americans, looking to a future transformed when he said, "The reign of tears is over. The slums will soon be a memory. We will turn our prisons into factories and our jails into storehouses and corncribs. Men will walk upright now; women will smile and the children will laugh. Hell will be forever rent."[32] He savored the moment, ending by saying, "Good-bye John. You were God's worst enemy; you were Hell's best friend. I hate you with a perfect hatred; I love to hate you."[33] While many sorrowful and soused bar goers spent their last night comforting themselves with a bottle in hand, a reporter noted, "Instead of passing from us in violent paroxysms, the demon rum lay down to a painless, peaceful" end.[34] John Barleycorn was dead.

Another group, a well-heeled bunch, gathered to send him off at the First Congregational Church in Washington, D.C. Wayne Wheeler was there, along with Andrew Volstead. Howard Hyde Russell, the founder of the Anti-Saloon League, joined them, along with Anna A. Gordon from the Women's Christian Temperance Union. These architects of Prohibition listened intently to fundamentalist politician William Jennings Bryan, who spoke for 40 minutes celebrating the moment many in the room had worked toward for most of their lives. As the clock struck midnight, the group sang hymns praising God, and Bryan finished his rousing and fiery speech by shouting three times over, of purveyors of liquor, "They are dead!"

Within two hours, the first arrest for Prohibition violations took place in Peoria, Illinois, when distillery workers were caught leaving their warehouse with two truckloads of whiskey in tow. Hundreds of thousands of arrests were still to come, making it increasingly evident that purveyors of intoxicating liquors and John Barleycorn were not, in fact, dead after all.[35] But many did start to drink less, especially away from the two coasts. Scholars estimate that the consumption of alcohol fell by 30 percent, which was not insubstantial. In the early days of this experiment, city officials and reformers reveled in lowering crime rates and noticeably less disorderly streets. But for many, the will to follow the rules of Prohibition soon cracked, and inevitably, perhaps, people continued to drink.[36]

Americans managed to get their alcohol in all sorts of ways after Prohibition became law. A network of small stills in Chicago, funded and supplied by gangsters, served that market. In New England, liquor was brought ashore by a bevy of small vessels that linked up with ships moored three miles off the coast. Moonshine spread throughout the south, coming from a variety of local stills in different states. Industrial alcohol produced by the chemical companies in Philadelphia was cleaned up and flavored, supplying eager drinkers there. In Detroit, not far from the Canadian border, the joke went, "It was absolutely impossible to get a drink . . . unless you walked at least ten feet and told the busy bartender what you wanted in a voice loud enough for him to hear you above the uproar."[37] The Yale Club in New York City had a 14-year supply of liquor when Prohibition went into effect.[38] President Harding and a host of other politicians enjoyed a steady flow of liquor in their own private homes, including booty taken in by the Justice Department in raids.

Americans also brewed beer and distilled moonshine in their homes in increasing numbers. The materials required for these efforts flew off the shelves. Hardware stores advertised supplies like copper cans and kegs, knowing the particular market for such goods. And grocers saw sales of yeast skyrocket. More often than not, these home operations existed in working-class, ethnic homes, and women did their share of the production. Their homes provided not only the alcohol but also the location in which to drink it. While risky, it was profitable.[39] Though, these mom and pop operations were small potatoes compared to the organized network of bootleggers who, for better or worse, brought liquor to the masses in the 1920s. Alcohol "factories" emerged in warehouses and barns and basements, serving a growing need in illicit establishments.[40] Few Americans felt the law was truly working as it was supposed to. But satisfaction in the law's very existence tided some supporters over. They believed it would take more than a decade for the country to adjust, but rather, a generation.[41]

While the nation waited for that adjustment, debate over Prohibition raged on along battle lines familiar in the ongoing culture war. The "drys" got their way, but not everyone was happy about it. Opponents to the amendment, wets as they were called, disagreed for different reasons. Immigrants felt targeted, and many vehemently opposed the total prohibition of alcohol, but they had little recourse in American life in the 1920s. Workers felt particularly aggrieved. The head of the New York State Federation of Labor complained that the American worker "resents this patriarchal attitude of the lessees of all goodness and morality, such as the Anti-Saloon League, and demands the liberty to shape his own standard of life."[42] Labor leaders like him rightly viewed the amendment as a class-based attack on the culture and values of workers, but they too held little political clout in Red Scare America. Liquor manufacturers vigorously opposed the law but they registered their opposition too late to make a real difference. And, in reality, fighting against Prohibition meant one would have to stand up for the saloon, which at this moment seemed crazy. Middle-class and elite Americans uniformly disapproved of saloon culture.[43]

This antagonism to Prohibition, and the ongoing culture war, kept the issue at the forefront of politics throughout the decade. In elections at all levels, the candidate's stance on alcohol played a role in their popularity. Al Smith served as the most prominent example. The presidential election of 1928 symbolized to many the national disagreement over Prohibition.

Smith, prominently known for his Catholicism, his ties to Tammany Hall, and his Irish mother, long articulated his disagreement with the war on alcohol. He cultivated deep ties to the urban, immigrant community in New York City. Smith seemed in some way to represent the rising prominence and power of that very group and that very place in the national imaginary. Here, the Prohibition debate clearly intersects with not only anxieties over nativism but also the deep tension between city and town.

His opponent in the election was Herbert Hoover, an old-stock native Protestant from Iowa who ran on his support for the seemingly besieged traditional, middle-class American way of life.[44] Unsurprisingly, then, he stood behind Prohibition. The race centered on this Prohibition stance, as well as on religion. Preachers regularly likened Al Smith to the devil, and groups like the WCTU and the Anti-Saloon League condemned him harshly. Hoover won the election with impressive numbers, taking 40 states with an Electoral College vote of 444 to 87. His victory was in no small part due to the wave of prosperity his Republican predecessors brought to many Americans, but his effort to ride the wave of the culture war mattered too.

Unsurprisingly, geographic location greatly influenced the debate over and success of Prohibition. People in rural areas associated the problem of alcohol with urban communities, populated by large immigrant groups. Those from the country saw cities as infested with corrupt machine politicians, unassimilated foreigners, and immorality, all things tied to the saloon in their minds. While many small-town residents applauded the outlawing of beer, a drink central to saloon life, the structure of the Volstead Act encouraged rural dwellers to maintain a hypocritical attitude toward drinking. Many continued to drink fermented cider and wine, items only classified as illegal if they proved intoxicating—a difficult standard to prove and one rarely monitored.

In many small cities and larger towns, evidence demonstrates that Prohibition was largely effective. Many activists in the WCTU and Anti-Saloon League hailed from such locales, while others there gave it up with Prohibition. The Lynds found that the dry behavior of Middletown's leaders discouraged drinking among the middle classes. It seemed that social pressure worked effectively in these places even in the absence of major law enforcement efforts.[45]

City dwellers proved significantly more resistant to the pull of the war on alcohol. Urban areas from coast to coast housed drinkers of all backgrounds, though it appears drinking more commonly persisted among the wealthy and the working class. This likely came down to the issue of access. The price of beer and liquor shot up exponentially after

Prohibition, and the ability to obtain it required either a great deal of money or the expertise to make it at home. Middle-class groups often had neither the money to buy nor the skill to manufacture alcohol.

Many shielded their eyes from the realization that opposition to the law created serious problems. Yes, the moral high ground reflected in the law could prevent the nation from becoming debauched, overrun with vice and drunkenness. But the very fact that many, many Americans simply went around the law—in effect becoming criminals when before 1920 they were not—was not lost. The vice and criminality unleashed by gangster bootleggers and speakeasies, some argued, lowered the nation's values significantly more than the prohibition on alcohol raised them.

Furthermore, enforcers of the amendment, in practice, demonstrated class bias as well as racial, ethnic, and religious discrimination. They targeted Catholic, ethnic, immigrant, and working-class Americans in significantly higher numbers, which was predictable given the virulent nativism streaming through the history of the temperance movement. A 77-year-old woman in a New York City courtroom in 1921, charged with having a cheap whiskey flask, argued in vain that a small sip each day gave her frail body strength. When the judge sentenced her to five days in jail, she said what no doubt many felt. "It is the poor people [Prohibition] drives hardest," she claimed. No one seemed to police the nation's wealthy elite, she argued, saying, "Those that are rich can have what they want."[46]

PROHIBITION ENFORCEMENT AND ITS IMPACT

Actually, setting up enforcement of the Volstead Act proved problematic straightaway. It fell to the U.S. Department of the Treasury, mostly because they were formerly charged with collecting taxes on alcohol before Prohibition. A Prohibition Unit formed within the department as a division of the Internal Revenue Service, with a national commissioner who oversaw 48 different state-level directors. The nation handed over the enforcement of every aspect of Prohibition to the unit, later known as the Bureau of Prohibition. This included blocking smuggling at the borders, overseeing legal production of industrial alcohol, managing the distribution of sacramental wine, and policing illegal alcohol sales with raids and arrests. Immediately, the bureau was overwhelmed.[47]

To make matters worse, early on the bureau operated on a meager budget, and without adequate manpower. In its first year, the Bureau of Prohibition had a budget of $4.5 million, with some 3,000 employees including both agents and administrative staffers. The federal government kept their funding and their numbers low because they expected a great degree of cooperation with local law enforcement agencies, U.S. Customs, the Coast Guard, and temperance groups. And there was some. But the bureau lacked the number of agents and the money to truly enforce a sweeping ban on alcohol. Faced with this lack of funds, the feds avoided raising taxes, knowing full well that Americans would lack the will to pay more than they expected. And groups like the Anti-Saloon League avoided calling for such increases, reluctant as they were to acknowledge how much they missed the mark in their assessment of Prohibition's real financial cost.[48]

The ability to uphold the ban on alcohol suffered more blows still in the form of corrupt enforcement agents. The press and the public realized the true nature of this problem amid splashy stories about agents gone bad. A Senate investigation in 1926 revealed some 875 agents to be "crooked," about 1/5th of the total force. These men, according to the testimony of an official, were "discharged for detected bribery, extortion, soliciting money, falsification of expense accounts, and so on."[49] And it did not get better over time. Most agents were poorly trained and vulnerable to bribes. They confiscated alcohol and then kept it either for their own use or sold it to others for a profit. They engaged in wanton violence that disregarded public safety. Car chases and crashes wounded civilians, raids went awry with deadly results, and shootouts like one on a crowded Harlem street in 1923 often put innocent bystanders in danger.[50] Enforcement agents killed at least 190 people by 1929, prompting alarm in the White House.[51] Some high-profile scandals led to the dismissal of agents, but overall this made little difference. The bureau failed to meet the monumental task of enforcing Prohibition, which only fostered the growing lawlessness of the population.[52]

Crime in the Prohibition Era

Prohibition proved to be a seismic moment of cultural transgression, one that captured average men and women and overturned Americans' values all over the country. As posh urbanites thrilled to the swinging nightlife created by Prohibition, the impact of their revelry spread far beyond city streets. The late nights, the flappers smoking cigarettes, the young sophisticates dancing with wild abandon, the jazz music, and the free flowing gin all made their way to the nation's smaller cities and towns in the flood of Hollywood films, in the sensational tabloid news, in novels and short stories, and by 1927, thanks to Columbia Broadcasting System, on the radio. As historian Lisa McGirr put it, the "cultural earthquake" that shook up a metropolis like New York "radiated, with perhaps even greater consequences, in the cultural shallows of America's smaller towns and cities."[53]

The nightlife spawned by Prohibition worked to reframe the nation's moral order by reframing leisure spaces around the country. The law forced legitimate and respectable watering holes to close, including bars, restaurants, and hotel lounges. The drop in income following the law's enactment made staying in business an unworthy enterprise. One by one, legendary establishments in cities such as New York City closed their doors after a few months, or a few years. Those that stayed afloat worked hard to provide patrons with liquor, while appearing to stay on the right side of the law. For example, at the Ritz-Carlton in Boston, waiters brought small flasks with them on the restaurant floor, fulfilling the drink orders of known patrons surreptitiously upon demand. But for respectable establishments this proved difficult and complicated.[54]

Speakeasies grew up in droves to fill the vacuum. A police commission in New York estimated that some 5,000 speakeasies operated in the city in 1927. And a 1928 investigation by an anti-vice organization discovered at least one speakeasy per block. Some were grand affairs and others were dank and dirty. Those that operated partially in the open found themselves at the mercy of crackdowns by authorities, even if they were paying someone to keep them in the clear. So, many night spots cropped up in out-of-the-way, hidden places like office spaces, lofts, and basements. A variety of measures operated to allow speakeasies to keep their cover, from requiring patrons to have entry cards to show a bouncer to simply giving each potential patron a keen looking over.[55]

In the west a new breed of speakeasy cropped up, often in the outer edges of town. In this restaurant-nightclub hybrid, men and women both felt comfortable coming together for food, gambling, dancing, socializing, and, of course, drinking. One patron in Butte, Montana, identified the shift, saying the new Prohibition era nightclubs "lack the vigor, the hairy chests and the call of the wild that you'll find in the city. Women may gamble side by side with their men and loll at the bars with them."[56]

Social and sexual morals bent and wavered too, then, in the mixed sex crowds that gathered in Prohibition era nightlife. Working-class youth and Greenwich Village radicals pushed the boundaries of propriety earlier in the 1910s by entering previously male spaces, eager to imbibe, but in a strange turn of events the outlawing of alcohol in those spaces ended their long-term association with rough masculinity and inappropriate sexual behavior. The nightlife that sprang forward after 1920 was toned down, in order to maximize profit, and it drew in middle- and upper-class women in significant numbers for the first time. Stanley Walker put it baldly in his reporting on New York in the twenties, saying, "Great raving hordes of women began to discover what their less respectable sisters had known for years—that it was a lot of fun, if you liked it, to get soused."[57]

It became for many young women a way to mark themselves off from previous generations, a sophisticated and edgy behavior. Young men and women around the nation, on college campuses and in rural small towns, sought to live the high life by emulating the cultural style of cities such as New York. Even in Butte, girls associated modern youth with drinking. Helen Harrington, a store clerk there, worried over her parents' response when she cut her hair short in the new style. "Ma, I got my hair bobbed," she said, and after her mother looked her over she responded, "I guess you'll be going to the roadhouses next." And, she did just that, along with lots of other women like her. Harrington was a "good" girl, doing what many other good kids did during Prohibition.[58] To them, freedom in the 1920s looked like bobbed hair, jazz dancing, and drinking with men. It may have been disreputable but to them it was not controversial.

The illegal gin joints dotting the landscape of marginalized neighborhoods also allowed for the growth of a black market in illegal drugs. In Harlem, New York, and on Chicago's South Side, the traffic of well-to-do white partygoers encouraged the availability of illicit drugs like cocaine, marijuana, and opium. The federal government strove to block the distribution and sale of drugs as it worked to enforce Prohibition, and the thriving black market helped achieve the opposite result when gangland bootleggers expanded their wares to include those drugs. Authorities showed less interest in policing areas with little political power, and so it was often those poor and black neighborhoods that became the center of both the illegal liquor and drug trade. Despite repeated complaints by inhabitants of Harlem throughout the decade, city officials did little about it and the neighborhood, like many others, became suffused with crime and vice.[59]

The spike in criminality in the Prohibition years therefore disproportionately impacted poor and black communities in urban enclaves such as Chicago. The conditions proved to be a boon to growing gangs and bootleggers. Slowly but surely these streets became a battleground between rival gangs, in clashes like the beer wars in Chicago. The city's different gangs threatened sellers in the city in an effort to market only their particular beer brand—hesitant shopkeepers invited bomb threats, which were carried out.[60] The fact that illicit substances substantially contributed to the violence and lack of safety on the streets of poor neighborhoods in the 1920s would echo into the future.

The gangs running city streets gained the most from Prohibition's arrival, one might argue. Organized crime, specifically, operated on a relatively small scale before the 1920s, largely in urban areas. And, it focused mostly on the threat or enactment of physical violence in support of money-making schemes like gambling and prostitution. Criminals enjoyed years of experience in the trade of illegal goods and services. Yet, in one fell swoop, when the government outlawed the manufacture and sale of liquor, it created a vast and profitable market for the criminal underworld. Bootleggers and distributors built complex organizations, employing a wide range of participants including thugs, lawyers, and truck drivers just to name a few. The political corruption plaguing American cities made the job of buying off influential men a relatively easy one. Criminals cultivated ties, through bribery, with politicians, judges, and police officers. A collection of criminal syndicates like these operated throughout the country, drastically increasing the level of criminality in the nation, and all the while throwing a spotlight on a new figure, one both menacing and compelling. Overnight, it seemed, Prohibition gave birth to the American gangster.[61]

The cooperation of government officials at all levels smoothed the way for his rise. When gangsters baptized children, or when they got married, politicians joined them in the party. State and national senators, mayors, judges, and police all over the country joined with bootleggers to provide illegal liquor. Reports even claimed policemen escorted trucks full of liquor as they made their deliveries.[62] In order to make it in the bootleg business, one required "protection" from other criminals or from the police, and this did not come cheap. Government officials estimated that men like Al Capone took in $100,000 per week in protection money, a figure that today equals more than a million dollars. This exorbitantly expensive scheme, one necessary to operation for the most part, meant that only the businesses with substantial profits could even afford to stay in the game. Everyone involved, from government officials to the gangsters themselves, made a lot of money.[63]

That quintessential gangster, Alphonse Capone, rose to prominence in gang-infested Chicago in the 1920s. Capone moved himself and his family from Brooklyn to the growing midwestern metropolis to assist a former mentor and fellow gangster in an expansion of his own criminal operation beyond prostitution and into bootlegging. Continuous turf wars erupted among rival gangs as they all jockeyed for power and resources. Capone's mentor survived an attack by rivals but gave him the reins afterward. In 1925, at just 26 years old, Al Capone took over the Outfit, a massive crime syndicate in Prohibition-era Chicago.

He expanded his illegal activities to include gambling and extortion in addition to prostitution and bootlegging. As his visibility grew, he purchased a custom-made Cadillac with bulletproof glass. No longer in the shadows, now, Al Capone emerged as one of the most powerful crime bosses in Chicago.

Consequently, a sharp rise in the number of murders stalked the Prohibition years. Thousands of people died in violence linked to the war on alcohol. Shootings among gangsters surged, with gory gangland deaths plastered all over the newspapers. The Valentine's Day massacre in Chicago in February 1929 stands out as one particularly brutal example of this violence. On the front page of the New York Times, a reporter called it the "most cold-blooded gang massacre in the history of this city's underworld."[64] Members of the Bugs Moran gang waited in a garage for a shipment of alcohol when Al Capone's men approached them dressed as police officers. Going through the routine of a typical raid, Capone's men easily lined up Moran's men along a wall before spraying them with bullets. All 7 men died, and the police reported finding some 100 discharged machine gun shells. But regular Americans died too in the crosshairs of gang violence.[65] And the number of reported homicides went from just over 5,800 in 1920 to 7,800 in 1928.[66]

The popularity of automobiles further exacerbated the problem, as vehicles both increased crime rates as a target of theft and served to ferry would-be criminals to and from their crimes more easily. The use of cars fostered a rash of bank robberies by gangsters in the 1920s, with a getaway now more possible than ever. An armed robbery at the Jefferson State Bank in the Illinois state capital in 1924 offers an example familiar to many at the time. Three men entered the bank, forced the employees into the vault, put nearly $30,000 into two bags and escaped in a car idling outside.[67] In just one year, 1926, the New York Times highlighted 43 major bank robberies across the nation. And news coverage of Prohibition violations only whetted Americans' appetites for more sensational reporting on crime.[68]

This issue of crime was at the forefront of national discussion, then. In the very early postwar years, concerns about criminality focused on widespread labor unrest, racial upheaval, and politically inspired radicalism, but now those concerns competed with the fallout from the Volstead Act. Even though many supported Prohibition, many others felt overwhelmed by the impact of the legislation. It was apparent to anyone who cared to notice that alcohol was widely available, and that it was unregulated and often dangerous to consume. The courts groaned under the high volume of arrests the legislation produced. And even so, average Americans joined gang members and police officers in widespread disregard for the law. People were worried. Numerous cities and states put together crime commissions, and investigators published more than 30 surveys and reports studying the crime problem.[69] And for the first time in the nation's history, in his inaugural address, the president prioritized crime "as a problem of national concern."[70]

Reshaping the Criminal Justice System

President Herbert Hoover made this statement in 1929, and he set in motion a searching investigation of the nation's law enforcement structures and practices. This national approach signaled a noticeable break from the past. Typically, Americans worried over and worked to combat crime on the local level. But this would be different. Hoover called for a national commission to study the criminal justice system. The National Commission on Law Observance and Enforcement, or the Wickersham Commission, so named after the group's chairman George Wickersham, set about studying and investigating the problems with and possible remedies for the nation's dysfunctional criminal justice system. Known for his belief in the value of this type of social science and expert analysis, Hoover's response to criminality and his particular type of governance laid the groundwork for what one historian calls our "modern penal state."[71]

This effort involved cooperation among policy makers and experts in local and state crime studies, fostering an expansion of the government apparatus that often goes overlooked in examinations of Prohibition. While the Progressive Era and the New Deal are characteristically known for the increasing degree of federal intervention into the lives of Americans, the rather conservative decade and a half in between those two political eras has stood somewhat apart. But historians now point out that Prohibition linked these two efforts chronologically. The vast and absorbing process of policing liquor in the 1920s, by necessity, dramatically enlarged the American state.[72]

In part, this was thanks to the work of the Wickersham Commission. The fundamental premise of the commission lay in their belief that it was no longer appropriate to leave the increasingly serious issue of crime to non-profits and local and state governments. Looking for more systematic change, 10 men and 1 woman brought their social science and legal experience together. They heard from and were counseled by many, many other prominent national experts, and after two years of exhaustive research and complicated wrangling among members, the group published 14 reports along with several more volumes of records. While Hoover initiated the effort, the commission held nothing back in their indictment of American society, even challenging some of Hoover's own policies.[73]

The commission helped spur an increase in information gathering as a crime-fighting tool. The busy Bureau of Investigation, soon to be renamed the Federal Bureau of Investigation, used information in new and exciting ways. The low bar set by the Prohibition Bureau compelled a young J. Edgar Hoover to run a tight ship at the Bureau of Investigation, leveraging his well-oiled machine against the failing department. His bureau, along with other law enforcement groups, collected and centralized reporting of crimes nationwide into a practical system of statistics to be used in facilitating policy decisions. One of the Wickersham Commission's fundamental criticisms of law enforcement in America was a plain lack of facts, and Prohibition transformed the collection of crime data going forward.[74]

The rise of a reconstituted FBI in 1924 reflected this interest in collecting information on criminality, and the organization's presence furthered Americans' sense that crime was an issue they needed to worry about. J. Edgar Hoover had notoriously high expectations of his agents and he purposefully moved them around so they did not fall prey to offers for preferential treatment.[75] But he propelled the agency into the spotlight by the 1930s, not by focusing on Prohibition, which Hoover saw as a possible tarnish to the agency's image, but by lionizing bank robbers like Bonnie Parker, Clyde Barrow, and John Dillinger. This was a crime problem Hoover felt the FBI could handle. He set up the notorious "Ten Most Wanted" list, a major vehicle for publicity, and collaborated with filmmakers to always portray "G-men" as the good guys who got their man. While the agency's star rose in the public's estimation and in the federal bureaucracy—doubling in size by 1940—the presence of crime nationwide seemed more palpable to average Americans.[76]

The development of the FBI also reflected the evolution of modern crime fighting. First, police officials felt the impact of a trend toward bigness, toward national culture over the intimacy of small-town culture. While policemen still walked the streets of many cities, increasingly they also relied on automobiles. And advances in technology meant that citizens reached out to police via the telephone, and headquarters dispatched them by radio. Technological developments fostered degrees of separation that crept in between the police and local communities. Second, these same developments changed the way authorities solved crimes. As gangsters used automobiles and telephones, law enforcement officials found ways to use this to their advantage. Police pulled over cars and trucks they believed could be transporting alcohol, and a 1925 Supreme Court case, *Caroll v. U.S.*, ruled that authorities did not need a search warrant in such cases. Furthermore, in 1927, the Court decided that authorities could wiretap suspects' telephones, as long as they did so off the suspect's private property. *Olmstead v. U.S.* allowed law enforcement officials to listen to phone conversations at the phone company's headquarters and treat that knowledge as if it was a conversation they heard in public. These, along with other decisions enabling entrapment, increased some Americans' discomfort with Prohibition and its enforcement as government overreach. Federal, state, and local law enforcement seemed to have a great deal of power.[77]

Efforts to stem the tide of criminality led officials to ratchet up penalty laws too, making punishments for Prohibition-related crime more severe. In some states, mandatory sentencing rules went into play. New York State ensured that a fourth felony would carry a mandatory life sentence. And Congress enacted the Jones Act in 1929, making a violation of the Volstead Act a felony with up to five years in prison and up to a $10,000 fine, even on the first go around.[78]

Unsurprisingly, prison overcrowding became a thorny problem in the 1920s as the number of people incarcerated tripled. The federal government held just several thousand prisoners in facilities leading up to World War I, but that number exploded to over 10,000 by the end of Prohibition. And the federal penal facilities needed to house this influx of criminals did not come close to meeting the demand. The same problem existed among state prisons, which found themselves woefully overcrowded in the 1920s. In Pennsylvania's Eastern Penitentiary, four prisoners bunked in a cell designed for one, a situation repeated around the country.

The need for more prison facilities in this moment actually spurred the growth of the prison system. President Hoover announced a request for $5 million "to end prison crowding" in 1929, and followed through with plans to expand existing prisons, build additional ones, and expand the probation system.[79] Prohibition demand ultimately led authorities to construct 11 new federal prisons and many more run by states.[80] At first, when Prohibition ended, the number of people incarcerated continued to rise, but ultimately this number fell through the 1970s. However, it is worth noting that beginning in the 1970s, and even more so in the 1980s, the nation's prison population skyrocketed once again. Americans in the last quarter of the century watched as a familiar trend, one from the 1920s, played out amid a new war on illicit substances—the war on drugs.[81]

Prohibition

In fact, the Prohibition era featured a simultaneous, while lesser known, attack on the use and sale of narcotics. A war on drugs formed alongside the prohibition of alcohol, and while the stigmatization of narcotics had more broad popular support, the movement lacked a similar grassroots push for enforcement. Yet, because many agreed on the general dangers of drug use, the effort found fewer obstacles and lasted much, much longer. The 1920s war on drugs, and its consequences, are with us still.

While efforts to crack down on drug abuse certainly predated Prohibition, the enactment of the Eighteenth Amendment intensified those efforts. In 1914, Congress passed the Harrison Narcotics Act to facilitate the prohibition of drug sales, but notably this measure did not criminalize drug use. Society tended to view addicted individuals as weak and in need of help, not necessarily as criminals. However, once the criminal justice system responded to alcohol prohibition and the wheels were turning at all levels, authorities and the courts became more and more willing to accept the abuse and distribution of drugs as a criminal act. The Eighteenth Amendment allowed for the growth of a drug enforcement agency, one that operated within the Prohibition Unit. Congress tightened up drug laws, making substances like opium and cocaine scarce. This led to an upsurge in the use and distribution of heroin, which was easier to transport and easier to obtain, creating a shift toward more powerful narcotics.[82] At the same time, marijuana became a growing concern linked to Mexican immigrants in the Southwest in the 1920s, and officials there convinced government authorities to add it to the list of illicit substances. The newspapers keyed in on stories of drug rings and seizures of opium at the nation's borders, highlighting the problem of narcotics in America.

The structural apparatus for combatting drug use emerged at this point, then. Herbert Hoover created the Federal Narcotics Bureau in 1930, independent of the Prohibition Bureau. Its director, well-known Prohibition enforcer, Harry Anslinger, worked to bring the federal drug laws into concert with state laws in order to coordinate drug designations and enforcement. He and his colleagues learned important lessons from the nightmare of Prohibition and made certain that as many states as they could push to do so passed consistent legislation to ensure smooth and effective application of the law. Prominent Anti-Saloon League lecturer Richmond Hobson founded the International Narcotics Education Association in 1923, a nonprofit focused on education and policy. Hobson framed the drug problem with flourish typical of his Prohibition efforts, claiming that over a million Americans suffered from narcotic addiction when government estimates numbered less than 150,000. And Anslinger used some enduring images to sell his efforts, claiming that "a significant majority of rape, assault, and murder cases" were linked with drug use.[83] At a narcotics conference in the Waldorf-Astoria in 1928, Hobson called for a Twentieth Amendment to the Constitution, providing the federal government with total police power to curb drug traffic. His effort rallied quite a few prominent supporters.[84] This did not come to pass, but he and others like him convinced anti-liquor crusaders in and out of government circles to uphold increasingly stringent enforcement and punitive efforts, especially when the Prohibition effort began to break down.

Prosecutions of drug violations began to fall after Prohibition ended, as the depression took its toll on appropriations for the Federal Narcotics Bureau. These numbers continued to decline over the next few decades, too. But when the revived war on drugs emerged in the 1970s and 1980s, historians argue that the framework for that effort, and the reasoning behind it, existed long before, thanks to Prohibition.[85] The expansion of law enforcement agencies, the growth of prisons, and the structure of Prohibition law set up the modern penal state. The moral arguments propping up Prohibition fostered national acceptance of a looming federal government. And a more coercive American state emerged from the culture wars of the 1920s.[86]

Prohibition exposed and exacerbated a profound division among Americans. Older Protestant bourgeois values like discipline and thrift, borne of the old economic order, clashed with newer more indulgent desires for instant gratification and leisure, synonymous with the new consumer culture. Immigrant patterns of social life and community building clashed with middle-class reformers' and nativists' views of a moral, upstanding society. While Prohibition did not spark these conflicts, it fanned the flames lit by war, urbanization, the decline in religion, mass immigration, and the development of mass culture.

When Prohibition legally compelled Americans to give up the leisure activities associated with alcohol, particularly in urban areas, trendsetters moved to willingly and proudly break that law. This outcome was due in no small part to the fact that middle- and upper-class drinkers were impacted by the law as well as poor men and women. Unlike in previous anti-vice crusades, which often targeted the marginal and weak, bourgeois Americans found their social lives limited. And their money and influence allowed them to disregard that effort in ways sanctioned by many. Furthermore, enforcement efforts came down disproportionately on marginalized communities of working-class and immigrant violators of the Volstead Act.

One observer in New York argued that Prohibition created a "state of civil war" in American culture, as those who supported the law upheld it and those who disagreed openly flouted it.[87] While the motivations behind the law reflected the hopes of culture warriors battling change, rather than rebuilding and reinforcing an older, more traditional moral code, the war on alcohol seemed only to hasten its demise. Nonetheless, Prohibition's impact proved potent and lasting.

CHAPTER FOUR

Searching for a "Full Life": The Modern Woman in 1920s America

"There must be a way out," cried the *Smith College Weekly*.[1] Facing down a perplexing future, the paper's editor acknowledged living in a world still governed by the double standard in 1919. Sure, the states were in the process of ratifying the Nineteenth Amendment, and more and more women entered college, and access to birth control became easier. Yet many, maybe even most, Americans felt it was not possible for a woman to combine home life successfully with a career in the 1920s. Among her peers, this writer felt a "rebellion" was "rousing." In a remarkable moment, it no longer seemed natural to these young women that they had to choose between a career and a family, particularly when men would naturally have both. "There must be a way out," the editor insisted, "and it is the problem of our generation to find" it.[2] But the way proved to be elusive in the 1920s.

Women activists established modern feminism in the early decades of the 20th century, and so it is no surprise that a pestering problem for many women in the present day—that complicated struggle to "have it all"—actually first emerged in the 1920s. Pioneering women in the 1800s and early 1900s often chose public service or careers instead of marriage and children, mostly out of necessity, and many failed to find conflict between the two life choices. They simply did not go together. But in the 1920s, self-professed new style feminists sought to combine work and family life. A "full life," explained feminist Dorothy Bromley, in 1927, "calls for marriage and children as well as a career."[3] Radical activist Crystal Eastman insisted that a modern woman was "not altogether satisfied with love, marriage, and a purely domestic career." Rather, she wanted "money of her own," "work of her own," and a "means of self-expression." And in addition to all of that, she wanted a "husband, home, and children, too. How to reconcile these two desires in real life, that is the question," she opined.[4]

Americans responded to this modern feminist desire with profound and lasting discomfort. Dr. Charles Eliot, public intellectual and former president of Harvard University, lectured the wives of Harvard alumni and faculty in 1927 with strong criticism of these "modern young women." He echoed the sentiments of many old guard traditionalists who resisted women's entry into the public sphere. The idea that "there is a healthier and happier career for women in these days than that of the mother" was, to Eliot, a "delusion."[5] Author and critic John Macy wrote in the pages of *Harper's* in 1926, "Let us be done forever with this nonsense about the equality of the sexes. They are not equal in nature and never can be."[6] By the end of the 1920s, as the Depression began and prominent, organized feminist activism began its long decline, these hopeful women bristling with ambition saw no way out. Their lingering disappointment and frustration at the seeming impossibility of realizing this ambition then moved forward through several generations in the 20th century. Eventually, it formed the very foundation of second wave feminism in the 1960s, which according to Elaine Showalter aimed "not for a 'free' choice, but for life in both dimensions."[7] The hope for a choice to combine career and family, a version of living life in both dimensions, is emblematic still of our contemporary society's enduring struggle to live up to a feminist vision first articulated in the 1920s.

A familiar script took shape in the 1920s, then, when political rights, economic opportunity, birth control, and changing sex and gender norms reframed the relationship between women and American society. Women, having secured the right to vote in 1920, agitated for more political and social equality in a push that had little to do with their traditional roles as wives and mothers. More and more professional women sought to join the workforce in this decade, seeking some degree of economic independence. In the face of these changing roles for women, coupled with shifting norms for sexual behavior among the young, marriage reformers worked feverishly to modernize marriage in the 1920s in order to save it. They wished to gird it against the winds of change by allowing it to bend. At the same time experts raised the bar for the work of mothers in modern America, sparking a surge of anxiety over the act of parenting. Meanwhile, the push for birth control begun before World War I continued apace, fundamentally shifting Americans' thinking on women and family life. Sherwood Eddy, a prominent progressive activist and youth leader, claimed in 1929 that "no other generation in this country ever faced the insistent demand for equality between the sexes, for the economic independence of women and the abolition of a false double standard of morals."[8] While familiar to us now, in the 1920s these felt new. And just as feminist women moved to expand their roles to include both a home life and a career, others took up the struggle to cast women only in their domestic roles as wives and mothers.

A changed society and culture in the 1920s seemed to explode the sanctity of family life in unavoidable ways, and people drew the battle lines in efforts to encourage or condemn these changes. Americans typically held the family in a space apart from the rough and tumble world of the public sphere, preferring to see it as impervious to change. But in the 1920s, this fiction became harder and harder to maintain. Birth control, shifting marital, maternal, and work patterns for women, and women's entry into formal politics had the potential to reframe family life, to blur the edges between the private and public spheres. A visible struggle materialized as an array of women's rights activists took up one side, and their opponents, a motley crew, took up the other. The right to shape the outline of family life, to alter women's roles within it or to grasp onto tradition, was the prize. Then and now, "in every generation," historian James Morone observed, "The family is ground zero of the culture wars."[9]

REPRODUCTIVE RIGHTS

In New York City, 8,000 people crowded outside the Park Theatre on an unusually warm November evening in 1921, straining to gain entry into a public forum titled "Birth Control—Is It Moral?"[10] After the doors opened at 7:30 P.M., the crowd pushed into the theater, a venue designed for 1,500, and when the doors closed at 8:00 P.M. police disbursed those remaining outside. But the officers stayed—they settled into the crowd with court stenographers to monitor the content of speeches by leading birth control activist Margaret Sanger and others, lining the aisles in an effort to very visibly keep the peace.

This police presence came on the heels of a starkly different scene, this one at Town Hall several nights earlier. After receiving a complaint from the office of prominent Catholic leader Archbishop Patrick Hayes, police arrived at the planned event to shut it down, arresting Sanger and a colleague in violation of their right to free speech as they began the meeting. Outrage at the shuttering of the lawful public event followed, for according to Sanger and her defenders, she had the right "to conduct clean, orderly, and peaceful discussion of the wisdom and morality of conscious regulation of parenthood."[11] She was released, and the event took place at the Park Theater a few nights later, this time with both police protection and intense monitoring.

Sanger thrilled at the publicity the ruckus offered her cause, because birth control still generated controversy in the 1920s and securing access to it still required years of hard work. She would find herself barred from speaking on numerous occasions in the coming decade. Conservative religious figures and those opposed to women's rights vociferously campaigned against the movement. Rev. Harry Emerson Fosdick, a leading progressive figure, demonstrated the divide when he called for an end of the effort to suppress birth control in 1929. Surveying the cultural landscape, he noted the great emotions still at play, saying there are "some flaming with ardor for it, some with wrath against it, and too few thoroughly studying it."[12] Reproductive rights—or, whether women should have them or not—ignited passions in the modern 1920s as women's roles underwent significant shifts. Birth control became one way to talk about these shifts, whether one was for or against access to it.

The Fight for Birth Control

In the 1920s, the controversy over reproductive rights focused on birth control specifically, for Americans stigmatized abortion decades earlier. At this point, abortion no longer seemed like a hot button issue. Early on in the nation's history, people viewed abortion through a different lens than some do now, demonstrating a kind of moral ambivalence that dated back to the Roman Empire. Not until the mid-19th century did a campaign begin to frame abortion as murder, an argument we are familiar with today.[13] In fact, up until that point abortion was legal and freely available in the United States, as long as quickening—the moment when a mother can feel fetal movement—had not taken place. But most failed to consider it an egregious crime even if the procedure took place after that point. As historian James Morone notes, "Neither politics nor morality defined abortion as a problem" in the early part of the 19th century. But after the Civil War, a movement stirred with the intention of demonizing it. Demographic shifts and social upheavals contributed to a climate that became less and less tolerant of the practice, particularly as abortion rates rose.

Physicians, religious officials, and other concerned citizens crafted a purposeful campaign that turned American thinking on abortion on its head in a stunningly short period of time.[14] Physician Horatio Storer launched a prominent crusade calling for the criminalization of abortion, fighting what he and the American Medical Association (AMA) called "a crime against life."[15] Their efforts found remarkable success, with 30 states prohibiting abortion between 1866 and 1877. In 1873, the Comstock Act declared that "any article or medicine for causing an abortion except on a prescription of a physician in good standing" was illegal. This would be the closest thing to a federal ban on abortion.[16]

The antiabortion campaign permanently reframed the narrative on the practice, but abortions continued. By 1900, every state had laws on the books making abortion at any stage of pregnancy illegal, unless it would spare the life of the mother.[17] And yet, a medical examiner in 1920 called frequent abortions an "open secret."[18] Studies of working-class patients at well-known clinics in the 1920s found that 20 percent of all pregnancies ended in abortion, while surveys of middle-class women in the same decade found that 10–23 percent of the survey's respondents had abortions.[19] These included women from all ethnic and religious backgrounds, including both the married and the unwed. And because these 19th-century physicians framed abortion as a moral concern requiring the expertise of a medical practitioner, the issue largely disappeared from public view in the 20th century as doctors quietly made decisions behind office doors.[20] Thus, while women continued to have both therapeutic and criminal abortions throughout the 20th century, including in the 1920s, the issue would not become a decidedly public concern once again until the rise of second-wave feminism in the late 1960s.[21]

In the 1920s, then, rather than abortion it was the controversy over a woman's ability to prevent pregnancy in the first place that shaped the public debate over reproductive rights.[22] Much like abortion, though, up until the mid-19th-century Americans enjoyed free and unfettered access to a range of methods of birth control, including condoms, pessaries, douches, and jellies. Information about these contraceptive technologies could be found in the pages of newspapers where they were widely, if discreetly, advertised, through word of mouth in one's neighborhood, or from a doctor or midwife. Condoms cost about six cents each in 1870 and diaphragms only a dollar, and so Americans from all social classes, including workers, had potential access to them.[23] Birth control, while not yet labeled as such, enjoyed a comfortable place in American life.

But by the 1870s, several pressing social issues triggered a move by Congress to limit access to birth control. Anthony Comstock, working through the newly established New York Society for the Suppression of Vice, crusaded against birth control as immoral and dangerous in his larger efforts to squash obscenity in America. With help from other concerned elites, Comstock successfully lobbied Congress in 1873 to pass a broad bill forbidding any obscene letter, photo, book, poem, advertisement, device, or medicine, just to name a few examples. The law also criminalized the sharing of information that would prevent conception or cause an abortion. The federal law forbade the passage of such information in the press or through the mail, and a New York law that Comstock bolstered later prevented even verbal communication of this information. An eager investigator, Comstock found obscenity everywhere, often using entrapment to arrest people.[24] He boasted of seizing 60,000 contraceptive devices by the end of 1874.[25] Comstock's motivations definitely stemmed from his extreme religiosity, but they also included broader concerns at the time. Fears of the women's rights movement, of women controlling their own sexuality, and of the national and racial cost incurred when white women limited their reproduction, loomed large.

Despite these difficulties, women continued to find ways to control pregnancy. Without prior knowledge of discreet supply channels, it took a great deal of courage to risk committing a criminal offense. Middle- and upper-class women sometimes successfully convinced doctors to give them information. Others restricted sexual activity with their spouses, or used folk remedies handed down through generations. Statistics demonstrate this: the number of children born to white women dropped from 4.4 to 2.1 between 1880 and 1940, while the number of children born to African American women dropped from 7.5 to 3.[26]

Through the 1910s, Americans underwent a sea change in popular thinking on birth control, reconstructing the framework for discussion. Unlike abortion, debate over birth control was pushed into public view. Anarchist feminist Emma Goldman agitated for birth control as early as the 1890s, but by the 1910s she made the call for birth control a staple of her lecture tours in an effort to publicize the issue. The substantial social hygiene program undertaken by the federal government during World War I profoundly publicized discussions of sex. The emerging mass consumer culture splashed sex all over movie screens and magazine covers. Sex, it seemed, was everywhere. And soon, a new crop of reformers began to insist that discussion of reproductive health in the form of birth control take place in public, not just in private. While the focus of their efforts may have been intimate, in order to affect change their work needed to take place in the light of day.

The movement began in earnest with Margaret Sanger's work in New York City. And Sanger, a nurse and socialist activist, espoused radical intentions. She first ran a rather explicit series on birth control titled "What Every Girl Should Know" in the socialist paper *The Call* in 1912. The government summarily banned it under the Comstock Law. From there she moved more and more purposefully into the exclusive realm of birth control activism. Historian Linda Gordon positions Sanger as having realized the potentially historic possibility inherent in freely available birth control information and technologies. Seen through the lens of class politics, birth control was "ameliorative," Gordon writes, but "seen in terms of sexual politics . . . birth control was revolutionary because it could free women entirely from the major burden that differentiated them from men and made them dependent on men."[27] Sanger aimed for revolution.

The movement's potential therefore invited great enthusiasm and opposition. Before Sanger's star began to rise, activists like Emma Goldman, Ben Reitman, and Elizabeth Gurley Flynn were arrested numerous times for publishing pamphlets or speaking publicly about birth control. Yet Sanger, more than the others, invited adoration by many, and she walked a line between militancy and charm that helped swell support for the movement. Her appeals were emotional, dramatic, compelling, and requests for birth control information came in from all kinds of women from all over the country. Her aggressive efforts led to her arrest, and she fled to Europe to avoid trial in October 1914.

The year Sanger spent in Europe altered the future of the birth control movement, as a grassroots movement grew up in her absence. William Sanger, her estranged husband, went on trial for distributing a birth control pamphlet she wrote, swelling support for him and his wife. An effort to help William brought together a group of committed activists in New York, all of whom felt the time was right to directly challenge the Comstock Act. In early 1915, Mary Ware Dennett and several others founded the first birth control organization in the country, the National Birth Control League.[28] Sanger returned to a changed environment later that year, in part thanks to the efforts of Dennett, and she capitalized on the publicity. Sanger made herself and her cause famous by embarking on a nationwide speaking tour, which led the government to drop charges against her as sympathy for her and her cause grew. Comstock himself died soon after William's trial. And by the time authorities arrested Sanger again in 1916 for opening a birth control clinic in a poor Brooklyn neighborhood, one that operated for just 9 days and served 400 women, the organized push for birth control in America was widespread.[29]

Opposition to this movement came from many directions. Many suffragists dared not back the movement publicly for fear of being branded as radicals. Both the League of Women Voters and the National Woman's Party refused to support birth control, perhaps sensing the ease with which it would allow opponents of women's rights to attack them as being against the family. In addition, some feminists chose not to undermine the female moral authority they felt supported their political legitimacy. Private matters should stay private, some felt.[30] Antifeminists firmly believed in traditionally arranged gender norms, with a woman maintaining her rightful place at the hearth of the home with as many children as God gave her, regardless of whether she could afford to sit at the hearth in order to feed them. And some worried that birth control would further foster male sexual license at the same time that it robbed women of the protective forces of marriage and monogamy.[31] Religious conservatives fundamentally opposed contraception for the most part in the 1920s, and though Sanger did win over some leaders with her argument that birth control could improve marriages, reduce abortions, and better women's health, Catholic officials worked hard to blunt her impact.[32] And doctors, as they did earlier in the movement to ban abortion, stressed their male professional prerogative to know what was best for women: pregnancy and motherhood. Sanger, they argued, a lowly nurse, and worse yet a "sexually liberated woman and outspoken political maverick" surely had no business in such affairs.[33]

But something changed by the 1920s, as two powerful forces in American life fostered acceptance of birth control. The first was the race and class anxiety of the middle class in the face of nativism and urban poverty. Middle-class women could access birth control by visiting their sympathetic physician, and many did so. They likely did not feel hindered by the trappings of the Comstock law.[34] But working-class women could not afford such access. In what historian Linda Gordon calls a "neo-race-suicide view," many felt if middle- and upper-class Americans used birth control anyway, to keep it from the poor was simply bad social policy.[35] Second, sex modernism permeated middle-class culture in this decade. Americans developed a certain degree of comfortability with sex, making more people amenable to the idea of legalized birth control.

The presence of sex modernism, even if contested by many traditionalists, meant that this effort for birth control would trigger a revolution in American sexual thought. Sexuality became commercialized. The common man's interpretation of Freud—widely popular—posited the healthy expression of sexual desire as a necessity. And heterosexual dating and marital practices crystallized in the 1920s. These developments allowed for the exploding birth control movement to forge a significant shift in thinking about sex in America. While previous calls for reform of birth control laws focused on the need for voluntary motherhood, by the 1920s this shifted to new ground entirely. Birth control radicals like Sanger and Emma Goldman insisted on women's right to both self-determination and pleasure. Women needed access to birth control because they should have the final say on their own reproductive future and because just like men, double standard be damned, they deserved to have sex on their own terms without the fear of pregnancy.

The birth control movement implicitly made a fundamental argument separating reproduction from sexual pleasure.[36] This had tremendous liberatory potential for women, something many people were profoundly uncomfortable with at the time. In essence, these reformers saw birth control as more than a medical issue—to them it was a potentially radical social revolution. Historian Linda Gordon asserts, "They believed that birth control could alleviate much human misery and fundamentally alter social and political power relations, thereby creating greater sexual and class equality."[37]

In Red Scare America, however, Sanger found herself needing to choose between her radical social activism and an alliance with the growing body of more conservative supporters, including male physicians and middle-class women. She chose to divorce herself from her radical past, also divorcing her husband in 1921 only to marry oil tycoon James Noah H. Slee, who would bankroll her work for decades to come. While activists such as Mary Ware Dennett fought into the early 1920s for alterations to the Comstock Law in an effort to decriminalize birth control altogether, Sanger sought approval for medical literature and prescription contraceptives to be granted exemption from the law.[38] Sanger focused now on organizing the American Birth Control League, founded in 1921. She associated it with medical professionals who did speaking tours to drum up support, distributed medical research in support of contraception, and closely documented over 5,000 doctors who approved of birth control even half-heartedly. Sanger also moved toward a eugenic platform and edged away from the claim that it was a woman's right to control her fertility.

And so, after 1920, the birth control movement became more widely accepted than ever, and it was distinctly less radical. Despite Sanger's earlier aspirations, only middle-class women had relatively easy access to contraception through doctors they could pay for. The potential for class equality through birth control slipped away.[39] But Sanger's contribution is undeniable.[40] When marriage reformer Judge Ben Lindsey came out in support of birth control in *Physical Culture* magazine in 1925, a man wrote to him pleading, "Give me the method of birth control taught by the lady in New York who has created such a stir."[41]

The most controversial aspect of the birth control movement in the 1920s was probably the degree to which the public embraced it, and this embrace lingered. By 1930, 55 birth control clinics operated in 23 cities in 15 states, and doctors often advised women on how to fit contraception into their daily lives. A host of progressive religious groups in the 1930s supported the efforts of numerous well-known political action organizations, including the Voluntary Parenthood League and the American Birth Control League.[42] In 1938, a *Ladies Home Journal* poll showed that 79 percent of women asked approved of birth control in some form.[43] Margaret Sanger continued her quest for a form of birth control women might control completely, and with the help of generous funders and courageous physicians in 1960 the FDA approved the birth control pill for contraceptive use. Within five years, 6.5 million American women took the pill. But controversy remained, as eight states banned the drug and Pope Paul VI publicly opposed it. It was not until the Supreme Court case of *Griswold v. Connecticut* in 1965 that a married couples right to "privacy," and thus to birth control, was upheld. Several years later the court ruled the same held for unmarried people.

The 1920s fundamentally altered the experience of women in America, as the weakening of the link between sex and reproduction had lasting implications throughout the remainder of the 20th century. The real tension over reproductive rights in the 1920s stemmed from concerns over those implications, over what reproductive rights might enable. The modern woman and those who supported her right to birth control found hope in changing sex and gender norms, shifting marriage trends, increased access to college, and easier entry into the professions. The tension over reproductive rights in this decade stemmed from concerns over what those rights might enable, a concern apparent then and now. But would their hopes be realized?

SHIFTING WORK AND FAMILY ROLES

A college girl in the 1920s "kisses the boys, she smokes with them, and why? Because the feeling of comradeship is running rampant." In fact, according to this young woman at the Ohio State University, coeds met "on common ground."[44] The upheaval in sex and gender norms on college campuses, in cities and towns, and in popular media became apparent by the 1920s, and it constituted perhaps the most significant "cultural revolution of the twentieth century."[45]

This unnerving development disrupted American culture as people struggled to reframe women's place in deep and meaningful ways. Our attention here is focused on white, educated, middle-class women, as this group probably felt the impact of these changes most dramatically in both their personal and work lives in the 1920s. Their experiences are also reflected most visibly in popular culture. Public hand wringing over sex and marriage and the contours of women's work offer snapshots into the various venues Americans used to hash out the changing place of the modern American woman.

Sex and Marriage

The shadowy outline of actress Colleen Moore moves across the screen with a gang of revelers as they take a skinny dip in the hit 1923 film *Flaming Youth*. Moore portrayed the scandalous young Patricia, lover of jazz and booze and bobbed hair, and advertisements promised visions of "pleasure mad daughters." People went to the theater in droves. No doubt about it, the flapper enthralled America in the years after World War I, and she received the lion's share of attention on shifting sex and gender norms. While most women in America were not flappers—they were older, or married, or mothers, or they lived far from urban areas where the pace of change moved much more slowly—it was the nation's obsession with youth in the 1920s that crowned the flapper as the symbol of change. In a marked break from the recent past, young people publicly and unapologetically overturned convention and pushed the boundaries of propriety. As one historian explained, "For the first time—and in a prelude to the Sixties—the nation's youth rather than their elders set the standards for American society."[46]

The nation's young people came of age in a unique cultural moment in the 1920s. First, social scientists only recently established a shared sense of adolescence as a life stage, marking this age as something distinct from childhood and adulthood. Educator and psychologist G. Stanley Hall developed adolescence study in the years leading up to the turn of the century, and other noted social scientists built on his ideas, arguing that modern youth faced unprecedented circumstances in an increasingly urbanized, industrialized, and commercialized culture. Adolescence was a different time, an age that required society's protection. At the same time, this generation grew up as the framework of separate spheres finally fell away. They gathered in mixed sex spaces and were expected to mingle.

Young people sought education in coeducational high schools around the country, where attendance doubled in the 1920s from 2.2 million to more than 5 million. Increasing numbers of men and women went on to college, and women made up 47 percent of the total college student population in 1920, more than double the percentage they made up in 1870.

This group was primarily white and middle class.[47] The lack of segregated school facilities meant that many black students—men and women—simply could not go to high school, and they were similarly underrepresented on college campuses. But the culture welcomed and encouraged middle-class women to get degrees, and a boisterous coeducational youth culture developed on campuses around the country. The numbers betray the singularity of this moment. For a variety of reasons that 47 percent declined steadily in the coming years and decades, not reaching such heights again until the late 1970s with the rise of feminism's second wave.

The sheer size of this youth group's cultural presence engendered conversations about an apparent "sexual revolution," marking the young as different from their elders, and as both troubled and troubling. Many mothers and fathers, and probably their children too, felt that an impassable gulf existed between generations.[48] And these intrepid explorers of sex and mass culture lived lives that were indeed different. In mixed-sex high schools and on college campuses, a new dating system developed, one with overt sexual overtones, including kissing, petting, and even sex before marriage. This was more pronounced among white middle-class youth in cities and suburbs, where young people had access to discretionary income, cars, and commercialized leisure. But on the whole, courtship moved outside the immediate purview of families and communities.

People began to talk about a new kind of relationship between young men and women, one seemingly based on equality of desires. Men said they wanted a woman they could talk to about the world. Women wanted to express their own individual freedom, sense of self, and sexuality—all afforded to them by a new and modern culture. Writer Frederick Lewis Allen claimed that young women understood that some men no longer wanted the burden of a "family or the companionship of mature wisdom." Rather, he wanted "excited play" and the "thrills of sex without their fruition."[49] His counterpart was, no doubt, the flapper.

Some say the flapper, beautiful and unorthodox, first appeared in America in the pages of F. Scott Fitzgerald's novel *This Side of Paradise*, published in 1920; he called her "lovely and expensive and about nineteen."[50] Dr. Charles J. Smith of Roanoke College made a buzz in the media when he said, "The world has never known the turning loose of such an army of hard-drinking, cigarette-puffing, licentious Amazons as walk our streets and invade our campuses today."[51] The flapper was young, urban, single, white, and middle class. She was a flirty, carefree, cigarette-smoking, drinking, dance hall loving kind of girl. She cared about having fun, and she pushed the envelope. And she became a stereotype for all kinds of women who challenged the status quo in the early 20th century.

In the time of a "revolution in manners and morals" then, the flapper served as the revolution's figurehead. Popular psychology in the 1920s claimed that sexual satisfaction allowed for good mental health, and as the birth control movement expanded, many women insisted on their own right to sexual pleasure for pleasure's sake. Mass culture challenged the Victorian sexual order on a daily basis. And so, while the flapper did not create this revolution, as one historian put it, she "inflated its notoriety by making it look like fun."[52]

The visual presentation flappers crafted mattered a great deal, as they threw the modest corseted style of the Victorian era aside. Flappers bobbed their hair, abandoning their mother's hairstyles that piled long locks neatly atop their heads. The bob swung freely as they danced. They rouged their cheeks and lips, a practice previously associated with prostitutes. Flappers sported shorter hemlines, just an inch below their knees. Their dresses typically had short sleeves, or worse yet, no sleeves at all. Gone were the corsets, the hats, long draping skirts. In fact, to many Victorians, flappers seemed nearly naked. But by the middle of the decade, the "flapper style" pervaded New York City, adorned by women of all ages. Pages and pages of advertisements in magazines and newspapers broadcast the new styles to more out-of-the-way places too, along with countless mass-market films like *It* (1927) and *Our Dancing Daughters* (1928).[53]

Flappers' personal style coupled with their social habits led many in American society to fear for their virtue. As jazz music moved into the mainstream in the 1920s, it shaped the ongoing dance craze, inspiring new, boisterous moves that clearly offended the senses of the older generation. A Parents League in Brooklyn, New York, landed on the front page of the *Washington Post* for setting up " 'blue laws' against their flapper daughters." These rules limited parties to weekend evenings, forbid short skirts and "improper" dancing, and ratcheted up parental supervision.[54] Moral crusaders such as Billy Sunday and Rev. John Roach Straton painted the lurid connection between dancing and sex, and their fears were not entirely unwarranted. In a culture saturated with sex, these girls knew more than their mothers and their grandmothers had at their age, and evidence shows that they did in fact engage in more sexual activity than their forebears. Later research demonstrates that higher numbers of women partook in premarital sex in the 1920s, though for most it was only acceptable as a prelude to marriage.[55]

Yet, for all the boundaries these young women appeared to push, the flapper expressed no real interest in feminism just a moment after the heyday of activism in the 1910s. In fact, cultural commentators placed the flapper in direct opposition to this political feminism. Sexologists, male sex reformers, and the media often framed the unmarried "new woman" of the early 20th century—suffragists and settlement house workers—as antagonistic to the new "liberated" flapper. The older feminists did their part in currying this sentiment. Prominent writer and feminist Charlotte Perkins Gilman commented on the great irony of so many young women, now with so much more opportunity than she had, focusing on dress, dance, and men, and doing so little politically. "This is the woman's century," she said, "the first chance . . . [for her] transcendent power to remake humanity, to rebuild the suffering world—and the world waits while she powders her nose."[56]

Significantly, the revolution in manners and morals was not a revolt against family life either. Despite growing numbers of women attending college, despite the wild popularity of the flapper and her disregard for tradition, marriage became more attractive than ever.[57] The marriage rate rose between 1890 and 1920. In fact, marriage rates increased for all classes and racial-ethnic groups. Where half of educated Victorian-era women declined to marry, from 1913 to 1923 "between 80 and 90 percent of female college graduates married."[58] People married younger, too. In urban areas, the age at marriage fell from 26.1 years in 1890 to 24.6 in 1920 for men, and from 22.0 years to 21.3 among women.[59]

Rather than a revolution against marriage, the rupture with traditional Victorian sexual and gender roles fostered "a revolution within marriage," setting up the 1920s as a decade that looked more like the 1990s than the 1890s.[60] Americans approached a sexual liberalism at this moment, where many embraced a growing acceptance of sex before marriage, of sex as separate from procreation, which served to celebrate sex for pleasure. In a very modern manner, then, sexual satisfaction became a marker of both individual happiness and a fruitful marriage.[61]

Marriage in the 1920s began to represent something a bit different, then, something new. The changing norms of this youth culture, paired with the popularity of sex theorists like Havelock Ellis and Ellen Key, the fading economic importance of the family, and the fight for birth control, permanently fractured an "older marriage ideal."

Fearful of the consequences of this fracture, physicians, social workers, social scientists and psychologists crafted a new, "modern" marriage ideal.[62] Reformers called these modern partnerships "companionate marriages." Here was a way to contain shifts in the sexual order and promote the family, while conceding to and perhaps even co-opting real liberal shifts in thought about sexuality. They purposefully adapted traditional sexual values to these new, emerging patterns, crafting an ideal as opposed to an accurate reflection of reality.[63] Mass media covered the concept of companionate marriage extensively in the 1920s, popularizing the ideal. Well-known judge and activist Ben Lindsey published a book titled *Companionate Marriage*, defending the concept in lectures around the nation.

Local political, religious, and social groups invited speakers to debate the benefits and drawbacks of such a marital scheme. Articulated in the popular press, prescriptive literature, local programs, and in marriage manuals, awareness of companionate marriage as a concept pervaded the nation.

This ideal appears radical in some respects but not entirely. First, companionate marriage included an acceptance of women's sexuality separate from reproduction—so a tacit acknowledgment of birth control. Second, by pushing early marriage, there was an attempt to accommodate adolescents experimenting with sex at an earlier age. Better to have young people engaging in sexual relations inside the marital relationship than before it. And lastly, reformers embraced a camaraderie between the sexes—this idea of equal partnership became part of modern marriage, making divorce acceptable if a couple was unhappy and, importantly, childless. The main tenets of companionate marriage acknowledged the need for good sex in a successful marriage and recognized women's bid for more equality. In some ways, the ideal was profoundly modern and is reminiscent of more contemporary views of marriage. Reformers upheld monogamy as the rule, however, and they still supported the family as the fundamental component of happiness and social cohesion.[64]

Marriage survived the 1920s but in altered form as it evolved into a more contemporary institution. Surveys of college students show that by the 1920s many accepted birth control and divorce as a part of married life. This is a marked difference from the views of previous generations. The 1920s youth unabashedly acknowledged their plans to limit children and delay their childbearing for several years after marriage and expressed a belief in the need for mutual satisfaction in a successful marriage. Without it, to them divorce seemed a reasonable solution.[65] In the 1920s, the United States was second only to the Soviet Union in rates of divorce, with one in six marriages splitting up in 1928, up from one in ten before the war. Helen and Robert Lynd noted in *Middletown*, their study of Middle America in the 1920s, that while women never used to openly discuss divorce, even in Middletown "now they are beginning to wonder."[66]

While rooted partly in changes already underway, these developments reflected contested, controversial practices, ones that horrified many Americans. Moreover, these norms reflected the actions and the aspirations of middle-class, white youth. The different leisure habits of working-class and black couples, as well as their limited access to contraception and relative lack of privacy, threw up barriers to this kind of latitude in marriage relationships in this decade.[67]

Ultimately, the reality remained that even women who embraced the flapper lifestyle, or this modern marriage, remained tethered to wifehood and motherhood in 1920s America. The freedom to engage socially and sexually with the opposite sex did not, it turned out, translate into significant economic or political freedom. And despite changing assumptions, the marital relationship remained fundamentally framed by a traditional morality, one where women remained more pure than men, where society expected most women to marry, to eventually have children, and finally, to forego a career to stay at home with them. The intense focus on the flapper and her supposed sexual freedom masked this reality, promoting the myth of a truly liberated woman for decades to come.[68] But this supposed liberation failed to create real equality between the sexes.

Women's Work

The status of women's work played a critical role in that failure. None other than the female governor of Wyoming, having won an emergency election after her husband's death in office, told women in 1926 to embrace motherhood over careers as their true mission. Nellie Ross told the *Atlanta Constitution*, "I am old-fashioned enough . . . to believe that no career for women is as glorious or as satisfying as that which wifehood and motherhood offers and it is there she fulfills her highest destiny."[69] There was no combining these things—women needed to choose one or the other. Women may have won the right to vote, and manners and morals surely changed, but professional women in the 1920s still faced a dilemma familiar to us today—they wanted but could not "have it all." If women wished to marry, and especially if they wished to have children, most of the time they dropped out of the workforce. More important, society expected them to do so and shamed them if they did not. Married women worked only if they had to, or so people assumed. Like women in the late 20th century, these "modern" women chafed against stubbornly persistent expectations that tied them to the home. Quite simply, they were disappointed. Furthermore, the "rules" of mothering underwent a significant transition in the 1920s, making the work of motherhood more complex and more anxiety producing than it had once been.

Science influenced parenting in new and sustained ways in the 1920s, changing the goals and expectations of parents in America. This development arose for several reasons. Science gained new currency in general in the 1910s and 1920s. The establishment of the Children's Bureau in 1912 created an apparatus to collect and then disseminate the latest research and information on health and childrearing practices. The national media allowed newspapers and magazines to provide millions of readers access to the work of social scientists and physicians, at a moment when many had no regular access to a physician in their day-to-day lives.[70] A child study movement underway since the late 1800s influenced, and no doubt capitalized on, the increasing emotional attention Americans lavished on their children. As one historian argues, with fewer and fewer children being born in the early 20th century, rather than economic helpmeets for the family they in turn became "priceless." Purveyors of this movement decried the lack of a scientific approach to children's health and well-being. They exalted the opinions and advice of experts over parents themselves. While advice literature for parents existed for many years already at that point, books and pamphlets typically struck a moral tone. By the 1920s, an entirely new kind of advice literature emerged, one rooted in and canonized by the tenets of modern science. No other than F. Scott Fitzgerald himself wrote for *Ladies Home Journal* in 1923, "Motherhood, as blind, unreasoning habit, is something we have inherited from our ancestors in the cave."[71]

This development beleaguered parents, and particularly mothers, birthing a decidedly modern age of anxious parenthood in the 1920s.[72] A "new generation of literature" emerged in that decade, focused most prominently on the problems that might befall the young. Notably, these problems were as often psychological as physical. In homing in on these potential problems, the new advice literature spoke to a shift in American conceptions of children. Whereas before, in the 18th and 19th centuries, people considered their children hearty and stalwart, the new 20th-century literature portrayed infants and children as inherently vulnerable. These fragile beings needed parents educated by experts in order to survive, let alone thrive.

The reach of this intellectual and cultural shift is impressive. A study in the 1920s found that 74 percent of mothers consulted this literature, compared to only 37 percent of fathers. Writers of this advice literature most often aimed their message at the white, middle class, which is the most likely population surveyed for the aforementioned study. A study in 1936 noted that while 80 percent of professional women read a book on child-rearing in the previous year, just 25 percent of women from the "laboring" class did so. However, the shift in the tone of discussions about parenting permeated the wider culture. By 1936, over 70 percent of all families in the survey referenced at least one pamphlet on parental advice.[73] Many social welfare agencies targeted potentially dysfunctional immigrant parents in the 1920s, with many non-English-speaking mothers being dragged to parenting classes at settlement houses. Child study clubs and "Better Babies" clubs proliferated in rural and urban areas, among different classes, races, and ethnicities.[74]

Motherhood became a consuming, anxiety-ridden role for many in the 1920s—this was no time for women to take their eyes off the prize. Much was expected of mothers, and the stakes were high. Surging fears about cleanliness and disease amplified in the wake of germ theory. The number of suggested baths increased. Doctors urged the practice of consistent checkups for children. Children's sleep position, place, and duration needed monitoring. Mothers had to guard their children's emotional well-being but avoid "smother love." Adolescence was acknowledged as a troubling time, and sex-appropriate morals and tasks were to be passed on to girls and boys. A motherhood fraught with modern fears plagued women in the 1920s, in a departure from the past.[75]

On top of this anxiety, the seemingly unavoidable trappings of domesticity frustrated many middle-class women's efforts to establish a career in the 1920s. Surveys offer statistics and stories of women convinced that their fulfillment lay in marriage and motherhood, but the tug of possibility presented by a life outside the home beckoned them still. In several studies, the same women who professed a commitment to domesticity expressed a clear wish for meaningful professional work when asked about it directly.[76]

These women were perhaps atypical, but their existence in the 1920s is well worth noting. Historian Elaine Showalter calls some of these women "avant-garde," for their " 'modernity,' their mobility, their choice of careers, and their control of their bodies."[77] Unlike the women the Lynds encountered in Middletown, they did not live in a "sexually segregated world," and at the same time most did not need to work to survive. At its inception, then, "having it all" was an urban, middle-class feminist dilemma.

The cultural obsession with this dilemma in the 1920s belied the radical potential of married women's economic independence. Magazines routinely carried articles with titles such as "Can a Woman Run a Home and a Job, Too?" and "The Home-Plus-Job Woman." Women's organizations entered the fray, devoting hours of study to uncover the impact of wives and mothers working outside the home. The Young Women's Christian Association, in association with the National Federation of Business and Professional Women, created a debater's manual devoted to the question "shall I go on with my job after marriage?"[78] Historian Nancy Cott called these 1920s discussions the "career-marriage" genre. Typically, these articles presumed a professional, middle- or upper-class audience; they framed marriage as an option rather than a necessity, and they insisted that all women should find marriage and motherhood available to them.[79] But a host of others disagreed. A survey of men's opinions on working wives showed that 65 percent believed those women belonged at home and nowhere else.[80] In 1926, the progressive journal *Survey* solicited responses to a story titled "How Should the Family Be Supported?" Only one out of four suggested that both parents should support their family through earned wages.[81]

Feminists and reformers sought structural change to support working mothers but found little success. Charlotte Perkins Gilman called for families to cooperate in sharing meals, housekeeping, and childcare. Henrietta Rodman tried to develop collective housing—a feminist apartment complex—with communal kitchens. Alice Beale Parsons suggested socialized housework schemes and went even further by arguing that both men and women would have to pitch in to make a modern household run smoothly. Cooking and cleaning were not naturally women's vocations, she noted. And yet, in the 1920s, to a nation steeped in antiradicalism, these reforms seemed parallel to changes established in Soviet Russia after the Russian Revolution. Such innovative programs, ones with great transformative potential in this historical moment, were stained the color red. This, coupled with Americans' long-standing reluctance to think outside the bounds of the private family, made such efforts untenable, just as they would decades later when President Richard Nixon cast universal daycare as a communist plot.

Still, despite the difficulties, many women worked. By 1930, the percentage of women over the age of 16 who worked was some 25 percent, a significant number. Few worked in professions—about 14 percent—including nurses, teachers, and social workers. Most were in agriculture, manufacturing, retail, and domestic or personal service. Many of these were black women, and relatively few were immigrants. Native-born girls more often found employment in the expanding field of white-collar work, a group glamorized by the media at the time. While almost 30 percent of those working women were married, overall, only 10 percent of married women worked. And while the uptick in employment for working women on the whole opened "new opportunities for non-procreative, non marital forms of sexual behavior," their employment failed to provide a substantial degree of power or economic self-sufficiency.[82]

And so, for most middle-class women, an environment hostile to working wives meant that marriage to a male breadwinner remained their primary source of support.[83] Popular marriage expert Ernest Groves wrote in 1925, "When the woman herself earns and her maintenance is not entirely at the mercy of her husband's will, diminishing masculine authority necessarily follows."[84] Historian Christina Simmons argued that even the iconic flapper's "equality lay in being a good sport about sex, not in making the same claim for a public work life as men."[85]

The foundations of modern marriage undoubtedly shifted, placing women on more equal footing through an emphasis on both emotional and sexual mutual satisfaction, but curiously, equality did not extend beyond the home.[86] While society presented the role of wife and mother as something of a choice in the 1920s, a new and modern development, more than ever before overwhelming numbers of women made that choice despite new opportunities afforded by a changing culture. One college woman demonstrated this trend, saying, "Yes, I'd be willing to marry while yet in college and pay whatever price the companionship costs."[87] Tellingly, even advocates of careers for married women stopped short of scrutinizing marriage as an institution, or the degree of husbands' financial and emotional power within it.[88] The emphasis on companionate family life ultimately offered no solution to the vexing problems of gender inequality in America.[89]

A number of professional women in the 1920s did in fact want to realistically have it all—marriage, motherhood, and a career—possibly for the first time in modern American history. To expect or even desire to "have it all" assumes two things: women are entitled to a career and economic independence if they wish, and women have a choice whether or not to have children. While the notion of the struggle to "have it all" ignores the realities and absence of choices experienced by working-class women for generations, in the 1920s the space existed for some women to consider the pursuit of a career if they wanted one. The persistence of sexism in American society hampered access to those careers then, and even today there is still no clear way to "reconcile" the "two desires" some professional women have in real life.[90] Women's continued lack of political equality plays some part in this.

THE POLITICS OF THE EQUAL RIGHTS AMENDMENT

The year 1923 marked the 75th anniversary of the Seneca Falls convention, where Elizabeth Cady Stanton outlined the demands of the first women's rights movement. National Woman's Party (NWP) leader Alice Paul commemorated the anniversary in June of that year by positioning herself and supporters of the new Equal Rights Amendment as "descendants" of the "little band who met at Seneca Falls." Paul and the NWP carried on the fight for equality, which Paul firmly believed still needed to be won despite the passage of the Nineteenth Amendment.[91]

The long battle for women's suffrage ended with the ratification of that amendment in 1920, when the large and diverse movement fractured. Despite deep divides after the Civil War, and strong disagreements about strategy in the 1910s, on the whole women's rights activists worked toward similar goals for decades, with the National American Woman Suffrage Association (NAWSA) taking the lead. However, once the unifying power of the suffrage fight evaporated, it became very clear that feminism and women's rights meant different things to different women. In a general sense, all women pushing for the right to vote were feminists, but the impulses motivating their activism differed. Two clear divisions stood out: social feminism and a more "ideology-based" feminism.[92] While social feminists typically organized around women's difference *from* men, ideological feminists focused on securing women's equality *with* men.

Many women viewed suffrage as a hurdle cleared, and they moved on to a broader feminist agenda based on equal rights for women. These women sought equal status in social, economic, and civic life, as well as in the home. Women could be mothers, or not, they argued, just as women could choose careers, or marriage, or both. Their goals seemed more possible than ever, thanks to the growing popularity of higher education for women, jobs and professions for many, and the possibility of birth control. This was a feminism concerned with social reform more generally but focused more on individual liberation through full gender equality. Many of these ideological feminists came from Alice Paul's National Women's Party, reflecting Paul's own brand of feminism.

Many others, often referred to by historians as social feminists, instead sought to use their new political power to further progressive goals of social reform and social justice, particularly in relation to poor women and children. They operated as women on issues of particular concern to women, including labor legislation and social welfare measures. In so doing, they did not challenge women's traditional role as mother and caretaker.[93] Believing that certain incontrovertible differences existed between women and men, social feminists sought protection for women over a seeming false acceptance of sameness. Many social feminists came from the ranks of NAWSA and had deep ties to progressive reform.

Social feminists' work after the suffrage win was steeped in an understanding of women as different from men, while more ideologically driven feminists worked to achieve the realization of their belief in equality between women and men. This tension between the view that women and men were fundamentally the same and the view that women and men were distinct beings with different social and economic needs created a massive divide in the feminist movement in the 1920s.

The struggle to decide how best to advocate for women, as men's equals or as different from men, posed significant problems in the advancement of women's rights at the time and in the future. Supporters of protective labor legislation for women, limiting the hours women could work in some industries, for example, sought to seize power for women from exploitative employers through claims of difference. But others saw this approach as potentially problematic. Organizing *as* women for women's concerns required an acknowledgment, perhaps even a tacit endorsement, of the idea that women were fundamentally different from men, with different needs and different circumstances. Others sought to secure legislation for equal rights to canonize once and for all equality between men and women in the law. Their efforts resulted in the first Equal Rights Amendment. The battle over its fate then and in the more recent iteration of our culture wars demonstrates a persistent divide in the way Americans envision women's role in society.

The Equal Rights Amendment

The National Woman's Party acted as the driving force for ideological feminism, and leader Alice Paul was no stranger to conflict. Paul headed NAWSA's Congressional Union, which she later reorganized as the NWP in 1916 after breaking with the leadership. In February 1921, after the suffrage win, the NWP held a convention on the future of the organization. Paul, a "general, a supreme tactician," according to radical activist Crystal Eastman, directed the NWP as a single issue suffrage party all along, ignoring issues like black women's voting rights. Critics called her elitist, and racist, and her narrow focus on the suffrage amendment coupled with her militant tactics alienated many. So, in an unsurprising move, Paul guided the convention toward an approval of her preferred goal—equality under the law. In doing so, the NWP convention attendees voted down calls for the organization to focus on more comprehensive issues like birth control, rights for economically marginalized women, and the movement for peace. While Paul believed these issues were important, she said, "I am not interested in writing a fine program, I am interested in getting something done."[94] The NWP disbanded and reorganized as a group in pursuit of equality, and Paul envisioned this as another constitutional amendment, which, like the vote, would offer one clear goal, to reenergize the dedicated troops of the suffrage movement.

Despite the disappointment of luminaries like Eastman and Jane Addams, the NWP would stay a single-issue organization—this was Paul's kind of feminism—undiluted by other issues that affected women, and focused on equality. An equal rights amendment (ERA) was formulated, and its simple aim was to remove all legal disabilities affecting women, which would then establish the principle of gender equality. Paul

Searching for a "Full Life"

drafted the legislation, a clear statement of her intentions: "Men and women shall have equal rights throughout the United States and every place subject to its jurisdiction. Congress shall have the power to enforce this article by appropriate legislation." The amendment appeared before Congress for the first time in December 1923.[95]

As soon as Paul drafted the ERA, feminists opposed to the measure found fundamental flaws. Trade unionists and social feminists like Florence Kelley homed in on the fact that such legislation would likely invalidate the special protective labor laws hard fought and won for women workers in the Progressive Era of the 1910s. Paul herself once supported such laws, but by the 1920s she thought they constituted one more barrier for women in the economic struggle for equality. Such laws were, in her view, a way for union men and employers to keep women workers out of well-paying jobs due to maximum hours laws, and to maintain low wages for women workers due to wage minimums that were often below union targets.[96] Paul cited women printers and streetcar conductors who lost their jobs because protective labor laws prohibited their working at night, or working overtime. While she stood for equality, Paul argued, other women asked "for protection instead of equality."[97]

Despite Paul's convictions, the NWP found itself isolated on the ERA in the 1920s. NWP membership suffered dramatic losses in the tens of thousands. The League of Women Voters, the Children's Bureau, the Women's Bureau, the Women's Trade Union League, and the National Consumer's League, all high-profile women's organizations, opposed the ERA. The Women's Bureau and labor organizations barraged Congress with attacks on the legislation, arguing that protective labor legislation did not in fact hamper women's ability to earn a living. One activist in favor of protective legislation resigned from a committee set up to study the efficacy of such laws, and she said to the press, "My experience with the National Woman's Party has shown me that it is composed mostly of women who never knew what it meant to work a day in their lives."[98] The struggle between these two factions only intensified. Florence Kelly resigned from the NWP, and Maude Wood Park told Paul, "You will divide the woman's movement."[99] And this she did.

Women such as Park and Kelley wanted equality, surely, but they appreciated the practical differences between women and men, and they worked to alleviate the real suffering those differences sometimes caused. They argued that women differed from men in ways that mattered. ERA opponents generally saw working women in their capacity as mothers, ever aware of their actual burdens. Many in this camp made up a formidable bastion of female social reformers in the first few decades of the

20th century, and they built their lives' work around an edifice of protection for working women. Kelley claimed, "So long as men cannot be mothers, so long legislation adequate for them can never be adequate for wage-earning women; and the cry Equality, Equality, where Nature had created Inequality, is as stupid and as deadly as the cry Peace, Peace, where there is no Peace."[100]

ERA opponents accused Paul of being an ideologue who would sacrifice real women on the altar of an abstract sense of equality. She did fashion her feminism around the need to establish gender equality first and foremost, sidestepping the struggles so many women faced as a result of their race and class. ERA supporters argued that protective labor laws ran counter to women's economic interests, that they diminished women's sense of self-worth, and encouraged women to see themselves as weak, less capable than men. NWP member Crystal Eastman stressed the significance of shedding a cultural and psychological belief in women's inferiority. She wrote in *The Nation*, "The equal rights amendment will have a wonderful effect not only on the attitude of men toward women, but of women toward women."[101]

Conservative critics of the ERA attacked the measure for a host of reasons, ones that tied into their consternation at women's rights more broadly. Journalist John Walker Harrington criticized the gargantuan goals of the ERA in the pages of the *New York Times*, calling the effort "the suffrage war after the suffrage war." NWP women, Harrington argued, pushed too hard for "literal equality" and were in danger of needing to surrender the "tender treatment" and "freely accorded privileges" they long enjoyed as women.[102] At a subcommittee meeting on the ERA in the Senate Judiciary Committee, senators heard from speakers representing prominent anticommunist organizations. Antifeminism featured strongly in the conservative agendas of many such groups in and after the Red Scare. A supporter of the Sentinels of the Republic, Mrs. Rufus Gibbs of Baltimore, called the amendment a "sinister attack on the American system of government by the Amazons of the Woman's Party." The conservative Massachusetts Public Interest League submitted a statement warning the amendment "would thrust women into ruthless competition with men and result in sex war."[103] The Alimony Payers Protective Association also protested the amendment, arguing that divorce and custody laws favored women already. The group telegrammed President Coolidge to complain that equal rights bills initiated by the NWP at the state level "operate against husbands and fathers."[104] Opposition was widespread.

Congress revisited the amendment again and again in the 1920s, but the coalition of forces arrayed against it kept it from ever being lifted out of committee. Americans continued to divide over the issue of equality versus difference when imagining social policy and political personhood for women.[105] The second wave of the feminist movement in the 1970s revived support for the ERA, and when Congress actually passed the amendment in 1972, Alice Paul was alive to see it. It then went to the states for ratification. In what many feminists assumed was a mere formality, the ERA at first found sweeping support, ratified by 30 states by the end of 1973.[106] Yet, as the ERA divided people in the 1920s, it did so again in the 1970s, and it did so along the same lines: equality versus difference. Anti-ERA forces pushed back against the passage of this legislation by arguing that, in their view, women were in fact fundamentally different from men. Conservative lawyer, mother, and writer Phyllis Schlafly mobilized this movement, dramatically slowed the momentum of the campaign, and ultimately sunk it. By the mid-1970s, the ERA stood as a glaring symbol of the fraught process of changing sex roles in America, both for feminists and their conservative opponents.[107] By the 1979 deadline set by Congress the ERA received only 35 state ratifications of the necessary 38. After an additional 39-month extension granted by Congress, despite a flurry of campaigning that included lobbying, marches, silent vigils, and a 37-day hunger strike, the Alice Paul Amendment fell short of the ratifications needed to become a constitutional amendment.[108]

Middle-class women's efforts to have it all, for the first time, with economic independence and the choice to have a family, the continuing push for reproductive freedom, and the controversial determination to seek political equality all mark the 1920s as the dawn of a truly modern era for women. The arrival of this modern woman sparked a great deal of debate over woman's place in American society. As sex became separated from reproduction, as women approached marriage with less traditional claims to wifehood and motherhood, and as feminist agitators sought legal equality, the ground seemed to be shifting underneath Americans' feet. The family, that stronghold of society, rocked with uncertainty in the wake of these developments. And although public debate over the implications of modern woman's arrival quieted through the years of Depression, war, and Cold War, by the 1960s and 1970s these issues burst through the surface of the nation's consciousness once again, and the reverberations echo around us still.

CHAPTER FIVE

The Dark Shadow of Darwin: Religion Battles Modernism

Americans heard from culture warrior Rev. John Roach Straton fairly often in the 1920s, usually in passionate opposition to the sins of modern culture. The head of New York City's Calvary Baptist Church spoke out frequently against drinking and dancing, but he also fought against the acceptance of evolution. Straton, like most Protestant fundamentalists, believed everything in the Bible to be literal truth, so evolution challenged his theological bedrock. And to him this attack on religion was just one part of a larger assault on all that he and others like him held dear. In an address at Harvard University in 1924, more than a year before the infamous Scopes Trial began, Straton explained, "Ever since the dark shadow of Darwinism came over the world, public morality has been progressing downward. The world must have a moral foundation and that foundation can only be found in religion. Take away religion and the whole moral structure falls."[1]

The challenges of modern life troubled Americans in the 1920s, and many felt profoundly shaken by the way scientific ideas tested religious faith. Antievolutionists mobilized around the country to shut down classroom instruction on Darwin's theories, prompting both outrage and relief. As the trial against John Scopes was about to begin in Tennessee in 1925, a mother wrote to the *Nashville Tennessean* to express her gratitude to all those safeguarding her kids from Darwinian science, "one of the destructive forces which . . . will destroy our civilization."[2] Even though the court convicted Scopes of teaching evolution, anxiety over the impact of scientific advances persisted. Reverend Straton visited Harvard once again in the months after the trial, where he claimed, "We see now the greatest wave of degeneracy and crime that has swept the world since the fall of the Roman Empire."[3] His evidence for this included climbing murder rates, more divorces, and a rise in circulation of pornographic material. And who was responsible for this degeneracy? None other than supporters of evolution.

Straton blasted men like Scopes's defense lawyers, Clarence Darrow and Dudley Field Malone, who he called "atheists and advocates of a degenerate cult."[4] These men came from vice-filled cities like New York and Chicago, and they brought their modern beliefs to good, old-fashioned towns like Dayton, Ohio. Straton condemned their corrosive values, arguing that they tried to "save from itself a community where women are still honored, where men are still chivalric, where laws are still respected, where home life is still sweet, where the marriage vow is still sacred."[5]

Here, we see the way antievolution advocacy lined up neatly with nostalgic ideals of community, chivalry, family, and monogamy. Morality could be salvaged, and even celebrated, if only evolution stayed out of the classroom. As historian Edward Larson put it, in this turbulent decade, "Antievolution promised a return to normalcy."[6] This issue became a fault line dividing the nation along familiar lines. Evolution was another battleground in the 1920s culture wars.

RELIGION IN THE MODERN 1920S: CHALLENGES AND REINFORCEMENTS

Most Americans welcomed religion into their lives in the 1920s, however, fewer people actively engaged with it on a day-to-day basis. Many belonged to one of the churches in their city or town but far fewer attended Sunday services every week, or volunteered their time and money on the church's behalf. Those who did tended to be women. Many parents who did not attend themselves still sent their children in their stead to well-established Sunday schools. Christian denominations dominated the scene, with the notable exception of Jewish congregants. Among Christians there were Catholics, who were still primarily immigrants, and Eastern Orthodox communities, but two-thirds of Christians affiliated with one of the many Protestant sects, including groups like Methodists, Lutherans, and Presbyterians.[7]

And so, religious-minded Americans did not constitute one unified community—in fact, a host of divisions separated out one religious group from another. Evidence of the splintered nature of American religion in the 1920s could be clearly seen in "Middletown", where a city of some 40,000 residents boasted 42 churches servicing 28 Christian denominations and 1 Jewish synagogue. Geographical splits found Baptists most prominent in the South, and Mormons mostly in the West. Sometimes doctrinal differences divided churches within one denomination or sect, while race acted as another concrete wedge. Hundreds of thousands of African Americans professed the Protestant faith in the 1920s, but they did so almost exclusively in segregated congregations.[8]

The most substantial divide in the 1920s arose from increasingly disparate ideas about the place of religion and the truth of the Bible in the modern world. From a theological perspective, religious individuals who disavowed modernity took up the mantle of "fundamentalism." This was a belief in the fundamentals of Protestant faith, including a literal interpretation of the Bible. Taking their name from a series of articles published early in the century titled "The Fundamentals," which focused on Protestant orthodoxy, this group accepted the Bible's story of creation and the virgin birth, among other things, as facts. They also believed the second coming of Jesus Christ was imminent, which significantly upped their intensity.[9]

Fundamentalists reacted to social and cultural change, perceiving an erosion of propriety and moral certainty, and a decline in spirituality and goodness.[10] Much like the anxieties that fueled prohibition and nativism, really, fundamentalists wanted to shore up an older cultural order, one that privileged them and their worldview. For some in the South it was also about race. If evolution explained the origins of man, then all humans shared a common origin. As editors of the black newspaper *Chicago Defender* noted wryly in 1925, this would force southerners "to admit that there is no fundamental difference between themselves and the race they pretend to despise."[11]

For all of these reasons, the fundamentalist movement coalesced in the 1910s as a community, an identity, one that was separate from others. What was first a way of thinking shared among elites became a broader movement thanks to purposeful planning and mobilization. In 1919, prominent pastor William Bell Riley helped put on the "World Conference on the Fundamentals of the Faith" in Philadelphia, an event that drew thousands.[12] Organizations like the World's Christian Fundamentals Association sprang up immediately afterward bringing this momentum to the rest of the country. Religion also ran through the radio waves, bringing fundamentalism to the masses. Revivalist preacher Paul Rader, who operated a sort of evangelical clearinghouse of information, ran the Chicago Gospel Tabernacle, a regular religious radio show for 14 hours on Sundays. It was the first of its kind, though he was not alone for long.[13] And public figures like political icon William Jennings Bryan and celebrity evangelist Billy Sunday further popularized the movement.[14]

Sunday's worldview neatly reflected the fundamentalist approach to the nation's problems in the 20th century. When assessing issues like poverty and vice, Sunday focused in on individual failings. Unlike the increasingly structural critique made by more liberal minded Protestants, people who took issue with the system and the ways it advanced some people at the expense of others, Sunday celebrated free market capitalism. He felt that the answer to the nation's ills was straightforward: individual men and women needed to be better, to do better. They needed to drink less, and work more. Women needed to embrace their roles as mothers over the lure of dance halls. Employers needed to pay workers more, not because of government-imposed wage minimums, but because it was the right thing to do. Crime and drunkenness were particularly the failings of immigrants, in Sundays estimation, which fit in with his steadfastly nativist worldview. In short, if individuals would curb their own moral failures in order to bring themselves closer to God, the country would be strengthened.[15] And so he sought to help the masses that flocked to his revivals, but through personal uplift, not reform.

On the other side of this conversation sat more liberal religious leaders, ones working to improve society by reforming cities and social institutions under the mantle of the "social gospel." Theologically, these men were more modern than their fundamentalist foes. To them, religion was a living thing. Borrowing from Darwin, it evolved over time. They thought the experiences of religious faith in the moment they lived in should be a guide instead of the memory of the birth of Christ.[16] Structural problems surrounded them in a world troubled by poverty, alcohol, and racial and ethnic strife. The social gospel believers found this too compelling to overlook and in their spirit of reform they portrayed more conservative standard bearers of Protestantism as uneducated, ineffectual, and ignorant.

Fundamentalists waved off these efforts as radical and troubling, and they instead homed their energies on building their own movement through networking and messaging. Movement leaders like William Riley and Frank Norris sought out connections between churches, seminaries, and a host of religious publications. And they built up their base of supporters through both the use of those publications and through a relentless circuit of speaking tours and conferences throughout the country, often including those same movement leaders as well as superstar supporters like William Jennings Bryan. Mobilizing interested supporters and donors in the early 1920s proved easy enough. Modernism's expansive reach permeated American culture at that point, prompting a broad backlash. But at the same time many others increasingly sought meaning and connection outside the bounds of organized religion.

Secularism and Meaning in Popular Culture

Secularism escaped no one's notice in the 1920s, as evidence of the loosening hold of religion appeared everywhere. The movie screens, automobile rides, and golf outings that called to Americans on Sundays made that clear. The war shook people's faith in deep and troubling ways. Changing sex and gender norms among the nation's young people proved yet another sign of the lack of religious belief. These were kids who gave in to pleasure with little regard for religious guidelines, or God's judgment. And a national obsession with wealth competed with religion as a driving force that captured the interest of certain Americans much more powerfully.[17]

But, scientific developments also rocked the foundations of faith in ways big and small in the early 20th century. Writer and critic Joseph Wood Krutch warned of this reality in the pages of his 1929 book *The Modern Temper*, claiming that science dislodged belief in God. He included both the social sciences, like psychology, and the natural sciences like physics and biology in his analysis. Krutch approached this development with some fatalism, but not all were so sullen. In fact, secularization had a varied impact. If science promoted questions about religion, some Americans simply moved on in their day-to-day lives accepting of uncertainty.[18] For many there was no existential crisis. But people's easy doubt of God, their willingness to swim in the unknowing waters of ambivalence, marks this modern decade as different. And in that difference we find the breeding ground for a culture war.

The seeds of cultural conflict pushed up on the surface of tradition in so many ways in the 1920s, but the rising popularity of science and social science shifted the very ways Americans interpreted the world around them. The ground of the knowable world quite literally seemed to be shifting beneath people's feet. Psychology, sociology, the theory of relativity, and evolutionary science all fostered an upsurge in secular thinking, challenging deeply felt and long-held religious beliefs. People with access to the media, be it print, radio, or the silver screen, were conversant with the ideas of Freud by the 1920s. Psychoanalysis made for a favorite parlor game among moderns in the Greenwich Village, and popular notions of Freudian psychology encouraged the need to live free from restraint in order to achieve well-being. The human mind seemed shadowy and maze-like, and a whole science was now needed if one hoped to unlock its mysteries. Men could not even confidently say they knew themselves.

Furthermore, knowing one's own culture no longer promised any insight into the rest of the world. Sociologists joined anthropologists in the 1920s in articulating the notion of cultural relativism, arguing that a people and the customs they enacted only had meaning in the context that produced them. Culture, in short, made people what they were and not the other way around. This meant that different societies around the world would have vastly different norms and standards and ideals. Writer Horace Kallen relished in this concept, calling for a cultural pluralism where difference would be celebrated as a strength. While to some this opened up opportunities for tolerance and blunted the message of concepts like scientific racism, it also made the world seemed less ordered, less knowable.

In the more abstract realm, Americans also internalized the findings of scientists like Albert Einstein and Charles Darwin. The media exposed Americans to Einstein's physics in the decade after the war. Though few laymen and women truly understood his theory of relativity, his cultural significance impressed upon people that the universe was vast and that truly understanding it required great knowledge and expertise. Darwin's theories existed for several decades by the 1920s, but they were becoming increasingly popular.

In the early decades of the 20th century, a series of fossil discoveries around the world, taken together, backed up Darwin's theories of evolution more strongly than ever. These findings in places like England, Germany, and Indonesia filled in an emerging picture of the stages of man's evolution over time. A skull fragment found in Piltdown, England, in the 1910s provided what the *New York Times* referred to at the time as a "missing link" between modern man and his ape-like early descendent. Other papers throughout the country carried similar stories, and discoveries only continued. The *New York Times* again declared the "missing link" found after another skull emerged in South Africa in 1924. These exciting bits of news came in a slow drip, built up a consensus around Darwin's ideas, and chipped away at the creation story of Genesis.[19] And to many intellectuals, the certainties of previous generations disintegrated. They faced a brave new world.

A generation of American writers articulated their own alienation as they experienced a rupture between modernity and tradition, between the fast-paced machine-fueled cities and the small byways of the nation's villages and towns. Here were the ideas animating the actors in the Scopes Trial, but in this case they spilled onto pages of poetry and prose. These disaffected writers were the "Lost Generation," as Gertrude Stein named her cohort. They condemned small town America's stranglehold on sexual propriety and modesty. They lampooned the ethos of cultural and intellectual conformity that structured the days and ways of so many Americans in the 1920s. They relentlessly critiqued what they believed was the hollow pursuit of money and material things. To them, the promise of civilization was being exposed as a sham. As ex-patriot Ezra Pound famously wrote, so many men of his World War I generation died, "For an old bitch gone in the teeth, for a botched civilization."

Much of the writing put forward by this "Lost Generation" was a direct response to the physical and psychological wounds of World War I. The senseless and catastrophic scale of death and deformity in the war shocked the senses of many people the world over. Americans experienced the aftermath of the war in a kind of stupor, feeling unmoored from the certainties they once held dear and ill-equipped to handle that. While some remedied this by desperately seeking a return to the world that existed before the war, Lost Generation writers satisfied themselves by mercilessly pointing up the problems of the old order, and with the war that exploded it. Most packed up and left the United States in disillusionment, but their work made its way back home and it sharpened the edges of the culture war.

For as much as novelists and poets like Stein, T.S. Eliot, and Ernest Hemingway defined the literary culture of the decade with their condemnation of the old ways, they also reflected the light of modernity with a spectacular brightness. Through their work they sought to create a new American culture, one that starkly contrasted the Victorian order of the previous century. They celebrated the breakdown of the old sexual order and the ties of repression that undergirded it. They advocated the search for meaning through authenticity and experiences rather than through the pursuit of material things. Individuality was prized over conformity.

Much of this literature included what historians have called a "revolt against the village," a nod toward a more progressive and tolerant cosmopolitanism. Many writers like E.E. Cummings and John Dos Passos experimented with rhythm and form, throwing off the old conventions in essential ways. This experimentation also emerged in jazz music, photography, painting, in plays, and in dance.[20] The modernist ethos suffused American culture with a sense of pessimism about the future, one framed resolutely by the tug of the new order but also by the grip of the old.

But it would be a mistake to assume that this alienated generation spoke for the country as a whole in the 1920s. Other Americans processed their nostalgia for the past and their hesitant flirtation with the future by fully embracing more conventional culture. They engaged in simple, apolitical pastimes, seeking an escape from the many tensions in American society rather than an acerbic critique of it. The 1920s proved to be a golden age of sport, as people packed baseball stadiums and football fields to watch men play. Sports heroes like boxer Jack Dempsey, football player "Red" Grange, and baseball great Babe Ruth dazzled anxious Americans, capturing millions in momentary fits of euphoria and collective experience.[21] People also escaped by turning their eyes to the sky, marveling over the feats of Charles Lindbergh as he piloted a single-engine plane, solo, across the Atlantic from New York City to Paris in 1927. Americans worshipped him for his bravery and ingenuity. He reinforced, in their view, what was good about America even though, since the war, the nation seemed more unsettled than ever. A writer in *Century* magazine perhaps put it best when he said, "Lindbergh served as a metaphor . . . we felt that in him we, too, had conquered something and regained lost ground."[22]

Americans interested in literature in the 1920s mostly focused on old-fashioned fare, overlooking the likes of Gertrude Stein or Ernest Hemingway. One historian notes that the most popular titles of the decade heavily featured frontier themes and "rural patterns of thought."[23] These authors typically reaffirmed a timeworn sense of morality and social cohesion. For example, one of the decade's most popular writers was Gene Stratton-Porter who wrote top-selling novels through the early 1900s and into the 1920s. Notably, many of her millions of sales came in the form of fifty-cent reprints—this was not a highbrow audience. Porter won her wide following by writing stories that placed her characters within nature, a nostalgic setting with few of the 1920s stresses on moral certainty. Her novels exuded courage, cheerfulness, and optimism, things many Americans felt were in short supply in the world around them. As historian Roderick Nash described her work, "In Porter one basked momentarily in an uncomplicated world where virtue triumphed and right prevailed."[24]

While the images of a flaming youth in novels and films enchanted some Americans, many others sought reassurance and comfort in a return to the past. The 19th century was more en vogue with 1920s popular readers than the modern age. Rather than critique the past, they chose to dwell in it. This tells us something important about the public perception of the clash between modernity and tradition and about popular understandings of the Scopes Trial. Secular thinking was on the rise, and most

Protestant Fundamentalism

Americans were reckoning with modernity on some level, but in cultural terms, it seemed many were ambivalent.

Protestant Fundamentalism

The division between fundamentalism and more liberal Protestant leaders would explode into the nation's consciousness in 1925 with the Scopes Trial, but for many Americans religion proved to be a far less controversial affair. The resilience of people's religious convictions was apparent.[25] When the Lynds asked Middletown's high school students if they believed Christianity to be the "one true religion" they overwhelmingly said yes, with 83 percent of boys and 92 percent of girls in agreement. Individuals turned to religion to affirm the beliefs they already held, and they relied on the institution of the church to provide rituals throughout their lives, including baptism and marriage. But religious leaders themselves tapped into the cultural divide wrenching American society apart. One of those leaders was Billy Sunday.

To Americans, Billy Sunday was right up there with their favorite baseball player, or their best loved siren of the silver screen. Sunday—his given name—actually was a professional baseball player turned revival preacher who used his renown to win souls over to fundamentalism. Reaching the height of his influence in the 1910s, he often addressed crowds in the tens of thousands. Sunday was an influencer, a powerful figure. Politicians and the nation's wealthiest industrialists helped to support his efforts, and in turn they enjoyed the goodwill curried by their public association with Sunday. Wilson received him when he preached in Washington, D.C., in 1915. John D. Rockefeller honored him with a luncheon at his home when Sunday held a huge revival in New York City in 1917. Almost 100,000 people brought themselves forward for conversion during his several months in that city, and his presence generated massive amounts of news coverage.[26] He was a phenomenon.

Sunday engineered his revivals with great care, with months of preparation, and the events themselves were quite a spectacle. Local volunteers laid the groundwork, motivated by sheer anticipation and adoration. Often, many different churches within a city organized to help prepare. And when Sunday finally came to town, for what would be a month or more, a boisterous crowd met him at the train station and paraded him through the streets. When he first dazzled them by taking the pulpit on the Sunday after his arrival, he offered only his words. No conversions were allowed. He held off on those, strategically, until the second week, at which point Sunday welcomed converts to come forward to shake his hand, and then pray with a local volunteer. By then the bubbling enthusiasm spilled forward and people lined up to engage with Sunday and to come home to Jesus.

But Sunday's fundamentalist message found competition in the marketplace of ideas. On the side of the liberal theologians was Harry Emerson Fosdick, who took up the charge from New York City's First Presbyterian Church. Fosdick moved into his education at New York's Union Theological Seminary with a deep sense that the Bible was not literal fact, but rather should be a guide. Christian experience mattered more than doctrine. This served him well when he experienced the ghastliness of urban poverty in New York at the turn of the century, as he aligned himself ideologically with those religious leaders who felt compelled to respond to social and intellectual change. First in a church in Montclair, New Jersey, then as a faculty member at Union Theological Seminary, and starting in 1918 at First Presbyterian, Fosdick preached, taught, and wrote in efforts to grapple with the place of religion in an astonishingly modern world. He was enormously popular, a sight to be seen in New York, and people lined up outside the church in hopes of admission as nonmembers.

Fosdick stepped into the fray of an already existing dispute between fundamentalists and liberal theologians, but his prominent presence at the pulpit in New York fanned the flames. He continued to insist that the Protestant faith needed to evolve, and he publicly accepted things like the virgin birth and the second coming of Christ as ideas or symbols, and not as facts. To this a host of fundamentalist leaders responded with a ready willingness to defend their faith. Men like Clarence Macartney from the Arch Street Presbyterian Church in Philadelphia and Princeton theologian J. Gresham Machen vigorously countered Fosdick with lectures, essays, pamphlets, and books. This religious modernism was, they argued, a godless ethos masquerading as Christianity.[27] Squabbles over doctrine and belief in the virgin birth proceeded behind the scenes in places like the General Assembly of the Presbyterian Church U.S.A. through the early 1920s.

These internecine debates hardly impacted the public, but the heightened emotions eventually pushed Fosdick to walk away from First Presbyterian, and John D. Rockefeller courted him to Park Avenue Baptist Church. At Fosdick's direction, the church moved uptown and became the non-denominational Riverside Church in 1930. He survived, thrived even, the struggles within Protestantism. But in the depths of the 1920s the stakes were still high in this conflict between fundamentalism and modernism. No instance made that more apparent to the nation than the Tennessee trial of school biology teacher John Scopes.

It seems safe to say the central figure in the Scopes Trial was not the teacher himself, but rather the venerable William Jennings Bryan, who stepped up to be a prosecutor in the trial. For many years Bryan was a beloved national figure, a progressive politician who ran unsuccessfully for president in 1896, 1900, and 1908. But his religious leanings were always more conservative, and he was tuned in to the conflict between modernists and fundamentalists. He himself played a part in the doctrinal response of the Presbyterian Church to the divide among theologians. Bryan actively fought the teaching of evolution in schools before Scopes broke the law in Tennessee, as the issue for him was plain. He believed in the story of Adam and Eve, in the Garden of Eden, and in original sin. This belief framed his sense of what was right in the world, and a deep belief in a moral universe guided his lifelong progressive activism. If there was no divine order, no creation story tracing human beings to God's work, then the world lacked a moral foundation. If people derived from apes then the brutal and unethical law of unreasoning animals also applied to humans. For Bryan, if evolution was real, there could be no clear right and wrong in the world.[28]

But it is important to acknowledge that Bryan's fundamentalist opposition to evolution was not necessarily inevitable among Christians at the time. It is true that intellectuals on both sides, by the mid-1920s, crafted a well-thought-out blueprint for a war between science and religion. Opinion among religious leaders varied after Darwin published *Origin of Species* in 1859. Some sought to validate Darwin, finding evolution and Christianity compatible if the process were overseen and guided by God. While often perceived as anti-science, not all fundamentalists divorced themselves from science per se, but many subscribed to older, 19th-century notions of scientific advancement.[29] Others simply dismissed Darwin from the outset, seeing his ideas as a direct challenge to the creation story in Genesis. But some conditions specific to the early 20th century provoked the coming war. A growing acceptance in the scientific community at the time held that simple genetic mutations moved evolution along, rather than any kind of design. God was being edged out of the equation. There was also a keen desire on the part of fundamentalists to save America's moral character in the aftermath of World War I. And so for several reasons this conflict came to a head in the 1920s, with Bryan as the most well-known participant.

Bryan's nickname, "the Great Commoner," reflected his concern for the average American, and his long career explains his national standing. He ran as both the Democratic and the populist People's Party candidate in 1896, calling for economic policy that would help farmers and workers. He lost to William McKinley, who then acquired colonial possessions as a consequence of the Spanish-American War in 1898. In 1900, Bryan ran against McKinley again, this time staking his candidacy on the unjust nature of that so-called splendid little war. Bryan found it unconscionable that the United States took countries like the Philippines and Puerto Rico from Spain as spoils of war, and that America held on to them as colonies without any regard for the will of those being governed. Filipino President Emilio Aguinaldo chastised the American government for refusing to give his people liberty, and a long brutal war between the United States and Filipino rebels killed as many as 200,000 fighters and civilians there. But many Americans glossed over these realities, savoring America's new position in the world, and McKinley won once again at the turn of the century.

Bryan put his lot in for the presidency one more time when powerhouse Republican Teddy Roosevelt left office. But in 1908, William Howard Taft was the chosen successor of the wildly popular Roosevelt. Bryan barely stood a chance. He later served as Woodrow Wilson's secretary of state, a remarkable position for an avowed pacifist at the dawn of World War I. And ultimately Bryan resigned because Wilson refused to observe complete and impartial neutrality toward both sides in 1915, after the Germans sunk the British passenger liner *Lusitania*. Evident here then are Bryan's credentials, which many Democrats and Republicans alike would surely have found impeccable when he took up the antievolution fight in 1919.

Bryan joined that fight for profound reasons. He became convinced that evolution led good Christian men to abandon their faith, an idea in part based on sociological studies that demonstrated higher numbers of college graduates lacking faith in God than among college entrants. Anecdotal evidence from parents around the country backed this up, as mothers and fathers complained about Johnny's spirituality being wrecked by atheistic college courses. Ministers echoed their complaints. This challenge to the religiosity of young adults threatened the very civilization Americans existed within, in Bryan's view.[30] More simply, he also believed Darwin's ideas were erroneous, untested as they were.[31]

Always willing to stand up for justice for the downtrodden, Bryan thought the consequences of accepting this untested Darwinism could be dire. Social Darwinism, a kind of socioeconomic survival of the fittest, justified astonishing discrepancies in wealth in America since the turn of the century. And the notion of survival of the fittest provided a backbone for then popular ideas of scientific racism. Bryan was attuned to these by-products of Darwin, as he saw them, and this also motivated his activism.[32]

For all of these reasons, then, Bryan committed to fighting the teaching of evolution in schools. He threw himself into the fight, speaking in several states in favor of antievolution legislation. He also authored "Bible Talks," newspaper columns that ran in more than 100 papers throughout the country, reaching millions.[33] Bryan set out to save the nation from the alarming trend of lost faith, and from what he saw as bad science.

Fundamentalists waged a campaign to influence educational policy in the United States in the 1920s that actually included more than just an antievolution platform. In fact, they found more success with other issues, like their quest to make the St. James Bible mandatory reading in public schools. Several states passed this legislation during the 1920s, as did the cities of New York, Washington, D.C., and Baltimore. But even some who neglected to pass the legislation claimed to support it wholeheartedly, feeling compelled to state publicly that they believed the issue was more appropriate for local school boards to determine on their own. Governor A. V. Donahey in Ohio, for example, vetoed a state law but urged local boards to "require the reading of the Holy Bible in the schools."[34]

Broader efforts were also underway in the 1920s. Some fundamentalists sought to prohibit any questioning of God at all, while privileging Protestantism within school curriculums. A Florida bill in 1927 was intended to outlaw any denial of "the existence of God," or any instruction that "contains vulgar, obscene, or indecent matter."[35] Fundamentalists also opened institutions of higher learning that would train future leaders of their movement, including Bob Jones University, still in operation today. So, they operated on more than one front.

The story is more complex than it seems at first glance, then, but fundamentalists also devoted a great deal of energy to efforts to stop the teaching of evolution. Evolution as an issue impacted the whole country because it impacted schools. And the campaign to stop evolution benefited from an easily identifiable target—the teacher who taught it.[36] Going after modernist theologians did not offer fundamentalists a lot of publicity. Going after teachers did. While fundamentalists drew in crowds because of the rising sentiment of antimodernism, keeping the masses in line, bound together, proved difficult. Organizing around evolution, in a pushback to scientific developments, provided the necessary glue, the unifying force the movement needed.[37]

THE SCOPES TRIAL

In the big picture, then, fundamentalists hoped to use this antievolution campaign to reframe public education in such a way that would prioritize their religious and even their social worldview, over and above any other. On the level of specifics, fundamentalist groups worked on more than 50 pieces of antievolution legislation in 21 states in the 1920s.[38] Within these efforts, the Scopes Trial garnered more publicity for fundamentalism than anything else.

For those opposed to the influence of fundamentalism, the Scopes Trial offered a chance to hit back at what they saw as the small-minded forces of conservatism running roughshod over the nation, evidenced by movements like prohibition and the Red Scare. Attorney for the defense Clarence Darrow perfectly reflected that cosmopolitan, urban, decidedly modern portion of the nation so taken with ideas like sexual freedom, racial equality, and cultural pluralism. These were the Americans left perplexed by the antievolution movement. And to them, the Scopes Trial was about more than a high school teacher in Dayton. It provided a public battlefield for the fight they hoped to wage against the ways of the village, the beliefs and ideals that animated the Red Scare, the resurgent Ku Klux Klan, prohibition, and nativism.[39]

As Protestant preachers like Sunday threw down the gauntlet for fundamentalism, their influence was not a given—the 1920s culture wars would come for them too. These fundamentalists engaged in a battle with religious modernists and secular scientists in splashy and public confrontations, ones they did not necessarily win. This was the start of a long public decline for fundamentalists, who would act behind the scenes, waiting on the sidelines of the nation's cultural and political center until the rise of the Moral Majority and the New Right in the last few decades of the 20th century.[40] But in 1925 they were quite sure of themselves.

Setting the Scene

Fundamentalist calls went out for a legislative solution to the "problem" of evolution in the early 1920s, and this changed the nature of the antievolution movement. In 1921, the Baptist State Board of Missions in the state of Kentucky advocated a ban on teaching evolution in the state's public school system, and this idea caught fire among fundamentalists across the country.[41] The University of Kentucky sought funding from the Kentucky legislature that year, and intense discussions over what the University taught—including evolution—swirled through the debate over how much money they should receive. University President Frank L. McVey worked to separate these discussions in the public mind, and skillfully argued that the University was not a bastion of immorality, however, it did teach science and would need to continue to do so in order to be an institution of higher learning. His careful tone and his cooperation with a sympathetic press garnered support in the state and across the nation, and the bill did not pass.[42]

But this hardly mattered in the big picture: the effort provided a sketch for an actionable campaign plan. By 1922, prominent defenders of fundamentalism like John Roach Straton and William Jennings Bryan marshaled their efforts and organized not only for state laws but also for national antievolution laws. These endeavors set the new tone for the antievolution movement, and activists found their first victory in Oklahoma in 1923 when the state legislature prohibited the use of textbooks that taught evolution rather than "the Bible theory of creation."[43] The governor signed it into law later that year. Tennessee followed suit in 1925 when the state legislature passed the Butler Act, making the teaching of evolution a misdemeanor offense. After some initial hesitation and disarray among state lawmakers, Billy Sunday rolled into Memphis for an almost three-week long revival, where he lambasted evolution and teachers of evolution, all while praising the tenets of fundamentalism to more than 200,000 Tennesseans. His influence mattered. One month later, in March of that year, the state Senate passed the bill and the governor signed it into law.[44]

Once fundamentalists employed this strategy, people on the other side began working to subvert it. The American Civil Liberties Union believed the Tennessee law was unconstitutional and they wanted the chance to prove it in court. The prominent group, newly formed in 1920, actively solicited test cases to challenge the Tennessee law by running advertisements in the state's newspapers. People in Dayton read these, and local businessman George Rappleyea came together with several others to enlist John Thomas Scopes as a potential test case. This group included people who genuinely wished to challenge the legality of the antievolution law as well as a few who hoped the media circus that might envelop such a trial would be good business for Dayton.

To the Dayton group, Scopes seemed ideal. He coached the high school football team, and occasionally substituted in other courses when needed. He recently taught biology in that capacity when the biology teacher was out on leave. Scopes was just 24 years old and had no family. While he opposed the antievolution bill, he was not one to purposefully capture the spotlight. He would never go about giving speeches, nor would he make the trial about him as an individual. While Scopes's father tended toward socialism, opponents could not tar Scopes himself as a radical. And in Red Scare America this was important. To Rappleyea and his friends, then, Scopes was a perfect fit.

The men called Scopes to a local drugstore to see if he was willing to be a test case, setting this historic trial in motion. Rappleyea showed Scopes the textbook used in the state's high schools, pointing to a section on evolution. He asked Scopes, "You have been teaching 'em this book?" And Scopes said, "yes." Again, he was not a biology teacher, so if he had used the textbook to prepare for class, he reasoned that he must have taught evolution. In May 1925, in Tennessee, this constituted breaking the law. Scopes agreed to step into the maelstrom. A warrant for his arrest was drawn up and served right then and there. The trial would happen. The press picked up the story the following day, eager as they were to come upon it, and soon everyone knew John T. Scopes by name.

Rather quickly the trial morphed into a massive public debate on the issue of evolution in the classroom. Defenders of Scopes discussed the possibility of luring H.G. Wells, a well-known British writer and supporter of evolution, to Dayton to help. He declined, but those worrying over the trial continued to dream big. William Jennings Bryan happened to be in Tennessee when Scopes was arrested. He was the speaker at a meeting of the World's Christian Fundamentals Association, and the group spent a great deal of time discussing the national and local issues at hand. After the meeting, concerned that those in Dayton seemed not to be taking the significance of the case into real consideration, the WCFA invited Bryan to join the prosecution, and he accepted. While he had not practiced law in several decades, at that moment there was no heavier hitter the prosecution could have drafted. When Bryan wrote a short note agreeing to serve in the case he dashed the hopes of those in the ACLU who planned to make the trial a narrow test case on individual liberty, on the constitutionality of the Butler Act.[45]

Now, Bryan's sweeping platform against evolution would infiltrate the courtroom and make this something much bigger than they bargained for. While some acquaintances mentioned the Tennessee evolution case to Darrow after Scopes's arrest, he had recently announced his retirement, and assumed the ACLU would prefer not to have a dedicated agnostic at the defense table. His assumption was correct, but after Bryan joined the prosecution, Darrow said, "At once I wanted to go."[46] While in New York City conferring with well-known radical attorney Dudley Field Malone, the two men decided to send a telegram to Dayton, which they then released to the press, offering their services free of charge in defense of

Scopes. John Neal, chief counsel for the defense, accepted their offer on behalf of Scopes, but never ran it by the ACLU. The organization tried numerous times to persuade Scopes that he might be better served by other high profile attorneys. But he persisted, finding Darrow to be his best bet. The situation so angered Roger Baldwin, head of the ACLU, that he skipped the trial. And needless to say, this moment proved to be a transcendent one for the trial and its legacy.[47]

Scopes headed to New York to confer with the ACLU and his lawyers before the trial began, where prominent liberal and radical intellectuals feted him. According to a *New York World* reporter, the kinds of people coming out to meet Scopes included "feminists, birth-control advocates, agnostics, atheists, free thinkers, free lovers, socialists, communists, syndicalists, biologists, psychoanalysts, educators, preachers, lawyers, professional liberals, and many others."[48] His support for evolution meshed with a litany of radical positions in the 1920s. A group of prominent evolution scientists also met with Scopes in New York, including president of the Museum of Natural History Henry Fairfield Osborn. All in all, despite the eclectic company, the media played up the image of Scopes as a good American, taking special note of his stop to visit the Constitution in Washington, D.C., on the way home.[49]

The public demonstrated a marked interest in evolution as the trial date neared, and both sides worked to capture their attention. The scientific community took advantage of the moment in order to educate the public more thoroughly. Researchers wrote columns in local newspapers, and books on evolution flew off the shelves.[50] Religious leaders also stepped into the fray, as all over the country ministers found their way into the headlines by broadcasting their stance on evolution. And crowds came out to watch men debate on the issue.

Religious leaders approached this publicity in different ways, belying the diversity of opinion in America at the time. Bryan threw down the gauntlet leading up to the trial, saying one was either for a fundamentalist interpretation on evolution or an atheist. But other ministers used their pulpits to argue that one could in fact be a good Christian and believe in science. Generally speaking, these individuals saw no issue with the ideas of evolution coexisting with their religious faith. As one religious expert put it, "I am thoroughly convinced that God created the heavens and the earth, but I find nothing in the Scripture that tells me His method." In other words, God very well may have created evolution in order to create man.[51]

This middle ground proved to be a space occupied by many, but noticed at the time by few. President Calvin Coolidge shrugged off any comment on the case by claiming it was a state matter, and most politicians on the national level did the same. It did not serve them to enter the fray on such a contested issue. Many local politicians in Tennessee publicly supported the Butler Act and condemned Scopes, but they too tried to distance themselves from the fanfare in Dayton. Few of them attended the trial. John Butler himself, the law's author, only agreed to witness the trial when a newspaper offered to pay him for his analysis. National unions mostly hesitated to get involved, as they saw both Clarence Darrow and William Jennings Bryan as allies. So they joined others in straddling the fence.

On the eve of the trial, the town of Dayton earnestly hoped to captivate the nation. One historian aptly referred to the trial as a "modern major media event."[52] Many businessmen and town boosters saw this as Dayton's opportunity to bask in the sun.[53] The town of roughly 1,800 people hoped to lure curious onlookers in addition to the throngs of press ensured by the trial's two lead attorneys. Officials sectioned off several blocks downtown with ropes to create a pedestrian mall. The thoroughfare, filled with local onlookers, resembled a "carnival in which religion and business had become strangely mixed, lined with soda-water, sandwich and book stalls."[54] A local progressive club created a souvenir coin with a monkey wearing a straw hat. Hotel capacity reached its limit, thanks to lawyers, experts, and the press, with cots set up in hallways. An airstrip was sectioned off in a nearby pasture.[55] The town fortified the physical structure of the three-story courthouse, adding toilets, lights, and telegraph lines. Once the trial began, a heat wave forced the proceedings outdoors on some days, further encouraging a festive atmosphere. The *New York Times* described the scene outside the courthouse, pointing out wandering evangelists, minstrels, and a string quartet. Although the throngs of out-of-town tourists never quite materialized, the town did happily welcome a crowd of people associated with the trial.

The press covered the trial with extraordinary attention, and their extensive reporting really turned this event into the "trial of the century." Newspaper reporters arrived before the trial began, and they pumped out story after story detailing the town, the defendant John Scopes, and the attorneys Bryan and Darrow. Coverage captured headlines around the country for at least a week. The *Chicago Tribune* set out to broadcast the trial along telephone lines to Chicago, where it would be sent out on WGN radio. They called the broadcast "the first of its kind in the history of radio." To shrug off any suggestion of impropriety, they assured their audience that it was not a criminal trial, after all. "The defendant, Scopes, is already a negligible factor," noted the *Tribune*, adding, "Nothing serious can happen to him. The contest is entirely over ideas."[56]

The town of Dayton did not necessarily conform to the stereotype northerners wished to ascribe to it.[57] Famous critic and reporter H. L. Mencken, writer for his magazine *American Mercury* as well as for the *Baltimore Evening Sun*, came into Dayton before the trial began. He said in one of his earliest dispatches from Dayton, "The town, I confess, greatly surprised me. I expected to find a squalid Southern village . . . pigs rooting under the houses and the inhabitants full of hookworm and malaria. What I found was a country town full of charm and even beauty." He noted paved streets, well-outfitted stores, and some nicely attired individuals. "Scopes himself, even in his shirt sleeves," he noted, "would fit into any college campus in America save that of Harvard alone."[58]

But not all coverage coming out of Dayton reflected well on the community, despite the town's efforts at hospitality. Many of those northeastern newspapermen could not see beyond their expectations for a small, southern town filled with simpletons, and they fed their audiences back home much of what they thought they might read. Mencken himself was a longtime critic of the village mentality, as well as much else in American culture at the time, and so despite his own surprise at what he found he still spared few feelings in his portrayal. He visited a Pentecostal prayer meeting nearby and characterized its participants as "pathetic."[59] He referred to Daytonites in dispatches as morons and as ignorant fools, calling religion "degraded nonsense" filling local "yokel skulls." Those same generous townsfolk met up to discuss Mencken's portrayal of them to the world, and they pushed for him to leave.[60] He stayed, though not for the full length of the eight-day trial. But the associations made so vividly, if at times unfairly, by reporters in Dayton created lasting images of Tennesseans, and Southerners more generally, as religious fanatics who were intellectually stunted and culturally backward.[61] This reflection of the American South would persist.

The calendar swiftly moved into mid-summer, and "the Great Commoner" took the fight to Dayton, arriving three days early to start making his case. Bryan had to handle a problem with strategy before the trial even began. His prosecution team decided they would oppose the use of expert testimony, believing it better for their side, but Bryan was not pleased. If they got their way, if the basic issue of whether evolution was a valid concept or not did not come up in the trial, then Bryan would not have a chance to stake out the validity of fundamentalism in the court room. This disturbed him. So he solved the problem with his early arrival.

He spent time meeting townspeople, spoke out against evolution to the local school board, and gave two public speeches. At one he laid out the coming fight as plain as could be: "The contest between evolution and Christianity is a duel to the death," he said.[62] When defense attorney Dudley Malone arrived two days later, he remarked to a reporter, "Am I too late for the trial? I rather suspected that I was. You see, I have been reading Mr. Bryan's speeches in the newspapers and I thought the trial had already begun."[63]

Darrow landed his own punches before the trial began, however. Boarding his train to Dayton he laid out the stakes for a reporter, saying bluntly, "Scopes is not on trial. Civilization is on trial."[64] Darrow arrived that evening on the last train into town, just in the nick of time. And then Bryan was no longer the only major player in Dayton. The trial was ready to begin.

The Trial

The trial opened the next day, on July 10, 1925, featuring pomp and circumstance. The room was packed well before the 9 A.M. start time, both with reporters and local onlookers. Judge Ralston arrived first, carrying a statute book and a Bible. While dressed in a new suit himself, he nonetheless allowed the lawyers to take off their coats and ties, given the extreme heat. He also banned smoking in the courtroom, which frustrated many, including most of the defense team. They arrived next. Dudley Field Malone appeared smartly dressed, and Clarence Darrow sported his customary colored suspenders, visible as he removed his jacket upon entering. When Bryan arrived with the prosecution shortly before 9 A.M., the crowd broke out in applause. The clapping started up again when Darrow and Bryan approached one another and shook hands. The men were friendly with each other, having worked on a host of issues together in the past. Without animosity, they stood together and posed for pictures with the judge. The image of these two, Darrow and Bryan standing there together, with all each man stood for in that particular moment, reflected the 1920s culture wars for all to see.[65]

After one last formality, a prayer delivered by none other than a fundamentalist minister, the work of the trial began. A procedural matter came first, as the grand jury needed to reindict Scopes due to a technicality with the original indictment. Jury selection followed. Darrow, known for his intense scrutiny of jurors, questioned them all in turn, though he probably knew most would lean toward fundamentalism. Most did, in the end. And as was the practice in Tennessee, all of the jurors were white men. Darrow pressed a few of them and had them disqualified, but overall he knew what he was going to get in Dayton.[66] The court then adjourned for the weekend.

When the trial convened again on Monday morning, the strategies employed by each side came into focus. At the outset, Scopes and his defense attorneys avoided litigating the issue of evolution's accuracy. They wished to let alone the validity of Darwin's theory right along with the thorny issue of how science and religion clashed on the issue. Instead, they decided to focus on proving that Tennessee's antievolution law violated the Constitution, highlighting the basic need for freedom of speech and for academic freedom in the classroom. But this approach did not last long. Darrow saw clearly the zeitgeist of the mid-1920s. People struggled with the fundamental questions at the heart of the case: what was more rational, more right? Should Americans believe in science, or in religion?[67] Which was to be believed—Genesis or Darwin?[68] And so Darrow shifted gears to focus on these issues he initially planned to avoid. He pushed the framework even farther, too, asking if less zealous, less radical Christianity could reconcile itself with evolution? If so, he probed, what was wrong with fundamentalists? These questions framed his defense of Scopes, and of science, over the remaining days.

The team pivoted once again when the trial's opening salvos called on the judge to decide to either allow or prohibit testimony from expert witnesses. Darrow now felt it critically necessary to determine the validity of evolutionary science in open court, and he wanted to hear from experts who would demonstrate the very real fact that Christians could accommodate such science into their worldview. Bryan countered that such expert testimony needed to have been brought before the Tennessee legislature back when they originally passed the Butler Act. He found it irrelevant to whether or not Scopes broke the law by teaching evolution. Despite dramatic performances by Dudley Malone, in particular, who cried, "We feel we stand with intelligence. We feel we stand with fundamental freedom in America. We are not afraid," the judge disagreed with the defense. No expert testimony would be admitted, though reporters summarized the work of would-be Scopes defenders and published it widely for the public to consider.

This left Darrow and Malone in a rough spot in the actual courtroom, in front of the jury, for ultimately they decided to try the case as one between progress and nostalgia, between modernity and stale traditions. If they could not hash out the significance of evolution in relation to fundamentalist belief they barely had a case at all. With few cards left to play, Darrow decided he would try to put fundamentalism on the stand anyway, and he did so by calling Bryan to testify on his interpretation of the Bible. In truth, Bryan had also hoped to make the trial a verdict on the intellectual worth of the Butler Act. He also planned to bring in expert witnesses, before the judge ruled against it, ones who would defend the fundamentalist interpretation of evolution and its clash with Protestantism. But, awkwardly, the prosecution had great difficulty finding such experts. Several outspoken so-called scientists who supported the fundamentalist cause in previous years proved, at this point, to be charlatans, much to Bryan's embarrassment.[69] And so he too needed to reframe the trial, in his case as one where the state passed a law and Scopes broke that law. Case closed.[70] Given that, members of the prosecution warned Bryan away from a potential embarrassment at the hand of Darrow, but in the end he agreed to go on the stand.

Bryan put himself in this vulnerable position for several reasons, not the least of which was his true conviction. But as the trial got underway in Dayton, a dialogue unfolded in the popular culture that loomed over the courtroom. Prominent paleontologist Henry Fairfield Osborn, who named the Tyrannosaurus Rex in 1905 and was president of the Museum of Natural History by 1925, published a justification for evolution in many of the nation's key newspapers. Osborn characterized Bryan as ignorant, as "unfamiliar with scientific evidence of every kind," and as one who "willfully and deliberately misrepresents the human evolution case." Osborn laid out the most up-to-date science for his readers, demonstrating that contrary to popular hype surrounding the trial, no evidence existed claiming apes or monkeys as direct human ancestors. Bryan and other fundamentalists made much of that claim, even though it was not quite the truth, because it helped their cause. It horrified some, and at the very least unsettled others, to hear that scientists claimed a direct link between men and apes. Osborn portrayed Bryan as a quack, whose efforts he found disingenuous at worst, and ill-informed at best.[71] Though the trial was not yet over, the national media was trying the case in the court of the public opinion. And evolution was winning.

Fundamentalism was on the ropes, then, and Bryan went on trial for it. After about a week, when proceedings had already been moved outside due to the heat, he was called to testify. Several thousand onlookers listened intently as the two lawyers engaged in a verbal sparring match. Darrow danced around the most likely traps he could lay for Bryan in his effort to make him admit his own understanding of the Bible's seeming impossibilities. For example, he asked Bryan to explain how it was that Jonah lived for three days in the belly of a whale. By doing this, Darrow and the other defense lawyers hoped for two things: to make Bryan admit

The Dark Shadow of Darwin

that he himself interpreted the Bible and to demonstrate Bryan's lack of genuine scientific knowledge. The first would allow Darrow to make the case that even this famous fundamentalist did not literally believe in every sentence of the Bible, and so others could interpret it as well. The words in the Bible were not literal truth. The second point would serve to make antievolutionists in general look stupid and uninformed rather than principled.[72]

Bryan treaded carefully, at first, pointing out figurative language in the Bible, but he stood by his beliefs. He claimed there were surely some things that were to be understood as symbolic. For example, he clarified that God did not believe people were—literally—salt, despite the phrase "Ye are the salt of the earth."[73] But Bryan took a stand on the matter of miracles. When Darrow pressed him on the story of Jonah and the whale, asking him if he really believed Jonah lived inside a sea-borne mammal for three days, Bryan replied that he did. He saw miracles as something man could not imagine, could not explain. They were simply, truly, an act of god. He said, "It is just as easy to believe in the miracle of Jonah as any other miracle in the Bible."[74] He stood his ground proudly, claiming his beliefs were shared widely by all kinds of Americans. And he chastised Darrow for his own skepticism. But even so, liberals gawked at his stated willingness to believe a man lived inside a whale, and in the end it was Bryan who looked foolish.[75]

His performance also wobbled when Darrow pressed him to account for the role of science in the world. He frankly expressed little interest in reconciling some of the challenges presented to religion by the advances of science, including one question Darrow returned to again and again: how old was the earth? Theoretical positions on this question existed, if Bryan cared to cite them, but he did not. He simply sidestepped it. He also appeared to lack any detailed knowledge about modern science, admitting his unfamiliarity with some tenets of geology, biology, and even history. The "Great Commoner" displayed a surprising lack of intellectual sophistication under Darrow's questioning.[76]

While Bryan made himself vulnerable, Darrow also failed to secure the higher ground in this very public and heated debate. Darrow stood up in a Tennessee courtroom and called Protestant fundamentalists "bigots and ignoramuses," ridiculing the Bible-based worldview of so many. Rather than attacking the extremes of fundamentalism, Darrow seemed intent on assailing all religious beliefs, a position sure to offend Americans. He mocked Bryan, coming across as bellicose and mean spirited. The skepticism, the sense of alienation, the scorn with which the lost generation viewed America seeped out of Darrow's pores in the sweaty Rhea County

Court. William Jennings Bryan, and many others, resented it. Progressive Christian leaders sympathetic to Scopes expressed their disappointment with Darrow. He did not win many converts to his cause.[77]

What the passionate exchange between the two men did do was fuel the sensationalism surrounding the trial. As Darrow peppered Bryan on the stand with questions about the Bible, the attorney general repeatedly interrupted him, urging the judge to intervene. When pressed on his motives, Darrow snapped, "We have the purpose to prevent bigots and ignoramuses from controlling the educational system of the United States, and you know it." Bryan retorted, "I am simply trying to protect the word of God against the greatest atheistic or agnostic in the United States." The audience thundered in applause. Each man baited the other, physically looming over one another as they went back and forth. Fearful of violence, the judge intervened and ended the day's proceedings.[78]

The following day when the trial began, the judge put an end to the Darrow and Bryan show. He instructed Darrow that he could not question Bryan further, and at the prosecution's urging he ordered Bryan's testimony from the previous day stricken from the record. All agreed that the jury should just go ahead and make their verdict. Darrow did so because he hoped for a quick move to an appeal. He expected to lose. In the end, Darrow had provided no real defense of Scopes—but rather tried to prove that the law was not a just one. Given this, all knew the verdict would be one of guilt, and it was. Scopes offered a withering statement, claiming he believed the Butler Act to be unjust. He stated his belief in academic freedom, as well as religious freedom, and said, "I will continue in the future, as I have in the past, to oppose the law in any way I can." The judge levied a fine of $100, one that Bryan himself offered to pay. And on July 21, 1925, the trial was done.

The Legacy of Scopes

Looking back, the 1920s trial of the century proves curious to the modern reader. After all, the defendant required convincing in order to participate. The prosecutor ended up on the stand. Both of the head lawyers physically menaced one another. The defense ultimately wanted a guilty verdict. Arguably, the nation's most prominent fundamentalist offered to pay the evolutionist schoolteacher's fine. And the whole thing was carried on the airwaves of WGN in Chicago. The events of the Scopes trial were undoubtedly remarkable.

But more remarkable is the unique moment the trial presents to those of us looking back at the 1920s. Here was a time when cultural crosscurrents pulled and strained on people's thoughts and beliefs. Suddenly, this cultural struggle was given a forum, a highly public stage, on which to play out. On this stage the cresting, antagonistic viewpoints presented by modernism on the one hand and nostalgia and tradition on the other smashed against one another, giving off sparks that the nation delighted to see. Scopes lost and the fundamentalists won, it seems, but the real victory in this case is far more complicated. If one considers which way of thinking won out, we are forced to revisit the trial's legacy. Bryan and the prosecution theoretically won the trial, and fundamentalist-inspired educational policy stood in Tennessee in 1925. Fundamentalists were generally pleased with Bryan's performance—after all, he was beloved after a long career as a public figure. But Bryan himself barely lasted a week after the trial's end. The way the trial closed, with all sides agreeing to bring in the jury for a guilty verdict, prevented Bryan from delivering a speech he'd spent a good deal of time preparing. Bryan was still well known for his "Cross of Gold" speech, delivered in favor of bimetallism back in 1896 and still considered one of the greatest political speeches ever. He hoped his concluding speech for the trial would rival that one and bring attention to the antievolution cause. And so he figured out how to give it anyway. He traveled several hundred miles to two nearby towns in the days after the trial to deliver the speech. He returned to Dayton for church on Sunday and afterward lay down for a nap. Bryan never woke up. He had a stroke in his sleep.[79] Five days after the conclusion of the Scopes Trial and the Commoner was dead.

 The legal matter of the case died along with Bryan, though it took a bit longer. The ACLU appealed to the Tennessee Supreme Court in 1927, and the court ruled in a way that cut off a higher appeal to the U.S. Supreme Court. The ruling had two distinct parts. First, the court upheld the constitutionality of the Butler Act. The state could prohibit the teaching of evolution in their classrooms. And, the state employed John Scopes. Given that, and given that he took such a position willingly, the state could legally tell him what he could and could not teach without infringing upon his academic freedom. The second part of the ruling actually overturned Scopes's conviction. The judge levied the fine in the summer of 1925, and technically the jury was supposed to have done so. Judge Raulston assessed the lowest possible fine, and when questioned at the time insisted it was common practice in a case such as that one. Citing the judge's decision to impose the fine himself, the Tennessee Supreme Court nullified Scopes's guilty verdict and asked the state attorney general not to refile the case. John Scopes was cleared of his conviction, but more important, and much to the outrage of the ACLU, without a conviction it was impossible for the group to continue to appeal the case.[80]

So the moderns lost the legal challenge to antievolution policy, but had they, for the time being, lost the larger culture war? It depended largely on who asked the question. In the immediate aftermath of the trial, it looked to some as if the opposite was true. Bryan died, and the antievolutionist cause lost its most famous leader. And, thanks to extensive media coverage of the trial in the nation's newspapers, many at the time felt that the trial had really only further exposed the outdated, regressive thinking of fundamentalists.

This worked against fundamentalists in significant ways. The popular narrative of the trial allowed liberals to portray fundamentalists as backward hillbillies, when in reality the movement was far more diverse, and interested in more than just antievolution activism. But after Scopes it hardly mattered. Fundamentalism simply lacked the respectability it once maintained.[81] In part, this was because of the negative associations made in the press, but it was also due to the prominence of science in popular culture at the moment of the trial. Media coverage boosted awareness of science, and of Darwin, making ideas that challenged traditional religious thinking even more widely accessible than before.

But, John Scopes and Clarence Darrow lost in Dayton, and William Jennings Bryan won. Didn't this matter? The simple answer is, yes, it did matter. It mattered very much, especially in the nation's classrooms. In the immediate aftermath of the trial, many fundamentalists felt emboldened to go farther in their efforts to shape educational policy. Few states passed restrictions like the Butler Act, but local school boards across the nation went on to restrict science education in practice with relative ease. Textbooks left out evolution for decades to come.[82] And the trial sensationalized evolution, making fewer teachers willing to go out on a limb in order to teach it.[83]

Furthermore, the widely shared notion that really, modernism triumphed in Tennessee actually dissuaded people from continuing their own efforts to bolster science and secular thinking. Maynard Shipley, president of the Science League of America, wrote a few years after Scopes that antievolution activism was still going strong, alerting fellow liberals that "the armies of ignorance are being organized, literally by the millions." He pointed out the folly of thinking the fight against evolution in schools went down with Bryan in Dayton.[84]

Antievolutionists came out of the Scopes Trial on top, then, even if fundamentalists themselves did not. But for a long time that is not how Americans remembered the trial. This curious misremembering of history came about largely for two reasons. First, in 1931, journalist Frederick Lewis Allen cemented the popular history of the 1920s for decades to come with his book titled *Only Yesterday: An Informal History of the Nineteen-Twenties*. In the book, one written for an audience subsumed by the Depression, Allen applied a veneer of nostalgia and certainty over the events of the previous decade. Rather than presenting a messy story of media bias and complex cultural and religious ideals, Allen reworked the tale as a simple one. All fundamentalists were antievolutionists, and Bryan stood in as the representative of all antievolutionists.

Scopes lost the trial, but won the day, Allen claimed. When Bryan died, fundamentalism died with him. Allen erased the memory of the antievolution policies that followed Scopes, erased the networking and building beginning to take place. Allen also helped construct the durable narrative placing Darrow as the valiant defender of modernism and Bryan as an ignorant buffoon. The truth of their dialogue was most certainly more nuanced, as we have seen. But his book sold over a million copies and laid a lasting foundation for popular memory of the 1920s.[85]

The second thing that framed the way Americans remember the Scopes Trial was the popular 1955 play *Inherit the Wind*, a fictional portrait of the events in Dayton. Historian Edward Larson calls it "the single most influential retelling of the tale."[86] The Broadway production ran for three years, a record for dramatic plays at the time. The show then traveled the country, only to become a smashingly successful film in 1960. In hindsight the film is clearly a product of the McCarthy era, in which it was created. It paints a portrait of the townspeople of Dayton engaging in a witch hunt for John Scopes. Participants from 1925 balked at the play's portrayal of the trial, claiming the real events were not so sinister. The play and then the film further lampooned Bryan's character, making his blunders on the stand more outrageous than they were. The retelling lionized Darrow's character, only building up the edifice of heroism around him. And the fictionalized version closed with Bryan's character collapsing in the courtroom, with tolerance vanquishing censorship and conformity. The Scopes character asks whether he won at the end of the play, and Darrow's character answers, "Millions of people will say you won. They'll read in their papers tonight that you smashed a bad law."[87] This narrative of the trial underwrote its popular history.[88]

But the trial plays an ambiguous part in our reckoning of the 1920s culture wars because this history was not quite accurate in ways that mattered. Did fundamentalism triumph, as Bryan hoped, or did it sputter out in the glare of media scrutiny, as Darrow believed it would? To many observers after 1925, it seemed as though modernists won the war. The trial marked the beginning of the end of 1920s-style fundamentalism, which went from a vibrant and powerful force with broad support among Protestants to a worldview tarnished and battered by the decade's end. The popular history seemed to be on target.

In the background fundamentalists continued to fight, and there were many of them. Critic H. L. Mencken complained after the trial that fundamentalists had not, in fact, been defeated, stating, "Heave an egg out of a Pullman window and you will hit a Fundamentalist almost anywhere in the United States to-day."[89] He was not wrong. But fundamentalists faced a difficult dilemma by the late 1920s. They could embrace the cultural representations of them made so popular by Mencken and others, and keep on with their agenda, an option that many went with. Or, they could more fully appreciate the conflict between modern science and their religious stance, and quietly begin to disassociate themselves from fundamentalist beliefs. Many took this route, too. But the former group soldiered on, despite the stereotypes crystallized by the trial. They were hardened, and determined, to maintain Protestantism's grasp on American culture.[90]

This committed group of fundamentalists found that the trial changed the contours of battles over education going forward. Americans had long haggled over what made up an appropriate education for all kinds of children. In the 19th century that fight typically raged between Catholics and Protestants, or between immigrants and natives. But the Scopes Trial reshaped the battle lines. The fundamentalist school controversies in the 1920s reflected the view of many Protestants in an increasingly modern world that public schools no longer provided a safe place for children to learn morality and decency. From that point on, and to this day, culture wars over school curricula tend to follow this framework. Liberals of a range of religious backgrounds battle with conservatives from a similar range of religious backgrounds.

This new framework positioned fundamentalists at the margins of the discussion over education, marking out space for them to see themselves as a distinct group in search of redress. They became a vocal and persistent interest group, outside the mainstream, seeking to influence educational policy.[91] As historian Adam Laats has argued, the transformation of fundamentalist school activism from a campaign to uphold what they saw as the majority's rights in a school curriculum to that of an embattled minority seeking inclusion has its roots in the unfolding of the Scopes Trial and its impact in the 1920s. The fundamentalist movement itself transformed in the aftermath of Scopes, and their tactics evolved, all of which helped establish the position of the Christian Right in our own contemporary culture wars.[92]

And so these outsiders did not go gently into the night after 1925. Pressure to keep evolution out of the nation's classrooms continued until the start of the Great Depression, which began an era scholars refer to as the "thirty year truce." The demands of Depression and wartime kept evolution out of the spotlight for some time. But interest in it blossomed again in the 1950s when anxieties over the Cold War bolstered revisions to America's science curriculum. Parents fought back against the inclusion of evolution, but this time teachers in many places held their ground. When the film version of *Inherit the Wind* debuted in 1960, interest in the trial reanimated the debate once again. Scopes reported getting phone calls from students writing school papers, and the Butler Act was still in place.

But evolution gained a foothold in the nation's schools in a way it had not before, and this was significant. In 1968, teacher Susan Epperson's case made it all the way to the Supreme Court, where she challenged her guilty conviction in Arkansas. Epperson taught biology and taught with a required textbook that included a chapter on evolution.[93] And yet she was convicted of breaking the state's laws for doing so. It seemed to many like a redo of the Scopes Trial some 40 years later. In this instance, the court ruled in Epperson's favor. The Arkansas state law was ruled unconstitutional. But this did not mean evolution won the day, even in the late 20th century.[94]

The explosion of fundamentalism with the Christian Right in the 1980s exposes the fallacy of the narrative of fundamentalism's decline. The resurgent right animated a new generation's culture war, seemingly revived from the dead. Given this reality, we must reconsider the years between 1925 and the 1980s. Fundamentalists may have retreated from public debate, giving up political ground, but they organized and fostered their identity as an outsider group through the decades of Depression, war, and social turmoil. Their work finally bloomed in politics and popular culture in the 1980s, when the same issues at stake in the struggles of the 1920s once again came to the fore.[95]

An emotional conflict over the public place of religion roared back into the spotlight. Dudley Malone, back during the Scopes Trial, urged his listeners in 1925 to "Keep your bible . . . keep it as your guide, but keep it where it belongs, in the world of your own conscience, in the world of your individual judgment."[96] With Ronald Reagan's election, the Christian Right went to battle to bring prayer back to public schools, to end abortion rights, to squash sex education, and to make room for creationism. In that moment Malone's words, spoken more than 50 years before, were more relevant than ever. The Bible, it seemed, belonged everywhere.

This became readily apparent when the battle over evolution in classrooms exploded again in 1981, in Little Rock, Arkansas, in a trial the press dubbed "Scopes II." Buoyed by the rise of the New Right and by the proliferation of independent fundamentalist and evangelical schools in the 1970s and 1980s, itself a product of the school controversies of the 1920s, creationism flourished in the last few decades of the 20th century. By 2001 a Gallup poll showed that slightly less than half of Americans believed "God created human beings pretty much in their present form at one time within the last 10,000 years or so."[97] Bryan's cause came roaring back with a vengeance, then, as creationists flipped the script and began battling for equal time in the classroom alongside evolution, which had become a regular classroom fixture by the 1980s. Creationism provided a human origin story friendly to Genesis, arguing that a divine being created life on earth rather than a natural process of evolution. And fundamentalist activists pushed for exposure to both models, urging public schools to give both "scientific" theories equal time. In 2008, the "Science Education Act" in Louisiana went so far as to protect teachers if they were critical of evolution in the classroom. The pendulum began swinging to the other side.[98]

Despite what we know about the rise of the religious right in the 1980s, the trial ultimately transformed 1920s fundamentalism in ways that troubled some and cheered others at the time. What started out as a robust movement peopled by men and women who felt certain of their position in the wider American culture ended the decade in a very different position. The blistering publicity of the Scopes Trial painted fundamentalists into a corner, into a negative stereotype framed by backwardness and lack of education. The trial created the rigid outlines of that stereotype, and soon fundamentalists who embraced science, ones who considered themselves respectable elites, did not know where to go. The movement ultimately faltered over the course of the decade because of the intensity of the antievolution campaign. And the stereotypes that materialized during this decade continued to frame conversations about the public role of religion in future culture wars.[99]

This trial mattered so much in the 1920s because it offered a powerful symbol of the brewing culture wars. Newspaper and radio coverage made it very difficult to miss the trial's details, so, as H. L. Mencken wrote after the trial, "The whole world has been made familiar with the issues, and the nature of the menace that Fundamentalism offers to civilization is now familiar to every schoolboy." This meant that the events in Dayton provided people with a narrative that helped construct their cultural framework in 1925. That narrative shaped the way they saw the world, and it shaped the way the world was, in essence, for them as individuals and as a larger society. Mencken continued, "On the one side was bigotry, ignorance, hatred, superstition, every sort of blackness that the human mind is capable of. On the other side was sense. And sense achieved a great victory."[100]

In this epic battle Darrow stood in as the harbinger of modernism, of the savvy and swagger of the city, of the intellectuals so critical of the old status quo. Bryan stepped up as the self-appointed defender of tradition, of the village, of the moral certainties of a nostalgic age that seemed to be slipping away. The assumed inherent conflict between these two sides likely hampered intelligent debate at the time—no conflict was so clear, so black and white. But individuals fall easily into such binary ways of thinking, especially when faced with thorny intellectual or cultural challenges to their sense of well-being. The very notion of a culture war holds such salience for exactly this reason.[101]

And so, the fireworks between these two sides, between Darrow and Bryan, reflected the growing polarization in American culture at that moment, as did the stunning ability of each side to view the trial as a win for their team. A great divide existed, even if it was not so totalizing, or so clear. Of course this was just one of several tensions flaring up all around Americans at the time, coinciding with and coalescing with other debates over immigration, race, sex, and alcohol. And here was one more example of resistant traditionalists seeking help from the state in their efforts to hold onto the status quo.[102] And, while they held back modernism in the classroom for a while, it would not last forever.

Epilogue

At the 1992 Republican National Convention in Houston, former candidate Pat Buchanan broadcast the existence of "a culture war" in America. It was, he claimed, "as critical to the kind of nation we will one day be as was the Cold War itself." To Americans at the time Buchanan's argument was not a revelation. For as long as Americans have shared a national community, they engaged in culture wars. The constant promise and threat of change has always cheered some, even as it challenged others who then worked to shut it down. And so, the 1920s do not reflect the true starting point of cultural battles in America. But they do provide the first real glimpse of our modern culture wars, the ones we are still living through today. The 1920s spawned the familiar narratives of conflict that we read in the paper, see on the television screen, and view on social media.

Yet, despite the fact that we can trace these familiar narratives back to the 1920s, many historians find the roots of our current culture wars in earlier eras. Deep cultural divisions over religion and the nature of the state erupted in the election of 1800. Bitter battles over religion broke out again in the 1800s between Catholics and Protestants and between Mormons and almost everyone else. But most often, historians find the source of our contemporary culture wars in a more recent era.[1]

As in the tumultuous 1920s, Americans in the 1960s experienced rapid social and cultural change. Between the early and later years of the decade spread an enormous gulf, where thoughts on race, patriotism, sexuality, gender, and politics appeared radically different. The "normative America" that existed in the 1950s, bought by mass consumerism and shadowed by the Cold War, was overturned.[2] As culture war historian Andrew Hartman put it, "The gulf that separated those who embraced the new America from those who viewed it ominously—those who looked to nurture it versus those who sought to roll it back—drew the boundaries of the culture wars."[3] But unlike the 1920s, in the 1960s Americans challenging the status quo brought that challenge to bear directly on the political order. Even as drastic transformations were underway in the 1920s, politically the nation remained largely conservative. While the decade brought forth discontent among women, immigrant groups, African Americans, urban and rural whites, and religious groups, people who felt marginalized or alienated in different ways, this was not quite identity politics as we know them today. In part, this is because only one set of culture warriors had access to mainstream political power. In the 1960s, a host of different groups clamoring for their rights brought their fight into the political arena, overtaking both the Republican and Democratic parties by the 1970s.

The two sides of these late 20th-century culture wars were not neatly defined by partisan politics, though. The battle featured two groups with different ways of seeing the world. James Davison Hunter, the sociologist who first canonized the culture wars in the early 1990s, argued that there was an orthodox worldview, which featured an inherent belief in some external, spiritual authority, be it in religion or nature or culture. Usually, these were people identified as conservatives, or neoconservatives. Then there was the progressive worldview, which denied existing systems of moral authority, was more secular, and instead based values on more subjective experiences in society. Liberals espoused this view, as did those on the left. The contest here then, according to Hunter, was between these two groups as they waged a "struggle over national identity—over the meaning of America."[4]

The rapid growth of Protestant evangelical churches in the 1970s and 1980s fueled the orthodox side, as they fought for the "soul of America," according to Hartman.[5] Religious conservatives sought to convert people to their faith and to infiltrate mainstream culture and society in order to beat back the impact of 1960s cultural radicalism.[6] The rising religious right found an organizational voice in the Moral Majority, founded in 1979, and with Ronald Reagan's election in 1980 they ascended to the highest office in the land. Religion was central to public life, just as it was briefly in the 1920s.[7] Yet, progressives continued to organize for feminism, freedom of expression, reproductive rights, multiculturalism, and gay rights. In 1981, famous television producer Norman Lear organized the People for the American Way in order to combat the growing influence of the religious right. And the battle waged on into the 1990s, when Buchanan called Americans to arms, and it rages still after the divisive presidency of the first black president, Barack Obama, and the current presidency of Donald Trump, one predicated in part on the culture war.

The legacy of this culture war is evident all around us. Today, the United States is fractured along many lines of division, but one of the most prominent is geographical. Conservatives and liberals whose skirmishes fuel our culture wars today tend to hail from "red states" or "blue states," from the supposedly elite coastal states or the conservative, working-class "fly over" states nestled in the country's middle. In a very real way, these are newer, updated terms that reflect the values of the small town in opposition to the values of the city. This divide still frames our political culture. Cities are synonymous with bustling streets, cosmopolitan values, progressive politics, queer life, and consumer culture. Alternatively, towns represent tight-knit communities rather than bastions of individualism. Towns are associated with traditional nuclear families, white picket fences, churches, and working-class men and women. It is worth noting that these working-class people are imagined to be white, almost always. Politically, people in the towns, or in red states, sway to the right. In the 2016 presidential election, Republican candidate and Texas senator Ted Cruz—a Southern Baptist—derided what he called "New York values" as a way to call out and condemn socially liberal policies and interest in superficial, material things. These were not the values of the town, he implied. This familiar narrative runs back to the 1920s, when this very same conflict first infiltrated the national conversation thanks to spreading consumer culture, modernizing sexual norms, shifts in racial demographics, and rapid urbanization.

Equally as striking in the late 20th-century and 21st-century culture wars is the association forged between black Americans and urban space. If segregated city neighborhoods appeared prominently in the 1920s, they mushroomed in the years that followed. Practices like white flight and the use of racial covenants persisted. The federal government further entrenched segregation and the clustering of African Americans in lower-income areas in cities with the practice of redlining. Franklin Delano Roosevelt's administration took up the task of helping to secure mortgage loans for Americans struggling under the weight of the Depression in the 1930s, and due to institutionalized racism the Federal Housing Administration typically backed loans only for white Americans. Housing stock deemed too risky to support would be encircled in red on zoning maps, and minority groups usually populated those areas. So federal money went disproportionately to white families looking to buy homes away from black neighborhoods in cities, often out in ever-expanding suburbs. And so, persistently, black America seemed to live in the city.

Segregation in the nation's cities and their surrounding suburbs exists still, propped up by white flight, social policy, and urban planning. In fact, a 2015 study published in *American Sociological Review* found that segregation increased rather than decreased over the last half century. While metropolitan areas have become less segregated, when looking at an area as a whole, including surrounding suburbs, overall segregation persisted. So while more minority groups live in the suburbs, they tend to live in suburbs populated mostly by people like them. The study's authors used Ferguson, Missouri, as one example, noting that between 1990 and 2010 the suburb of St. Louis went from being 25.1 percent black to 67.4 percent black. Over time, they found, the area became increasingly known as a black neighborhood, which plays a key role in fostering continued segregation. But as this happened, local decisions on the level of policy mattered too. White flight sparked the approval of construction on low- and mixed-income apartment buildings, while investment firms bought homes in foreclosure not to sell them to new owners but to rent them to minority groups. Furthermore, predominantly white areas sometimes choose zoning laws that do not allow for affordable housing in efforts to grow their tax base.[8]

More than 100 years after the Great Migration first began to pull the nation's African Americans into the nation's cities, urban poverty is rife, and it is often accompanied by compulsory segregation and racial stigma.[9] The race riots that pulled communities apart in 1919 appeared again, en masse, in cities such as Watts, Detroit, and Newark in the 1960s. President Lyndon Johnson's Kerner Commission, convened to study the causes of the riots, found a separate black and white America still in existence. Committee members wrote, "Our nation is moving toward two societies, one black, one white—separate and unequal." Today's culture wars over race still rage, when groups like Black Lives Matter, born out of the shooting of Trayvon Martin in 2012, call for an end to anti-black racism in all aspects of American society. Their focus on extrajudicial killings of black people by members of law enforcement has spawned an angry backlash from many white conservatives, leading to tense protests and occasional violence in cities like Chicago, Charlottesville, and Baltimore. The 1920s first established the stereotypical image of the troubled or disorderly black city—a space constructed by white racism—and today this image still frames understandings of racial conflict and determines social policy.

The presence of nativism, or anti-immigrant sentiment, is also most clearly still at the center of national debates over American identity and American values. Nativism was not new in the 1920s—it reaches back to the nation's beginnings, expanding and receding over the years depending on the rise and fall of national moods and tensions. For example, nativism swelled amid the influx of famine Irish in the late 1840s, in the tumultuous years preceding the Civil War. But it reached a crescendo in the 1920s, and today, once again conversations about immigrants reflect an urgency and an anger over who gets to be an American.

While regulations set up in the 1920s drastically limited immigration to America through the middle of the century, restrictions loosened in the decades after World War II. In 1968, President Johnson revamped immigration policy, effectively opening the nation's gates to millions of people who were purposefully excluded for a very long time. Thus, the ethnic and racial makeup of America transformed in the 1970s, 1980s, and 1990s, making immigration an integral part of the culture wars when they erupted at that point. Partisan battles echoed long-held concerns about immigrants who refused to assimilate, about the potential loss of a majority white population, about immigrants draining welfare funds, and most recently, about concerns over terrorism. Today, we see a resurgent xenophobia as the nation is embroiled in a bitter battle over immigration laws. The president of the United States is ratcheting up deportations, while calling for travel bans from predominantly Muslim countries as well as the building of a wall to cut off undocumented immigrants at the nation's southern border with Mexico. Despite a decrease in immigration on that border, many politicians and pundits have called for increased regulation and heightened enforcement, in decisions seemingly not based on real needs. In this political moment, Americans witnessed white supremacists and neo-Nazi's march on Charlottesville, Virginia, in opposition to the removal of General Robert E. Lee's statue in a local park. The deep disagreement over multiculturalism in America and a persistent tendency to associate Americanness and patriotism with whiteness is starkly reminiscent of America in the 1920s.

The antiradicalism that marked the decade after World War I resonated throughout the century that followed, too. Americans engaged with communism as a real political entity in Russia for the very first time in this decade, and the Cold War that developed after 1945, stretching into the latter years of the century, maintained a script written decades before. We must remember that the post–World War II "Red Scare" associated with Senator Joseph McCarthy and the infamous House Un-American Activities Committee hearings had a powerful precedent in the 1920s. The antiradicalism that coalesced in the 1920s leaves a lasting legacy. In these increasingly turbulent times, we still deploy narrow conceptions of fellowship and patriotism, and we continue to question just who truly deserves to be American.

Prohibition, both the way people conceived of it and the way they tried to enforce it, also has lasting implications that play into today's culture wars. This is evident in Prohibition's legacy for narcotics. Concerns about drug use existed before the 1920s, but the Prohibition law encouraged efforts to systematize regulation of narcotics. Drug users, once seen as victims in need of assistance, were now viewed as criminals. Laws prohibiting narcotics, and international regulations spearheaded by American officials, set up a formal system of regulation. While those regulations faltered once the Depression set in, the framework still existed. Furthermore, the power of the criminal justice system grew exponentially with the arrival of Prohibition. The technology and tactics of enforcement sharpened police efforts, while surging criminality led to more people in prisons than ever before. And when a war on drugs emerged, one that purposefully targeted minorities in the 1970s and beyond, primarily in cities, the edifice of our modern drug laws and the concurrent mass incarceration they triggered was constructed on this foundation.[10]

Prohibition's fueling of state growth represented an important step in the development of a powerful and coercive federal government. The enforcement needs brought on by the law included more bureaucracy, the use of Border Patrol, the growth of federal prisons, and the concurrent growth of the Federal Bureau of Investigation. Altogether this created a mass of information and might, what historians refer to as the "surveillance state."[11] The modern day relationship between Americans and their government is one that wavers between reverence and fear, and while many histories point to the bigger government that emerged from the Progressive Era, or more commonly the New Deal, Prohibition facilitated this growth in significant ways.[12]

The consequences of this shift are evident even beyond the current structure of drug laws or the prison system. More and more, Americans looked to the federal government for aid, changing the nature of their relationship with that government. And at the same time, more and more citizens resented the intervention of a government they feared was too large. Raging debates in the early 21st century about Obamacare, over the right of the federal government to force people to buy health insurance, are part of this very same conversation Americans had throughout the Prohibition Era. Exactly what role should the federal government play, and how far could it impinge upon Americans' liberties?

The profound legacy of America's first modern women is perhaps even more evident. For despite white, middle-class American women's efforts to stake claims for political equality, economic independence, reproductive freedom, and family life, these dreams proved elusive by the end of the twenties. And years of Depression and war kept those dreams on the back burner for decades more. Only after a run of economic prosperity, in an era of social tumult, did second-wave feminism arise to make these very same claims once again. Some historians credit their challenge to the sexual and gender order with the outbreak of the contemporary culture wars themselves, seeing second-wave feminism's real and imagined revolution as the primary catalyst for a coalescing conservative New Right. But whether it was women's rights, or race, women and the family remained at the center of America's culture wars when they surfaced again in the latter half of the 20th century, and they still sit there now.

Mobilization against the revived Equal Rights Amendment (ERA) spawned the mainstream political career of Republican Phyllis Schlafly, one of the architects of the New Right. Through her groups Eagle Forum and STOP-ERA, Schlafly celebrated the Judeo-Christian civilization she claimed was built around the biological and seemingly clear differences between women and men. Schlafly laid claim to the privileged position she felt American women enjoyed as she conjured sensational possible consequences of the amendment, arguing that the ERA would strip social security benefits from widows, make child support and alimony unconstitutional, subject women to the military draft, and create unisex bathrooms. However disingenuous Schlafly's claims were, her effectiveness as a speaker and a political strategist cannot be denied, and her anti-ERA stance gained traction.[13] Other women shared her concerns about whether men would uphold their "traditional" responsibilities if women abandoned the role of housewife and stay-at-home mother.[14]

By the mid-1970s, the ERA stood out as a symbol of the fraught process of changing understandings about sex roles in America, both for feminists and their conservative opponents. Conservatives folded the ERA into what they viewed as a larger assault on traditional notions of womanhood, manhood, and the family. They wondered, what did it mean to be women and men in America in the 1970s? Thanks to many forces beyond the purview of the women's movement, including an economic slowdown and the work of reformist lawyers to change divorce laws, it seemed as though more marriages were ending and more women were in the workforce. The traditional lines blurred and definitions that were rock solid in the 1950s were now up for debate. While this spurred on those challenging the old order, it terrified those whose power or sense of security depended on that old order.

By the late 1970s, the rise of that political entity labeled the "New Right" built upon the marriage of politics with social concerns. Growing consternation about issues like divorce rates, female-led households, and most significantly, abortion, became fodder for conservatives to politicize the very issues second-wave feminists seized upon—the family, gender norms, reproductive rights, and sexuality. Rising conservatives established a platform of "family values" to bolster their economic and political bedrock, widening the gap that already existed between cultural conservatives and cultural liberals since the Civil Rights Movement.[15] By then Ronald Reagan sat in the Oval Office and American political culture responded to the demands of feminism with a deep and very real backlash. Feminism of course survived the 1980s, and efforts to promote women's rights took new directions in hostile times, including calls by lesbians and women of color to reimagine feminism, but many prominent women's right activists lost power and the political tone of the era kept them on the defensive.[16]

Placing women's rights at the center of conservative rhetoric and symbolic imagery, the 1980s laid the groundwork for what many refer to today as a conservative "war on women." In fact, many conservative voters report making electoral decisions based mostly on their desire to overturn *Roe v. Wade*. With reproductive rights currently at stake in many states around the nation, with access to birth control a hot button political issue, with no equal pay for equal work, and still without an ERA, the emblematic role of women in both eras of culture war is undeniable. The challenge presented by the push for equal rights for women in the 1920s has only grown, and it is a challenge many in America still wish to beat back.

While our contemporary culture wars are driven in no small part by the religious right, who vociferously oppose abortion rights and gay marriage, we must remember that Protestant fundamentalism was born in the 1920s. At the time the movement sought to battle the influence of Catholics and liberal Protestants, and they were thoroughly antimodern, seeking to stop the advance of modern culture in all its forms. This manifested most visibly in the trial against John Scopes, but fundamentalist ideas animated many of the "wars" this book covers. Protestant fundamentalism moved out of the spotlight by the end of the 1920s, but it hardly disappeared. Instead, they spent the middle years of the century building up institutions and mechanisms of influence. It surprised some but not all when fundamentalists roared back into national prominence with the rise of the New Right. The coalition that buoyed opposition to issues spurred by the 1960s, things like the ERA, *Roe v. Wade*, the separation of church and state, and the gay liberation movement, was eventually cross-denominational and inclusive of Protestants, Catholics, and even Orthodox Jews. This was different from the 1920s. But their focus on "modernism" in the form of personal autonomy and identity politics, two products of the 1960s, feels very familiar as these religious conservatives seek to defend the place of religion in American public life.[17]

While the battles in both eras seem in some ways the same, the tactics of the 1920s religious right shifted as they geared up to wage what they saw as a culture war. Fundamentalists could not garner the dedicated attention of either political party in the 1920s, and so their efforts to reinsert Christianity into American life and identity were met with mixed success. But in the mid-20th century, Christian leaders courted the Republican Party for its stand against communism, a system they saw as hostile to religion. And by the late 1970s, major players like Jerry Falwell allied themselves with the Republican Party by focusing on the brewing culture wars, an effort to put up a fight against the vast transformations sweeping across the country since the late 1960s. Here, they found great success, and ultimately through well-organized groups like the Moral Majority, these religious leaders took over the agenda of the Republican Party by Ronald Reagan's election in 1980.[18] But the role of a religious right battling the eclipse of religion from the public arena began well before then. And still today, a loosely defined group of evangelicals mobilize consistently at the polls, working hard to keep some semblance of control over American culture.

The surprising election of Donald Trump in 2016 demonstrates the salience of all of these issues still. Americans can be powerfully moved by culture war concerns. Surveys, polls, and interviews reflect an abiding concern with cultural values and a divide between rural white voters and urban white voters. When asked about their motivations in pulling the lever for Trump, white rural voters who often live in tightly knit, small Christian communities pointed to a war they felt being waged on their religious freedom. Here, in particular, we can see the power of the culture war, as 81 percent of white evangelical voters cast a ballot for an irreligious man who violates all of their moral convictions. Why? Because he expertly constructed his campaign as a staunch defense of historically white, Protestant cultural values, ones we are familiar with, including restricting access to reproductive rights and protections on the role of religion in the public arena.

Furthermore, polls of rural Trump voters revealed that while they typically did not live among immigrants, they felt immigrants failed to assimilate and found that they weakened the country overall. They argued black and Hispanic Americans unfairly took government aid, a claim found far less frequently among urban white voters.[19] And in the wake of the white supremacist fight over Confederate statues, the lines that can be drawn from the Klan in the 1920s to our political climate today seem even more striking. Trump's campaign and subsequent election seemed to pour gasoline on the culture wars, then, adding fuel to battles over immigration, reproductive rights, racial equality, the city versus the town, the role of religion in public life, and drug and prison policies. In a continuing battle over whose vision of America should prevail, the culture wars live on.

In the 1920s, white, middle-class Protestant Americans keenly felt the "acids of modernity."[20] They felt as though they were losing their grip on the reins of their country, and they sought ways to enforce homogeneity on a nation that was already so heterogeneous that their task would prove impossible. The challenge to their power and influence stemming from urbanization, modern sex norms, increasing diversity, secular values, and consumer culture felt like a war being waged upon them. And so they fought back. They fought through antiradicalism, antifeminism, nativism, Prohibition, fundamentalism, white supremacy, and an opposition to modernism in their efforts to coerce fellow Americans into conforming to a way of life and a worldview that was already passing out of existence. The 1920s culture war was their concerted—though diffuse—effort to stop change in a newly modern culture.[21]

What can we learn from this formative struggle in the 1920s "over the meaning of America"? To start, geography still matters. The cultural divide spanning the distance between cities and small towns reflected and still does reflect an enduring tension between notions of America as fertile ground for the pursuit of happiness, and America as a grand moral experiment. The heady twenties romance with consumer culture, with self-satisfying indulgence, looked misguided to those still holding tight to a pious morality. And this tension only festered over the next century as evangelicals regrouped and asserted their will on electoral politics from their typically "red" states.

Americans still wrangle over the warp and woof of cultural identity. Some reject diversity and multiculturalism as threats to a white, Protestant America, promoting a racist and anti-immigrant narrative woven into the fabric of American culture in the 1920s, despite many challenges. Furthermore, the expansion of citizenship to include women on equal footing in 1920 forced a restructuring of Americanness, one the country is still yielding to. Political power for women, coupled later with more fully realized claims for economic power and sexual equality, seemed to fundamentally challenge visions of the American way, spurring on culture warriors.[22]

Epilogue

And lastly, our current attitude toward the evolution of cultural change clearly echoes the temper of the "Roaring Twenties." A polarized nation casts off the possibility for compromise amid calls for ideological purity, characterizing the success of the "other" side as a threat to civilization as we know it. Each side eyes the other with suspicion. Change continues its long march, unabated, while some still cling to a mythic past secured by old hierarchies of race, class, and gender. Perhaps the most substantial conclusion we can draw from the dawn of our culture wars in the 1920s is that these divisions are not new. They are a prominent feature of the 20th and 21st centuries. The culture wars are not an aberration, but rather, they are definitive of modern America. Coming to terms with this reality seems like an important step toward an eventual cease-fire. But in the meantime, the culture war rages on around us.

Notes

Introduction

1. Mary Fisher Torrance. "Yesterday's Daughters," *The New York Times*, February 20, 1921, BRM4.
2. Willa Cather. *Not Under Forty* (New York: Alfred A. Knopf, 1936), prefatory note.
3. Robert Lynd and Helen Lynd. *Middletown: A Study in Modern American Culture* (New York: Harcourt Brace & Co, 1929), 5.
4. Stephen Prothero. *Why Liberals Win the Culture Wars* (New York: Harper One, 2016), 9–10.
5. *Sunday Constitution Magazine, Atlanta Constitution*, January 15, 1922, 1.
6. "Klansmen, Raise Your Visors!" *The Fiery Cross*, Friday, April 13, 1923, 4.
7. Howard Kelly. "Prohibition and the Medical Fraternity," *North American Review* 222, no. 828, September–November 1925, 56–57.
8. John Thomas Scopes. *The World's Most Famous Court Trial: Tennessee Evolution Case: A Complete Stenographic Report of the Famous Court Test of the Tennessee Anti-Evolution Act, at Dayton, July 10 to 21, 1925, Including Speeches and Arguments of Attorneys* (1925), 316.
9. Lynds, 495.
10. Elizabeth Benson. *Vanity Fair*, September 1927, 104, quoted in *The American New Woman Revisited: A Reader, 1894–1930*, Martha H. Patterson ed. (New Brunswick, NJ: Rutgers University Press, 2008), 241–42.

Chapter 1 The City Challenges Main Street

1. *Sunrise: A Song of Two Humans*, directed by F. W. Murnau (1927; Fox Films).
2. Lawrence Levine. *The Unpredictable Past: Explorations in American Cultural History* (New York: Oxford University Press, 1993), 196.
3. Ibid., 196–97.

4. Ibid., 199–200.

5. Victoria W. Woolcott. *Race, Riots, and Roller Coasters: The Struggle over Segregated Recreation in America* (Philadelphia: University of Pennsylvania Press, 2012), 13–20.

6. Charles W. Eagles. "Urban-Rural Conflict in the 1920s: A Historiographical Assessment," *The Historian* 49, no. 1, November 1986, 26–48, 28.

7. Ibid., 28.

8. Karen L. Cox. "The South and Mass Culture," *The Journal of Southern History*, 75, no. 3, August 2009, 677–90, 677.

9. Eagles, 29.

10. Ibid., 30.

11. Ibid., 37–38.

12. Ann Douglas. *Terrible Honesty: Mongrel Manhattan in the 1920s* (New York: Noonday Press, 1995), 17.

13. Ibid., 5.

14. Quote from Anne Douglas in Douglas, 20.

15. Donald L. Miller. *Supreme City: How Jazz Age Manhattan Gave Birth to Modern America* (New York: Simon and Schuster, 2014), xi.

16. Douglas, 16.

17. Ibid., 14–15.

18. Miller, 257–60.

19. Tom Sitton and William Deverall, eds. *Metropolis in the Making: Los Angeles in the 1920s* (Berkeley: University of California Press, 2001), 2.

20. Ibid., 7.

21. Ibid., 2.

22. Ibid., 2–3.

23. Ibid., 3.

24. Ibid., 5.

25. Ibid., 3.

26. Lynn Dumenil. *The Modern Temper: American Culture and Society in the 1920s* (New York: Hill and Wang, 1995), 57–58.

27. Ibid., 85.

28. Ibid., 89.

29. Ibid., 89–90.

30. Tom Lewis. " 'A Godlike Presence': The Impact of Radio on the 1920s and 1930s." *OAH Magazine of History* 6, no. 4, Spring 1992, 26–33, 26–27.

31. Ibid., 27.

32. Ibid., 28.

33. Dumenil, 82–83.

34. John Kasson. *Amusing the Million: Coney Island at the Turn of the Century* (New York: Hill and Wang, 1978), 38.

35. Ibid., 39–40.

36. Ibid., 97–98.

37. Woolcott, 18.

38. Ibid., 14–20.

39. Dumenil, 82–83; for well-evidenced examples of this see Lizbeth Cohen. "Encountering Mass Culture at the Grassroots," *American Quarterly* 41, no. 1, March 1989, 6–33.

40. "Sex O'Clock in America," *Current Opinion* 55, August 1913, 113–14.

41. Kevin Mumford. *Interzones: Black/White Sex Districts in Chicago and New York in the Early Twentieth Century* (New York: Columbia University Press, 1997), xviii.

42. Ibid., xviii.

43. Ibid., xv.

44. White, 13–14.

45. Kasson, 42–43.

46. Mumford, 134.

47. Colin R. Johnson. *Just Queer Folks: Gender and Sexuality in Rural America* (Philadelphia, PA: Temple University Press, 2013), 76. Also, see Introduction.

48. Ibid., 79.

49. Ralph G. Giordano. *Satan in the Dance Hall* (Lanham, MD: Scarecrow Press, 2008), 14–15.

50. Lisa McGirr. *The War on Alcohol: Prohibition and the Rise of the American State* (New York: W.W. Norton, 2016), 108–10.

51. Natalie Zarrelli. "In the Early 20th Century, America Was Awash in Incredible Queer Nightlife," *Atlas Obscura*, April 14, 2016. Accessed April 18, 2016. http://www.atlasobscura.com/articles/in-the-early-20th-century-america-was-awash-in-incredible-queer-nightlife; Vicki L Eaklor. *Queer America* (New York: The New Press, 2008), 59.

52. McGirr, 110.

53. *Sunday Constitution Magazine*, in the *Atlanta Constitution*, January 15, 1922, 1–2.

54. Giordano, 22.

55. Ibid.

56. Ibid., 95.

57. Ibid., 34–35.

58. Robert S. Lynd and Helen Merrell Lynd. *Middletown: A Study in Modern American Culture* (San Diego, CA: Harcourt Brace & Co, 1929), 121.

59. Lynd and Lynd, 137–40.

60. Bailey, 16.

61. Kathy Peiss. *Cheap Amusements: Working Women and Leisure in Turn-of-the-Century New York* (Philadelphia, PA: Temple University Press, 1986), 51–52.

62. Bailey, 18.

63. Ibid., 19.

64. *Chicago Defender*, August 2, 1919, p. 1.

65. *Chicago Whip*, June 28, 1919.

66. Wolcott, 25–27.

67. Grace Elizabeth Hale. *Making Whiteness: The Culture of Segregation in the South, 1890–1940* (New York: Vintage Books, 1998), 123.

68. Isabel Wilkerson. *The Warmth of Other Suns: The Epic Story of America's Great Migration* (New York: Vintage Books, 2011), 272.

69. David J. Goldberg. *Discontented America: The United States in the 1920s* (Baltimore, MD: The Johns Hopkins University Press, 1999), 89–90.

70. Goldberg, 101–2.

71. Ibid., 92.

72. Ibid., 93, 106.

73. Ibid., 106–7.

74. Dumenil, 286.

75. See Jim Grossman. "The White Man's Union: The Great Migration and the Resonance of Race and Class in Chicago, 1916–1922," in *The Great Migration in Historical Perspective*, Joe William Trotter Jr., ed. (Bloomington: Indiana University Press, 1991), 83–105.

76. Goldberg, 106–7; Dumenil, 287.

77. Goldberg, 107. Quote taken from Richard Wright's *Black Boy*.

78. Ibid.

79. Douglas S. Massey and Nancy A. Denton. *American Apartheid: Segregation and the Making of the Underclass* (Cambridge, MA: Harvard University Press, 1993), 18, 24; David M. Cutler, Edward L. Glaeser, and Jacob L. Vigdor. "The Rise and Decline of the American Ghetto," *The Journal of Political Economy* 107, no. 3, 455–506: 456, 463.

80. Douglas S. Massey and Nancy A. Denton usefully define ghettos as a "set of neighborhoods that are exclusively inhabited by members of one group, within which virtually all members of that group live." Their definition does not reference the class composition of the group in question—merely the "racial makeup of the neighborhood." Massey and Denton, 18–19; Cutler, Glaeser, and Vigdor, 469.

81. Thomas Sugrue. *Sweet Land of Liberty: The Forgotten Struggle for Civil Rights in the North* (New York: Random House, 2008), 16–17.

82. Goldberg, 115.

83. Massey and Denton, 32. Since Myrdal's 1944 book segregation was understood to be a central component of racial oppression and helps explain poverty and unrest in cities. But by the 1980s that recognition was gone in these authors' views. They argue that segregation—most notably in the black ghetto—is critical to understanding these issues.

84. For example, see Kevin Boyle. *Arc of Justice: A Saga of Race, Civil Rights, and Murder* (New York: Henry Holt & Company), 2004.

85. See ibid.

86. Ibid.

87. Ibid.

88. Heather Bourbeau. "Dr. Ossian Sweet's Black Life Mattered," *JSTOR Daily*, June 17, 2015. https://daily.jstor.org/ossian-sweet-black-lives-matter/. Accessed on August 3, 2017.

89. Boyle, 24, 138.

90. Shannon King. "'Ready to Shoot and Do Shoot': Black Working-Class Self-Defense and Community Politics in Harlem, New York, during the 1920s," *Journal of Urban History* 37, no. 5, September 2011, 757–74: 758–59.

91. Ibid., 768.

92. Stanley B. Norvell and Victor F. Lasson, in William Tuttle, ed., "Views of a Negro during the Red Summer of 1919," *Journal of Negro History* 51, July 1966, 211–18.

93. Alain Locke. "Enter the New Negro," *Survey Graphic*, March 1925, 2, http://nationalhumanitiescenter.org/pds/maai3/migrations/text8/lockenewnegro.pdf. Accessed November 26, 2017.

94. Ibid.

95. Ibid., 5.

96. Steven Watson. *The Harlem Renaissance: Hub of African-American Culture, 1920–1930* (New York: Pantheon Books, 1995), 8–13.

97. Goldberg, 113–14.

98. Donald L Miller. *Supreme City: How Jazz Age Manhattan Gave Birth to Modern America* (New York: Simon & Schuster, 2014), 516–17.

99. Watson, 124–28.

100. Ibid., 134.

101. Dumenil, 288–300.

102. Gregory Holmes Singleton. "Birth, Rebirth, and the 'New Negro' of the 1920s," *Phylon* 43, no. 1, 1982, 29–45.

103. Ibid., 42.

104. New York, Los Angeles, Chicago, and Philadelphia, as per the 2010 census. Houston is the fourth most populous city and is located in a "red" state.

Chapter 2 Who Belongs in the Nativist 1920s?

1. "Curb Immigration to Halt Crime," *The Public Ledger*, December 4, 1920, 1. It should be noted that there was some debate over crime statistics at the time. See "Is the Melting Pot a Fallacy?" *The New York Tribune*, November 26, 1920, 1.

2. *New York Tribune*, December 4, 1920, 18.

3. Langdon Mitchell. "The New Secession," *The Atlantic Monthly*, August 1926, 169–82.

4. David J. Goldberg. *Discontented America: The United States in the 1920s* (Baltimore, MD: Johns Hopkins University Press, 1999), 140–41.

5. Ibid., 141.

6. For example, see Noel Ingnatiev. *How the Irish Became White* (New York: Routledge, 1995).

7. Goldberg, 141.

8. Theodore Roosevelt. "America for Americans: Afternoon Speech of Theodore Roosevelt at St. Louis, May 31, 1916," in *The Progressive Party: Its Record*

from January to July, 1916. Compiled by the Executive Committee of the Progressive National Committee.

9. Ibid.

10. Erica Ryan. *Red War on the Family: Sex, Gender, and Americanism in the First Red Scare* (Philadelphia, PA: Temple University Press, 2015), 6.

11. Ibid., 6.

12. Ibid., 64.

13. *Union Record*, February 4, 1919, 1.

14. Bill Bryson. *One Summer: America, 1927* (New York: Doubleday, 2013), 278–79.

15. *Ogden Examiner*, May 2, 1919, 1.

16. Bryson, 277.

17. Arthur Sears Henning. "Clash with Labor Looms Over Strike," *Chicago Daily Tribune*, November 1, 1919, 1.

18. Lara Vapnek. *Elizabeth Gurley Flynn: Modern American Revolutionary* (Philadelphia, PA: Westview Press, 2015), 71.

19. Paul Avrich. *Sacco and Vanzetti: The Anarchist Background* (Princeton, NJ: Princeton University Press, 1996), 167.

20. Ryan, 24.

21. Vapnek, 79.

22. John Higham. *Strangers in the Land: Patterns of American Nativism, 1860–1925* (New Brunswick, NJ: Rutgers University Press, 1988 [1955]), 259–63.

23. Ibid., 330.

24. Goldberg, 152.

25. Lathrop Stoddard. *The Rising Tide of Color against White World-Supremacy* (New York: Charles Scribner's Sons, 1921).

26. Goldberg, 156–57.

27. Ibid., 160.

28. Ibid., 161.

29. Albert Johnson. "The Coming Immigration Law," *Outlook*, January 23, 1924, 140.

30. Goldberg, 162–63.

31. "The Sacco-Vanzetti Case," *Albuquerque Morning Journal*, February 6, 1922, 6.

32. Ibid.

33. David E. Kyvig. *Repealing National Prohibition* (Kent, OH: Kent State University Press, 2000), 177; Bryson, 274–75.

34. Bryson, 275.

35. Vapnek, 83.

36. Art Shields. *Are They Doomed: The Sacco and Vanzetti Case and the Grim Forces Behind It* (New York: New York Call Printing Company, 1921), 4.

37. Ibid., 29.

38. Vapnek, 82–83.

Notes

39. Bryson, 287–89. Historians still disagree on the guilt or innocence of Sacco and Vanzetti to this day.

40. Ibid., 290–93.

41. Kyvig, 177.

42. Felix Frankfurter. *The Case of Sacco and Vanzetti: A Critical Analysis for Lawyers and Laymen* (Boston, MA: Little, Brown, 1927), 101.

43. The *New York Times*, August 23, 1927, 1.

44. "Klan Crosses Delaware," The *New York Times*, February 23, 1925, 8.

45. "The Klan Walks in Washington," *The Literary Digest*, August 22, 1925, 7–8.

46. Dumenil, 235.

47. Goldberg, 128–29.

48. Leonard J. Moore. *Citizen Klansmen: The Ku Klux Klan in Indiana, 1921–1928* (Chapel Hill: University of North Carolina Press, 1991), 2.

49. Ibid., 7.

50. Baker, 10.

51. Tom Rice. "Protecting Protestantism: The Ku Klux Klan vs. The Motion Picture Industry," *Film History* 20, no. 3, 2008, 367–80, 368.

52. Goldberg, 118.

53. Lynd and Lynd, 485.

54. Goldberg, 119.

55. Ibid., 127–28.

56. Moore, 2.

57. Goldberg, 130–31.

58. Ibid., 120–23. This anti-Catholicism was notably not linked to the fundamentalist Protestant outrage over evolution in schools.

59. Ibid., 123–24.

60. Hiram Evans. "The Klan's Fight for Americanism," *North American Review*, March 1926, 223.

61. Ibid.

62. Chris Romberg. "White Nativism and Urban Politics: The 1920s Ku Klux Klan in Oakland, California," *Journal of American Ethnic History* 17, no. 2, Winter 1998, 39–55, 50.

63. W.E.B. Du Bois. "The Ku Klux Are Riding Again!" *The Crisis*, March 1919, 229–31.

64. Nancy MacLean. *Behind the Mask of Chivalry: The Making of the Second Ku Klux Klan* (New York: Oxford University Press, 1995), 26–27.

65. Goldberg, 125–26.

66. See Kevin Boyle. *Arc of Justice: A Saga of Race, Civil Rights, and Murder in the Jazz Age* (New York: Henry Holt, 2004).

67. Henry P. Fry. *The Modern Ku Klux Klan* (Cambridge, MA: Small, Maynard, and Co, 1922), 185–87.

68. Rice, 369.

69. Ibid., 370.

70. MacLean, 32.
71. Goldberg, 126.
72. Kathleen Blee. "Women in the 1920's Ku Klux Klan Movement," *Feminist Studies* 17, no. 1, Spring 1991, 55–77, 57–58.
73. Ibid., 58.
74. Ibid.
75. William Robinson Pattangall. "Is the Ku Klux Un-American?" *The Forum*, September 1925, 321–32.
76. Ibid., 132–35.
77. Ibid., 135–37.
78. Moore, 9–10.
79. MacLean, 24.
80. Moore, 10–11.
81. Kelly Baker. *Gospel According to the Klan: The KKK's Appeal to Protestant America, 1915–1930* (Lawrence: University Press of Kansas, 2011), 10.

Chapter 3 Prohibition

1. Edward Behr. *Thirteen Years That Changed America* (New York: Arcade Publishing, 2011), 82–83.
2. James Morone. *Hellfire Nation: The Politics of Sin in American History* (New Haven, CT: Yale University Press, 2004), 281. Drinking levels did not rise to pre-1920 numbers again until the early 1970s.
3. Ibid., 281.
4. Ibid., 308.
5. Dumeil, 202.
6. Ibid., 226.
7. Ibid.
8. Ibid., 228.
9. Lisa McGirr. *The War on Alcohol: Prohibition and the Rise of the American State* (New York: W.W. Norton, 2016), 5.
10. Morone, 302–6.
11. Ibid., 306.
12. Ibid., 307.
13. Ibid., 292–97.
14. Quoted in Morone, 297.
15. Morone, 297–302.
16. Ibid., 308.
17. Excerpt from Willard speech titled "Everybody's War." Carolyn De Swarte Gifford and Amy R. Slagell, *Let Something Good Be Said: The Speeches and Writings of Frances E. Willard* (Urbana: University of Illinois Press, 2007), 5.
18. Dumenil, 229.
19. Ibid.
20. Ibid., 229–30.

Notes

21. Morone, 290.
22. Ibid.
23. Ibid., 308–9.
24. Ibid., 310–11.
25. Ibid., 311.
26. Ibid., 312–13.
27. Dumenil, 230; Barry Hankins. *Jesus and Gin: Evangelicalism, the Roaring Twenties and Today's Culture Wars* (New York: St. Martin's Press, 2010), 26; Kyvig, 11.
28. Daniel Okrent. *Last Call: The Rise and Fall of Prohibition* (New York: Scribner, 2010), 111.
29. Dumenil, 230–31.
30. Okrent, 110–11.
31. "Billy Sunday Preaches John Barleycorn's Funeral," The *Christian Advocate*, January 22, 1920, 124.
32. These often-quoted lines are in Morone, 325.
33. "Billy Sunday Speeds Barleycorn to Grave," The *New York Times*, January 17, 1920, 1.
34. "John Barleycorn Died Peacefully at the Toll of 12," The *New York Times*, January 17, 1920, 1.
35. Okrent, 117–18.
36. Ibid., 119.
37. Ibid., 128–29. The joke came from Malcom Bingay, editor of the *Detroit News* and later the *Detroit Free Press*, quoted in Okrent.
38. Dumenil, 233.
39. McGirr, 52–53.
40. McGirr, 53–54. Addams is quoted in McGirr from an article titled "'I Will' Is Chicago's Motto."
41. Dumenil, 233–34.
42. James P. Holland, "The Workingman's View of Prohibition," *North American Review*, Summer 1925, 611–614, 612.
43. Dumenil, 231.
44. Ibid., 232.
45. David Kyvig. *Repealing National Prohibition* (Kent, OH: Kent State University Press, 2000), 20–21.
46. Michael Lerner. *Dry Manhattan: Prohibition in New York City* (Cambridge, MA: Harvard University Press, 2007), 96.
47. Ibid., 64.
48. Ibid., 65.
49. The *New York Times*, April 7, 1926, 22.
50. The *New York Times*, July 20, 1923, 1.
51. The *New York Times*, April 6, 1929, 1.
52. Lerner, 69–71; McGirr, 209.
53. McGirr, 115–16.
54. Ibid., 104–5.

55. Ibid., 106–7.
56. Mary Murphy. "Bootlegging Mothers and Drinking Daughters: Gender and Prohibition in Butte, Montana," *American Quarterly* 46, no. 2, June 1994, 174–94, 184–85.
57. McGirr, 108.
58. Murphy, 187–89.
59. McGirr, 114–15.
60. Ibid., 57–58.
61. Marc Mappen. *Prohibition Gangsters: The Rise and Fall of a Bad Generation* (New Brunswick, NJ: Rutgers University Press, 2013), 5–6.
62. McGirr, 54.
63. Ibid., 56.
64. The *New York Times*, February 15, 1929, 1.
65. Morone, 326–27.
66. Ibid., 326–27; U.S. Department of Commerce, Bureau of the Census, Mortality Statistics 1928, 8. https://www.cdc.gov/nchs/data/vsushistorical/mortstatsh_1928.pdf.
67. The *New York Times*, September 4, 1924, 1.
68. McGirr, 193.
69. Ibid., 197.
70. Ibid., 190–91.
71. Ibid., 189–91. Quote comes from 191.
72. Ibid., 192.
73. Ibid., 199.
74. Ibid., 199–201.
75. Ibid., 210.
76. Kyvig, 179–80.
77. Ibid., 180–81.
78. McGirr, 197.
79. The *New York Times*, August 7, 1929, 1.
80. McGirr, 202–3.
81. Ibid., 203–4.
82. Ibid., 213.
83. Ibid., 218.
84. The *New York Times*, November 24, 1928, 13.
85. McGirr, 219.
86. Ibid., 221, 228.
87. Ibid., 104. The quote is taken from a meeting of anti-Prohibitionist women in 1930.

Chapter 4 Searching for a "Full Life"

1. "The Old Order Changeth," *Smith College Weekly*, December 3, 1919, 2.
2. Ibid.

Notes

3. Elaine Showalter, ed. *These Modern Women: Autobiographical Essays from the Twenties* (Old Westbury, NY: Feminist Press, 1978), 4.

4. Ibid., 5.

5. Charles W. Eliot. "Dr. Eliot Speaks Up for Old-Style Marriage," *New York Times*, February 22, 1925, XX6.

6. John Macy. "Equality of Woman with Man: A Myth—A Challenge to Feminism," *Harper's Magazine*, November 1926, 705–13.

7. Showalter, 5.

8. Christina Simmons. *Making Marriage Modern* (New York: Oxford University Press, 2009), 113.

9. Morone, 256.

10. "Birth Control Talk Guarded by Police," *New York Times*, November 19, 1921, 1.

11. "See Plot by Police to Bar Free Speech," *New York Times*, December 10, 1921, 14; "Hayes Denounces Birth Control Aim," *New York Times*, November 21, 1921, 1.

12. "Fosdick for Candor on Birth Control," *New York Times*, November 20, 1929, 25.

13. Kristin Luker. *Abortion and the Politics of Motherhood* (Berkeley: University of California Press, 1984), 14.

14. Ibid., 15.

15. Morone, 251.

16. Ibid., 251.

17. Luker, 15.

18. Leslie J. Reagan. *When Abortion Was a Crime* (Berkeley: University of California Press, 1997), 45.

19. Ibid., 23.

20. Luker, 39.

21. Ibid., 8. Abortion plays such a prominent role in our current culture wars because, as historian Kristin Luker argues, it relates to some of the "most critical and rarely examined parts of social life: the meaning of life and death, the meaning of parenthood, the role of sexuality, what is 'natural' for men and women, and how morality is formed and experienced."

22. Reagan, 110–11.

23. Morone, 249.

24. Constance Chen. *The Sex Side of Life* (New York: New Press, 1997), xviii–xxv.

25. Morone, 249.

26. Rickie Solinger. *Pregnancy and Power* (New York: New York University Press, 2005), 95.

27. Linda Gordon. *Moral Property of Women* (Urbana-Champaign: University of Illinois Press, 2002), 145.

28. Chen, 181.

29. Gordon, 153–55.

30. Solinger, 82–83.

31. Gordon, 160.

32. Nancy Marie Robertson. "'Churches in the Vanguard': Margaret Sanger and the Morality of Birth Control in the 1920s," M.A. Thesis, Indiana University Department of History, 2015.

33. Nathan Miller. *New World Coming* (Cambridge, MA: DeCapo Press, 2003), 268.

34. Luker, 79.

35. Gordon, 127.

36. Ibid., 128.

37. Ibid., 139.

38. Ibid., 183–84; Chen, 233–38.

39. McCann, 128.

40. Tone, 125.

41. Ibid., 152.

42. Solinger, 102.

43. John D'Emilio and Estelle Freedman. *Intimate Matters: A History of Sexuality in America* (Chicago, IL: University of Chicago Press, 1988), 248.

44. Frederick Lewis Allen. *Only Yesterday* (New York: Bantam Books, 1946), 129.

45. Arlene Skolnick. *Embattled Paradise* (New York: Basic Books, 1991), 41.

46. Miller, 259.

47. Immigration Commission report in 1911 finds that of all female students at 63 colleges across the country, 23.8 percent had immigrant parents. See Barbara Miller Solomon. *In the Company of Educated Women* (New Haven, CT: Yale University Press, 1985), 76.

48. Ibid., 262.

49. Allen, 129.

50. Kevin White. *The First Sexual Revolution* (New York: New York University Press, 1993), 1.

51. "Why Criticize the College Girl?" The *Washington Post*, January 27, 1924, EA2.

52. Stella Ress. "Finding the Flapper: A Historiographical Look at Image and Attitude," *History Compass* 8, no. 1, 2010, 118–28, 120.

53. Ralph Giordano. *Satan in the Dance Hall* (Lanham, MD: Scarecrow Press, 2008), 114–16.

54. "To Curb Brooklyn Flapper," *Washington Post*, June 2, 1922, 1.

55. Dumenil, 136.

56. Jean Matthews. *The Rise of the New Woman* (New York: Rowman and Littlefield, 2004), 176.

57. Skolnick, 46.

58. Stephanie Coontz. *Marriage: A History* (New York: Penguin Books, 2006), 207. Furthermore, it should be noted that as this ratio flipped, the number of women attending college dropped precipitously.

Notes

59. Paula Fass. *The Damned and the Beautiful: American Youth in the 1920s* (New York: Oxford University Press, 1977), 66.
60. Ibid., 75.
61. D'Emilio and Freedman, 241; Skolnick, 43.
62. D'Emilio and Freedman, 265.
63. See Rebecca Davis. "'Not Marriage at All, but Simple Harlotry': The Companionate Marriage Controversy," *Journal of American History* 94, no. 4, March 2008, 1137–163.
64. Simmons, 108, 114.
65. Fass, 80.
66. Miller, 271.
67. D'Emilio and Freedman, 270.
68. See Estelle Freedman, "The New Woman: Changing Views of Women in the 1920s," *The Journal of American History* 61, no. 2, September 1974, 372–93.
69. "Motherhood True Mission of Woman, Says Nellie Ross," *Atlanta Constitution*, March 28, 1926. http://americainclass.org/sources/becomingmodern/modernity/text2/colcommentarymodernwoman.pdf Accessed June 14, 2018.
70. Jodi Vandenberg-Daves. *Modern Motherhood: An American History* (New Brunswick, NJ: Rutgers University Press, 2014), 86.
71. Ibid., 77.
72. See Peter N. Stearns. *Anxious Parents: A History of Modern Childrearing in America* (New York: New York University Press, 2003).
73. Vandenberg-Daves, 93.
74. Ibid., 92. She notes that the "willingness to embrace scientific advice varied significantly with class, race and ethnicity." So adoption of the methods espoused at these events was not monolithic.
75. Stearns, Chapter 2: The Vulnerable Child.
76. Nancy F. Cott. *Grounding of Modern Feminism* (New Haven, CT: Yale University Press, 1989), 183–84.
77. Showalter, 8.
78. Cott, 181–82.
79. Ibid., 193.
80. Ibid., 195.
81. Ibid., 191.
82. D'Emilio and Freedman, 173; Dumenil, 113–22.
83. Simmons, 148.
84. Dumenil, 122.
85. Simmons, 150.
86. Fass, 81.
87. Ibid., 82.
88. Cott, 194.

89. Skolnick, 47.
90. Quote by Crystal Eastman in Showalter, 5.
91. Alice Paul, "An Approaching Anniversary," *The Christian Science Monitor*, June 2, 1923, 20.
92. Christine Lunardini. *Alice Paul* (Boulder, CO: Westview Press, 2012), 138.
93. Ibid., 139.
94. Dawn Keetley and John Pettegrew, eds. *Public Women, Public Words: A Documentary History of American Feminism, 1900 to 1960*, Vol. II (Lanham, MD: Rowman and Littlefield, 2005), 241.
95. Lunardini, 150.
96. Ibid., 153.
97. Alice Paul. "An Approaching Anniversary," The *Christian Science Monitor*, June 2, 1923, 20.
98. Lunardini, 154.
99. Cott, 124.
100. Ibid., 138.
101. Matthews, 172.
102. John Walker Harrington. "Woman's Rights Would Become Woman's Wrongs," *New York Times*, January 22, 1922, 84.
103. "Equal Rights Plan Heavily Attacked," *New York Times*, February 2, 1929, 10.
104. "Oppose Amendment for Women's Rights," *New York Times*, July 17, 1927, S12.
105. Alice Paul and the NWP persisted in their lobbying for the amendment, and after the strides made in legislation protecting all workers in the 1930s, many women's organizations opposed to the ERA eventually came around to support it.
106. Lunardini, 169.
107. Gail Collins. *When Everything Changed* (New York: Little, Brown, and Co., 2009), Chapter 9 "Backlash."
108. Sara Evans. *Tidal Wave* (New York: Free Press, 2003), 177.

Chapter 5 The Dark Shadow of Darwin

1. "Evolution Root of All Evil-Straton," *The Harvard Crimson*, March 26, 1924. https://www.thecrimson.com/article/1924/3/26/evolution-root-of-all-evil-straton-psome/. Accessed June 18, 2018.
2. Mrs. Jesse Sparks, Letter to Editor. *Nashville Tennessean*, July 3, 1925. http://historicalthinkingmatters.org/pdf/Scopes-docset.pdf. Accessed June 18, 2018.
3. "John Roach Straton Condemns Evolution as Degenerate Cult." *The Harvard Crimson*, October 16, 1925. https://www.thecrimson.com/article/1925/10/16/john-roach-straton-condemns-evolution-as/. Accessed June 18, 2018.

Notes

4. Ibid.

5. "The Most Sinister Movement in the United States," *American Fundamentalist*, December 26, 1925. http://historicalthinkingmatters.org/pdf/Scopes-docset.pdf. Accessed June 18, 2018.

6. Edward Larson. *Summer for the Gods: The Scopes Trial and America's Continuing Debate over Science and Religion* (New York: Basic Books, 1997), 49.

7. David E. Kyvig. *Repealing National Prohibition* (Kent, OH: Kent State University Press, 2000), 149–52.

8. Ibid., 150–52.

9. George Marsden. *Fundamentalism and American Culture* (New York: Oxford University Press, 2006), 158–64; Dumenil, 185–86.

10. Dumenil, 185.

11. "If Monkeys Could Speak," *Chicago Defender*, May 23, 1925. http://moses.law.umn.edu/darrow/documents/Chicago_Defender_Scopes_trial_May_23_1925_cropped_opt.pdf. Accessed June 18, 2018.

12. Michael Lienesch. *In the Beginning: Fundamentalism, the Scopes Trial, and the Making of the Antievolution Movement* (Chapel Hill: University of North Carolina Press, 2007), 33–36.

13. Barry Hankins. *Jesus and Gin: Evangelicalism, the Roaring Twenties, and Today's Culture Wars* (New York: Palgrave Macmillan, 2010), 56–62.

14. Kyvig, 153.

15. Hankins, 47–52.

16. Ibid., 64–65.

17. Dumenil, 170–74.

18. Ibid., 173–74.

19. Larson, 11–14, 28–30.

20. Dumenil, 157–58.

21. Roderick Nash. *The Nervous Generation: American Thought, 1917–1930* (Chicago, IL: Elephant Paperback, 1990), 127–30.

22. Ibid., 136.

23. Ibid., 137.

24. Ibid., 138.

25. Dumenil, 169.

26. Hankins, 44–45.

27. Ibid., 69–71.

28. Harding, 84.

29. Adam Laats. *Fundamentalism and Education in the Scopes Era: God, Darwin, and the Roots of America's Culture Wars* (New York: Palgrave McMillan, 2010), 89.

30. Lienesch, 64–66.

31. Hankins, 89–90.

32. http://www.pbs.org/godinamerica/people/william-jennings-bryan.html. Accessed on June 27, 2017.

33. Dumenil, 188.

34. Laats, 3.

35. Ibid., 5.
36. Lienesch, 72.
37. Ibid., Chapter 2.
38. Laats, 5.
39. Dumenil, 188.
40. Hankins, 62.
41. Ibid., 90.
42. George E. Webb. *The Evolution Controversy in America* (Lexington: University Press of Kentucky, 1994), 72–73.
43. Webb, 74.
44. Larson, 54–59.
45. Ibid., 96–100.
46. Ibid., 101.
47. Ibid., 101–3.
48. Ibid., 112.
49. Ibid., 112–13.
50. Ibid., 115.
51. Ibid., 119.
52. Dumenil, 187.
53. Laats, 80.
54. The *New York Times*, "Cranks and Freaks Flock to Dayton," July 11, 1925, 1.
55. Larson, 140.
56. Ibid., 142.
57. Laats, 80.
58. The *Baltimore Evening Sun*, July 9, 1925. https://archive.org/stream/CoverageOfTheScopesTrialByH.l.Mencken/ScopesTrialMencken.txt. Accessed June 18, 2018.
59. Laats, 81.
60. Hankins, 94–95.
61. Laats, 82.
62. Larson, 144.
63. Ibid., 145.
64. Ibid., 146.
65. Laats, 2.
66. Larson, 148–53.
67. Hankins, 94.
68. Dumenil, 189.
69. Laats, 94–95; Larson, 130.
70. Laats, 83.
71. The *New York Times*, "Osborn States the Case for Evolution," July 12, 1925, XX1.
72. Laats, 84.
73. Ibid., 84.
74. Ibid., 85.
75. Hankins, 97–99; Laats, 85.

76. Larson, 189–90.
77. Hankins, 99.
78. Ibid., 100; Laats, 78.
79. Hankins, 101.
80. Larson, 220–21; Hankins, 100.
81. Laats, 79.
82. Ibid., 196.
83. Dumenil, 190.
84. Laats, 86.
85. Hankins, 102.
86. Larson, 239.
87. Ibid., 246.
88. Larson, 239–44; Hankins, 103–4.
89. Laats, 87.
90. Ibid., 89, 191.
91. Ibid., 191–92.
92. Ibid., 199.
93. Larson, 250.
94. Peter Vacarro. "Distant Echoes: The Scopes Trial," unpublished capstone thesis, Rider University, 2017, in author's possession, 22–25.
95. Laats, 198–99.
96. Hankins, 105.
97. Laats, 194.
98. Vaccaro, 27.
99. Laats, 7.
100. *Baltimore Evening Sun*, September 14, 1925. https://archive.org/stream/CoverageOfTheScopesTrialByH.l.Mencken/ScopesTrialMencken.txt. Accessed June 18, 2018.
101. See Adam R. Shapiro. *Trying Biology: The Scopes Trial, Textbooks, and the Antievolution Movement in American Schools* (Chicago, IL: University of Chicago Press, 2013); see also Vacarro, "Distant Echoes."
102. Dumenil, 191.

Epilogue

1. Stephen Prothero. *Why Liberals Win the Culture Wars (Even When They Lose Elections): The Battles That Define America from Jefferson's Heresies to Gay Marriage* (New York: HarperCollins, 2016).
2. Andrew Hartman. *A War for the Soul of America: A History of the Culture Wars* (Chicago, IL: University of Chicago Press, 2015), 5.
3. Ibid., 2.
4. Robert Collins. *Transforming America: Politics and Culture during the Reagan Years* (New York: Columbia University Press, 2007), 172–73. See also Jonathan Zimmerman. *Whose America?: Culture Wars in the Public Schools* (Cambridge, MA: Harvard University Press, 2002), 3; James Davison Hunter and Alan Wolfe.

Is There a Culture War? A Dialogue on American Values and Public Life (Washington, DC: Pew Research Center, 2006); and Irene Taviss Thomson. *Culture Wars and Enduring American Dilemmas* (Ann Arbor: University of Michigan Press, 2010).

5. Hartman, 71.
6. Collins, 173.
7. Hankins, 4.
8. Alana Semuels. "White Flight Never Ended," *The Atlantic*, July 30, 2015. https://www.theatlantic.com/business/archive/2015/07/white-flight-alive-and-well/399980/ Accessed on June 13, 2018.
9. Alana Semuels. "Rethinking America's Dark Ghettos," *The Atlantic*, November 22, 2016. https://www.theatlantic.com/business/archive/2016/11/rethinking-americas-dark-ghettos/508400/ Accessed on June 13, 2018.
10. Tom LoBianco. "Report: Aide Says Nixon's War on Drug's Targeted Blacks and Hippies," CNN.com, March 24, 2016. http://www.cnn.com/2016/03/23/politics/john-ehrlichman-richard-nixon-drug-war-blacks-hippie/index.html. Accessed on August 24, 2017. On mass incarceration see Heather Anne Thompson, "Why Mass Incarceration Matters: Rethinking Crisis, Decline, and Transformation in Postwar American History," *The Journal of American History* 97, no. 3, December 2010, 703–34.
11. Lisa McGirr. *The War on Alcohol: Prohibition and the Rise of the American State* (New York: W.W. Norton, 2016), 221.
12. Ibid., 228.
13. Stacie Taranto. *Kitchen Table Politics: Conservative Women and Family Values in New York* (Philadelphia: University of Pennsylvania Press, 2017), 99–101.
14. Sara Evans. *Tidal Wave: How Women Changed America at Century's End* (New York: Simon and Schuster, 2010), 171.
15. Taranto, 164.
16. Evans, 176.
17. Hankins, 223.
18. Daniel K. Williams. *God's Own Party: The Making of the Christian Right* (Oxford: Oxford University Press, 2010), 1–3.
19. Jennifer Rubin. "Trump Exploited the Cultural Divide, Not Economic Unfairness," *The Washington Post*, June 19, 2017. https://www.washingtonpost.com/blogs/right-turn/wp/2017/06/19/trump-exploited-the-cultural-divide-not-economic-unfairness/?utm_term=.bc357f5db4dc. Accessed on November 4, 2017.
20. Walter Lippman. *A Preface to Morals* (New Brunswick, NJ: Transaction Publishers, 1960), 51. Lippman originally published the book in 1929.
21. Dumenil, 202–3, 225–26.
22. Nancy Cohen. *Delirium: The Politics of Sex in America* (Berkeley, CA: Counterpoint, 2012).

Bibliography

Allen, Frederick Lewis. *Only Yesterday.* New York: Bantam Books, 1946.
Bailey, Beth. *From Front Porch to the Back Seat.* Baltimore, MD: Johns Hopkins University Press, 1988.
Baker, Kelly. *Gospel According to the Klan: The KKK's Appeal to Protestant America, 1915–1930.* Lawrence: University Press of Kansas, 2011.
Behr, Edward. *Thirteen Years That Changed America.* New York: Arcade Publishing, 2011.
Blee, Kathleen. "Women in the 1920's Ku Klux Klan Movement." *Feminist Studies* 17, no. 1 (Spring 1991): 55–77.
Bourbeau, Heather. "Dr. Ossian Sweet's Black Life Mattered." *JSTOR Daily,* June 17, 2015. https://daily.jstor.org/ossian-sweet-black-lives-matter/. Accessed on August 3, 2017.
Boyle, Kevin. *Arc of Justice: A Saga of Race, Civil Rights, and Murder in the Jazz Age.* New York: Henry Holt, 2004.
Bryson, Bill. *One Summer: America, 1927.* New York: Doubleday, 2013.
Cather, Willa. *Not Under Forty.* New York: Alfred A. Knopf, 1936.
Chen, Constance. *The Sex Side of Life.* New York: New Press, 1997.
Cohen, Lizbeth. "Encountering Mass Culture at the Grassroots." *American Quarterly* 41, no. 1 (March 1989): 6–33.
Collins, Gail. *When Everything Changed.* New York: Little, Brown, and Co., 2009.
Collins, Robert. *Transforming America: Politics and Culture during the Reagan Years.* New York: Columbia University Press, 2007.
Coontz, Stephanie. *Marriage: A History.* New York: Penguin Books, 2006.
Cott, Nancy. *Grounding of Modern Feminism.* New Haven, CT: Yale University Press, 1989.
Cox, Karen L. "The South and Mass Culture." *The Journal of Southern History* 75, no. 3 (August 2009): 677–690.
Cutler, David M., Edward L. Glaeser, and Jacob L. Vigdor. "The Rise and Decline of the American Ghetto." *The Journal of Political Economy* 107, no. 3 (1999): 455–506.

Davis, Rebecca. "'Not Marriage at All, but Simple Harlotry': The Companionate Marriage Controversy." *Journal of American History* 94, no. 4 (March 2008): 1137–1163.
D'Emilio, John and Estelle Freedman. *Intimate Matters: A History of Sexuality in America*. Chicago, IL: University of Chicago Press, 1988.
Douglas, Ann. *Terrible Honesty: Mongrel Manhattan in the 1920s*. New York: Noonday Press, 1995.
Dumenil, Lynn. *The Modern Temper: American Culture and Society in the 1920s*. New York: Hill and Wang, 1995.
Eagles, Charles W. "Urban-Rural Conflict in the 1920s: A Historiographical Assessment." *The Historian* 49, no. 1 (November 1986): 26–48.
Eaklor, Vicki L. *Queer America*. New York: The New Press, 2008.
Evans, Sara. *Tidal Wave*. New York: Free Press, 2003.
Fass, Paula. *The Damned and the Beautiful: American Youth in the 1920s*. New York: Oxford University Press, 1977.
Freedman, Estelle. "The New Woman: Changing Views of Women in the 1920s." *The Journal of American History* 61, no. 2 (September 1974): 372–393.
Giordano, Ralph G. *Satan in the Dance Hall*. Lanham, MD: Scarecrow Press, 2008.
Goldberg, David J. *Discontented America: The United States in the 1920s*. Baltimore, MD: Johns Hopkins University Press, 1999.
Gordon, Linda. *Moral Property of Women*. Urbana-Champaign: University of Illinois Press, 2002.
Grossman, Jim. "The White Man's Union: The Great Migration and the Resonance of Race and Class in Chicago, 1916–1922." In Joe William Trotter Jr., ed., *The Great Migration in Historical Perspective*. Bloomington: University of Indiana, 1991, 83–105.
Hale, Grace Elizabeth. *Making Whiteness: The Culture of Segregation in the South, 1890–1940*. New York: Vintage Books, 1998.
Hankins, Barry. *Jesus and Gin: Evangelicalism, the Roaring Twenties, and Today's Culture Wars*. New York: Palgrave Macmillan, 2010.
Hartman, Andrew. *A War for the Soul of America: A History of the Culture Wars*. Chicago, IL: University of Chicago Press, 2015.
Higham, John. *Strangers in the Land: Patterns of American Nativism, 1860–1925*. New Brunswick, NJ: Rutgers University Press, 1988 [1955].
Hunter, James Davison and Alan Wolfe. *Is There a Culture War? A Dialogue on American Values and Public Life*. Washington, DC: Pew Research Center, 2006.
Ignatiev, Noel. *How the Irish Became White*. New York: Routledge, 1995.
Johnson, Colin R. *Just Queer Folks: Gender and Sexuality in Rural America*. Philadelphia, PA: Temple University Press, 2013.
Kasson, John. *Amusing the Million: Coney Island at the Turn of the Century*. New York: Hill and Wang, 1978.

Keetley, Dawn and John Pettegrew, eds. *Public Women, Public Words: A Documentary History of American Feminism, 1900 to 1960*, Vol II. Lanham, MD: Rowman and Littlefield, 2005.

King, Shannon. "'Ready to Shoot and Do Shoot': Black Working-Class Self-Defense and Community Politics in Harlem, New York, during the 1920s." *Journal of Urban History* 37, no. 5 (September 2011): 757–774.

Kyvig, David E. *Repealing National Prohibition*. Kent, OH: Kent State University Press, 2000.

Laats, Adam. *Fundamentalism and Education in the Scopes Era: God, Darwin, and the Roots of America's Culture Wars*. New York: Palgrave MacMillan, 2010.

Larson, Edward. *Summer for the Gods: The Scopes Trial and America's Continuing Debate over Science and Religion*. New York: Basic Books, 1997.

Lerner, Michael. *Dry Manhattan: Prohibition in New York City*. Cambridge, MA: Harvard University Press, 2007.

Levine, Lawrence. *The Unpredictable Past: Explorations in American Cultural History*. New York: Oxford University Press, 1993.

Lewis, Tom. "'A Godlike Presence': The Impact of Radio on the 1920s and 1930s." *OAH Magazine of History* 6, no. 4 (Spring 1992): 26–33.

Lienesch, Michael. *In the Beginning: Fundamentalism, the Scopes Trial, and the Making of the Antievolution Movement*. Chapel Hill: University of North Carolina Press, 2007.

Luker, Kristin. *Abortion and the Politics of Motherhood*. Berkeley: University of California Press, 1984.

Lunardini, Christine. *Alice Paul: Equality for Women*. Boulder, CO: Westview Press, 2012.

Lynd, Robert S. and Helen Merrell Lynd. *Middletown: A Study in Modern American Culture*. San Diego, CA: Harcourt Brace & Co., 1929.

MacLean, Nancy. *Behind the Mask of Chivalry: The Making of the Second Ku Klux Klan*. New York: Oxford University Press, 1995.

Mappen, Marc. *Prohibition Gangsters: The Rise and Fall of a Bad Generation*. New Brunswick, NJ: Rutgers University Press, 2013.

Marsden, George. *Fundamentalism and American Culture*. New York: Oxford University Press, 2006.

Massey, Douglas S. and Nancy A. Denton. *American Apartheid: Segregation and the Making of the Underclass*. Cambridge, MA: Harvard University Press, 1993.

Matthews, Jean. *The Rise of the New Woman*. New York: Rowman and Littlefield, 2004.

McGirr, Lisa. *The War on Alcohol: Prohibition and the Rise of the American State*. New York: W.W. Norton, 2016.

Miller, Donald L. *Supreme City: How Jazz Age Manhattan Gave Birth to Modern America*. New York: Simon and Schuster, 2014.

Miller, Nathan. *New World Coming*. Cambridge, MA: DeCapo Press, 2003.

Moore, Leonard J. *Citizen Klansmen: The Ku Klux Klan in Indiana, 1921–1928.* Chapel Hill: University of North Carolina Press, 1991.

Morone, James. *Hellfire Nation.* New Haven, CT: Yale University Press, 2004.

Mumford, Kevin. *Interzones: Black/White Sex Districts in Chicago and New York in the Early Twentieth Century.* New York: Columbia University Press, 1997.

Murphy, Mary. "Bootlegging Mothers and Drinking Daughters: Gender and Prohibition in Butte, Montana." *American Quarterly* 46, no. 2 (June 1994): 174–194.

Nash, Roderick. *The Nervous Generation: American Thought, 1917–1930.* Chicago, IL: Elephant Paperback, 1990.

Okrent, Daniel. *Last Call: The Rise and Fall of Prohibition.* New York: Scribner, 2010.

Prothero, Stephen. *Why Liberals Win the Culture Wars.* New York: Harper One, 2016.

Reagan, Leslie J. *When Abortion Was a Crime.* Berkeley: University of California Press, 1997.

Ress, Stella. "Finding the Flapper: A Historiographical Look at Image and Attitude." *History Compass* 8, no. 1 (2010): 118–128.

Rice, Tom. "Protecting Protestantism: The Ku Klux Klan vs. the Motion Picture Industry." *Film History* 20, no. 3 (2008): 367–380.

Robertson, Nancy Marie. "'Churches in the Vanguard': Margaret Sanger and the Morality of Birth Control in the 1920s." M.A. Thesis, Indiana University Department of History, 2015.

Romberg, Chris. "White Nativism and Urban Politics: The 1920s Ku Klux Klan in Oakland, California." *Journal of American Ethnic History* 17, no. 2 (Winter 1998): 39–55.

Ryan, Erica. *Red War on the Family: Sex, Gender, and Americanism in the First Red Scare.* Philadelphia, PA: Temple University Press, 2015.

Shapiro, Adam R. *Trying Biology: The Scopes Trial, Textbooks, and the Antievolution Movement in American Schools.* Chicago, IL: University of Chicago Press, 2013.

Showalter, Elaine, ed. *These Modern Women: Autobiographical Essays from the Twenties.* Old Westbury, NY: Feminist Press, 1978.

Simmons, Christina. *Making Marriage Modern.* New York: Oxford University Press, 2009.

Singleton, Gregory Holmes. "Birth, Rebirth, and the 'New Negro' of the 1920s." *Phylon* 43, no. 1 (1982): 29–45.

Sitton, Tom and William Deverall, eds. *Metropolis in the Making: Los Angeles in the 1920s.* Berkeley: University of California Press, 2001.

Skolnick, Arlene. *Embattled Paradise.* New York: Basic Books, 1991.

Solinger, Rickie. *Pregnancy and Power.* New York: New York University Press, 2005.

Solomon, Barbara Miller. *In the Company of Educated Women.* New Haven, CT: Yale University Press, 1985.

Stearns, Peter N. *Anxious Parents: A History of Modern Childrearing in America*. New York: New York University Press, 2003.

Sugrue, Thomas. *Sweet Land of Liberty: The Forgotten Struggle for Civil Rights in the North*. New York: Random House, 2008.

Taranto, Stacie. *Kitchen Table Politics: Conservative Women and Family Values in New York*. Philadelphia, PA: University of Pennsylvania Press, 2017.

Thompson, Heather Anne. "Why Mass Incarceration Matters: Rethinking Crisis, Decline, and Transformation in Postwar American History." *The Journal of American History* 97, no. 3 (December 2010): 703–734.

Thomson, Irene Taviss. *Culture Wars and Enduring American Dilemmas*. Ann Arbor: University of Michigan Press, 2010.

Vacarro, Peter. "Distant Echoes: The Scopes Trial." Unpublished capstone thesis, Rider University, 2017, in author's possession.

Vandenberg-Daves, Jodi. *Modern Motherhood: An American History*. New Brunswick, NJ: Rutgers University Press, 2014.

Vapnek, Lara. *Elizabeth Gurley Flynn: Modern American Revolutionary*. Philadelphia, PA: Westview Press, 2015.

Watson, Steven. *The Harlem Renaissance: Hub of African-American Culture, 1920–1930*. New York: Pantheon Books, 1995.

Webb, George E. *The Evolution Controversy in America*. Lexington: University Press of Kentucky, 1994.

White, Kevin. *The First Sexual Revolution*. New York: New York University Press, 1993.

Williams, Daniel K. *God's Own Party: The Making of the Christian Right*. Oxford: Oxford University Press, 2010.

Wilkerson, Isabel. *The Warmth of Other Suns: The Epic Story of America's Great Migration*. New York: Vintage Books, 2011.

Woolcott, Victoria W. *Race, Riots, and Roller Coasters: The Struggle over Segregated Recreation in America*. Philadelphia: University of Pennsylvania Press, 2012.

Zimmerman, Jonathan. *Whose America?: Culture Wars in the Public Schools*. Cambridge, MA: Harvard University Press, 2002.

Index

Abortion, 98–99, 150, 160, 175n21
Academic freedom, 144–45
Addams, Jane, 116
Adolescence, 105, 112
Advertising industry, 10
Advice literature, 111
African Americans, xii; artists and intellectuals, 29–32; birth rates, 100; black culture and the "new negro," 28–33; education, 106; employment, 23–24, 49, 113; home ownership, 25–28; as Klan targets, xiii, 56, 61–62, 66; marriage, 109; mass culture and, 12–13; myth of black male rapist, 22, 72–73; political activity, 28–29, 31, 65, 72–73; Prohibition and, 72–73; in rural South, 22–23; sex modernism and, 15; in urban areas, 3–4, 7–8, 20–33, 85, 155–56; women's voting rights, 116; in World War I, 23. *See also* Racial segregation; Racism
Agrarian movement, 5
Agrarian tradition, 2, 4–5. *See also* Rural areas; Sharecropping
Aguinaldo, Emilio, 132
Albuquerque Morning Journal, 51–52
Alcohol, possession of, 78
Alcohol consumption: attitudes toward, xiii–xiv, 70–71, 121; blacks and, 72–73; at nightclubs, 15; during Prohibition, 79–82; rates of, 79, 172n2; in rural areas, 81; in urban areas, 81–82. *See also* Prohibition
Alienation, 58, 126–27
Alimony Payers Protective Association, 118
Allen, Frederick Lewis, 106; *Only Yesterday*, 147
American Birth Control League, 103–4
American Civil Liberties Union (ACLU), 135–37, 145–46
American Defense Society, 46
American exceptionalism, xii
American Federation of Labor (AFL), 49
Americanism, xii–xiii, 38–40, 43, 56, 61, 64, 67. *See also* Patriotism
Americanization, 38–40, 46, 48
American Legion, 43–44
American Medical Association (AMA), 99
American Mercury, 139
American Railway Union, 40
American Unity League, 65
Amusements, public, 1–4, 12–20, 32; racial segregation in, 13, 21, 32. *See also* Dance halls; Jazz music; Leisure activities; Mass culture; Nightlife

Anarchists, 43, 52–53
Anslinger, Harry, 91–92
Anthropology, 126
Anti-Catholicism, xiii, 56, 59–60, 64, 66, 171n58. *See also* Catholics
Anticommunist organizations, 118
Antievolution activism, xiv–xv, 121, 131–35, 145–47, 150–51; town culture and, 5. *See also* Evolution; Scopes Trial
Antifeminism, 102, 118, 162. *See also* Feminism
Anti-immigrant sentiment. *See* Nativism
Antilynching bill, 22
Antimodernism, 58, 133, 162; of the Klan, 62–63, 66; Prohibition and, 69
Antiradicalism, xii–xiii, 42–48, 54, 58, 113, 157, 162; town culture and, 5; urbanization and, 8. *See also* Radicalism
Anti-Saloon League (ASL), 57, 74–77, 79–81, 83, 91
Anti-Semitism, 49, 60
Anxieties, cultural, xv; of fundamentalists, 123; parenting and, 96, 110–12; urbanization and, 6–9
Arch Street Presbyterian Church, 130
Arkansas, 21, 57, 149–50
Armenians, 49
Artists: black, 29–32; Lost Generation, 127; writers, 31, 126–27
Astaire, Fred and Adele, 15
Astor family, 16
Atheism, 136, 144. *See also* Secularism
Atlanta, Georgia, 58, 61
Atlanta Constitution, 16
Atlantic Monthly, 54

Automobiles, 2, 18, 125; crime and, 87, 89; dating and, 20; urban areas and, 8
Ayers, Edward, 73

Backwardness, 139, 146, 150
Baldwin, Roger, 137
Baltimore, 8, 133, 156
Baltimore Evening Sun, 139
Bank robberies, 87, 89
Baptist State Board of Missions, 134
Barney's (nightclub), 15
Barrow, Clyde, 89
Baseball, 128
Bay City, Texas, 62
Beer, 76–78, 85
Bella Donna (1923), 62
Benson, Elizabeth, xv
Berardelli, Alessandro, 52
Better America Federation, 8
Bible: literal interpretations of, 121, 123, 142–43; in public schools, 133. *See also* Creation story (Genesis)
Bimetallism, 145
Birth control, 18, 96–97; fight for, xiv, 97–104, 108, 116; pill, 104; sexual pleasure and, 107
Birth of a Nation (1915), 56
Black Bottom (Detroit), 25
Black intellectuals, 29–32
Black Lives Matter (organization), 156
Black male rapist, myth of, 22, 72–73
Black market, 85
Black newspapers, 20, 65, 123. *See also specific newspapers*
"Blue" states, 14, 32, 155
Bobbed hair, 85, 105, 107
Bob Jones University, 133
Bob-Lo Island (Detroit), 13
Bolshevism, 35, 41, 43, 45–47, 49, 64
Bombings: by gangs, 85; by radicals, 43, 45, 47, 52, 54

Bootleggers, 80, 82, 85–87
Border Patrol, 158
Boston, 38, 44, 84
Braintree, Massachusetts, 52–54
Brewing industry, 76. *See also* Beer
Bribery, 86
British immigrants, 48, 60
Bromley, Dorothy, 95
Brooklyn, New York, 12, 86, 101, 107. *See also* Coney Island
Brooks, Louise, 7
Bryan, William Jennings, xv, 4, 79; antievolutionism, 131–33, 135; "Cross of Gold" speech, 145; fundamentalism, 123–24; Scopes Trial, 136–47, 151; unions and, 138
Bryant, Louise, 42
Buchanan, Pat, 153–54
Buffalo, New York, 38
Bureau of Investigation (later, FBI), 46, 89, 158
Bureau of Prohibition, 82–83
Butler, John, 138
Butler Act (Tennessee), 135–36, 138, 141–42, 144–46, 149
Butte, Montana, 84–85

California, 8, 57, 61
The Call, 101
Calling, social system of, 18–19
Calvary Baptist Church, 17, 121
Capitalism. *See* Industrial capitalism
Capone, Al, 86–87
Caroll v. U.S., 90
Cather, Willa, xi
Catholics, 60, 81, 153, 160; birth control and, 102; immigrants, 3, 37–38, 122, 148; opposition to the Klan, 64. *See also* Anti-Catholicism
Censorship, 147
Census data (1890), 50–51
Century, 128
Charlottesville, Virginia, 156–57

Chicago: drug use, 85; gangsters, 79, 85–87; industry, 7; Klan in, 58, 65; population, 6, 169n104; race riots, 21, 28; racial violence, 26, 156; radio stations, 13; as vice-filled, 122
Chicago Daily Tribune, 44
Chicago Defender, 20, 24, 123
Chicago Gospel Tabernacle, 123
Chicago Tribune, 138–39
Chicago Whip, 20
Children, ideas on, 111. *See also* Parenting
Children's Bureau, 110, 117
Chinese Exclusion Act, 37
Chinese immigrants, 37
Chivalry, 122
Christian Advocate, 78
Christian denominations, 122–23
Christian Right, 149. *See also* New Right; Religious right
Chrysler Building, 7
Cincinnati, 13
Citizenship, 50, 60, 162
City *versus* town narrative, xi–xv, 1–33; alienation and, 126–27; antievolutionism and fundamentalism, 122; culture and values, xi–xv, 1–6, 32–33, 155; dating, 17–20; Klan and, 58–59; mass culture and, 9–13; Prohibition and, 69, 72, 81, 92–93; sex and, 13–17; urbanization and, 6–9. *See also* Culture wars; Rural areas; Towns; Urban areas; Urbanization
Civil liberties, 46
Civil rights, 31
Civil War, 2
Clam House (nightclub), 31
The Clansmen (Dixon), 56
Class bias, 82
Class segregation, 24. *See also* Racial segregation

Cleanliness, 112
Cleveland, 44
Club Abbey, 15
Club Pansy, 15
Coast Guard, 83
Cocaine, 85, 91
Cold War, 149, 153, 157
Collective housing, 113
College campuses, 20, 104–6, 109; women at, 176n47, 176n58
Colonies, U.S., 132
Colorado, 57, 59
Columbia Broadcasting System, 83
"Come Out of the South," 24
Communism, 6, 40–47, 113
Communist International, 41
Communist Labor Party (America), 45
Communist Party (America), 45
Communist Party (Russia), 41
Community life, 2–3, 122. *See also* City *versus* town narrative
Companionate marriage, 108–10, 114
Comstock, Anthony, 99–100
Comstock Law, 100–101, 103
Condoms, 99
Coney Island, 12–13, 15
Confederate statutes, 157, 161
Conformity, 39, 127, 147
Congress: drug laws, 91; Equal Rights Amendment, 118–19; House Un-American Activities Committee, 157; immigration restriction, 48–51; Klan investigations, 57; laws on access to birth control, 99–100; Prohibition and, 75–78; protective labor legislation, 117; Senate Committee on Bolshevism, 45–46; Senate Judiciary Committee, 118
Connecticut, 21, 77
Conservatism, 8–9, 43–44, 134, 154–55, 160. *See also* New Right
Conservatives, religious, 160–61; contraception and, 102

Constitution, 141; Eighteenth Amendment, 70, 76–77, 91; Fifteenth Amendment, 56; Nineteenth Amendment, xiv, 95, 114; proposed Twentieth Amendment, 92; Sixteenth Amendment, 76
Consumer culture, xi, xiv, 67, 155, 162; Klan and, 62; Prohibition and, 92; sex and, 14, 102; urbanization and, 2–3. *See also* Mass culture
Coolidge, Calvin, 44, 51, 118, 137
Corporatization, 8, 66
Corruption, 60–61, 66, 69, 74–75, 83, 86
Cott, Nancy, 112
Cotton Club, 30
Courtship, traditional, 18–19. *See also* Dating
Cox, Ida, 13
Cox, James M., 10
Creationism, 150. *See also* Antievolution activism
Creation story (Genesis), 123, 126, 131, 135, 141, 150
Crime: data collection, 89; immigration and, 51–55, 169n1; Klan opposition to, 66; obscenity as, 100; during Prohibition era, 60, 74, 79, 83–88; in urban neighborhoods, 85
Criminal justice system, xiv, 70, 88–93, 158
The Crisis, 30–31
Cruz, Ted, 155
Cultural diversity, 39
Cultural pluralism, xi, 32, 134
Cultural relativism, 126
Culture wars: 1800s, 153; 1920s, xi–xv; 1960s, 153–54; late 20th and early 21st centuries, xv, 150–51, 153–63. *See also* City *versus* town narrative

Index

Cummings, E. E., 127
Customs, U.S., 83

Dallas, Texas, 62
Dance halls, 2, 14–17, 106
Dancing: dangers of, 16–17, 121; sex and, 107. *See also* Jazz music
Danger, urban, xii
Dangers of the Dance, 17
Darrow, Clarence: Scopes Trial, xv, 122, 134, 136–44, 146–47, 151; Sweets case on racial discrimination, 27
Darwin, Charles, xiv, 121, 124, 126, 132, 141; *Origin of Species*, 131
Dating, 17–20, 106; birth control and, 102
Daughters of the American Revolution, 39, 46
Daycare, universal, 113
Dayton, Ohio, 122, 135–36, 138–39
Debs, Eugene V., 40–41, 45
Democratic Party, 32, 56, 132, 154
Dempsey, Jack, 128
Dennett, Mary Ware, 101, 103
Denton, Nancy A., 168n80
Deportation, 43, 46
Depression. *See* Great Depression
Detroit, Michigan, 6–7, 26–27, 38, 79, 156
The Devil's Ball, 17
Dewey, John, 4–5
Dillinger, John, 89
Discrimination: against immigrants, 37–38; Prohibition and, 82; racial, 4, 23, 25–27, 32
Disease, 112
Divorce, 17–18, 109, 159
Dixon, Thomas, *The Clansmen*, 56
Domestic service, 23–24
Domestic violence, 73–74
Donahey, A. V., 133
Dos Passos, John, 127
Douches (birth control), 99

Drag balls, 16
Drugs: attitudes toward, 70, 75, 91–92, 158; black market, 85; war on, 90–92, 158
Drunkenness, 73–74, 82, 124. *See also* Alcohol consumption
"Drys," 77, 80
Du Bois, W.E.B., 29, 31, 61
Dumenil, Lynn, 74

Eagle Forum, 159
Eastern European immigrants, 38, 71–72
Eastern Orthodox communities, 122
Eastman, Crystal, 95–96, 116, 118
Eddy, Sherwood, 97
Educational policy, xv, 131–34, 145–50
Eighteenth Amendment, 70, 76–77, 91
Einstein, Albert, 126
Electrification, 9, 12
Eliot, Charles, 96
Eliot, T. S., 127
Elites, 80, 116
Ellington, Duke, 7, 30
Ellis, Havelock, 108
Emergency Immigration Act, 48–50
Employment, 23–24; African Americans, 23–24, 49, 113; competition with immigrants, 49; women, 23, 95, 113
Engels, Friedrich, 40
Enid, Oklahoma, 62
Epperson, Susan, 149
Equal Rights Amendment (ERA), 114–19, 159–60, 178n105
Ethnic identities, 11–13, 38. *See also* Immigration/immigrants
Eugenics, 49, 103
Evans, Hiram Wesley, 58, 60–61, 67
Everest, Wesley, 44

Evolution: faith and, 132, 137; "missing link," 126; teaching of, xv, 131–36, 150–51. *See also* Antievolution activism; Scopes Trial
Extortion, 87

Falwell, Jerry, 161
Family, xiv, 159–60; antievolutionism and, 122; modern, 18; women's work and, 95–97, 110–14. *See also* Marriage
FBI. *See* Bureau of Investigation (later, FBI)
Federal government, power of, xiii, 70–71, 75, 88–93, 158
Federal Housing Administration, 155
Federal Narcotics Bureau, 91–92
Feminism, xiv, xv, 64, 95, 102, 107–8, 113, 154; "ideology-based" (equality), 115–19; second wave, 96, 99, 119, 159–60; social (difference), 115–19. *See also* Antifeminism
Ferguson, Missouri, 156
Fiery Cross (Klan paper), 62
Fifteenth Amendment, 56
First Congregational Church, 79
First Presbyterian Church (New York), 130
Fitzgerald, F. Scott, 7, 31, 111; *This Side of Paradise*, 106
Flaming Youth (1923), 105
Flappers, xii, 14, 63, 83, 105–9, 113; as Klan targets, xiii
Florida, 133
Flynn, Elizabeth Gurley, 45, 101
Football, 128
Forum, 64
Fosdick, Harry Emerson, 98, 130
Frankfurter, Felix, 54
Fraternal orders, 13, 57
Freedom of expression, 154
Freedom of speech, 141

Free enterprise, xii, 124. *See also* Industrial capitalism
Freud, Sigmund, 102, 125
From the Ball Room to Hell, 17
Fundamentalism, Protestant, xiv–xv, 121–25, 129–31, 134, 160, 162; antievolutionism, 131–51; biblical literalism and, 121, 123; protests against urban nightlife, 17; town culture and, 5

Galleani, Luigi, 52
Gambling, 86–87
Gangsters, 79, 82, 85–90
Garden of Joy (nightclub), 31
Garry, Elbert, 49
Garvey, Marcus, 31
Gay and lesbian communities: liberation movement, 154, 160; nightlife, 15–16, 31
Gender norms, xi–xv, 15; cities and, 4; colleges and, 104; modern, 17–20; "pure womanhood," 63–64; secularism and, 125; traditional, 102, 159; Victorian, xiv, 108; women and, 96. *See also* Sex norms
Genesis. *See* Creation story (Genesis)
German immigrants, 37–38, 40, 48, 50, 60
German propaganda, 45
Germ theory, 112
Ghettos, 25–26, 33, 168n80, 168n83
Gibbs, Mrs. Rufus, 118
Gilded Age, 40
Gilman, Charlotte Perkins, 108, 113
"G-men," 89
Goldman, Emma, 14, 46, 100–101, 103
Goodyear Tire, 8
Gordon, Anna A., 79
Gordon, Linda, 101–3
Grange, "Red," 128
Grant, Madison, 50; *The Passing of the Great Race*, 49

Index

Great Depression, 96, 147, 149, 155, 158
Great Migration, xii, 4, 6–7, 20–22, 24–33, 62, 156
Greek immigrants, xii, 38
Greenwich Village radicals, 84, 125
Griffith, D. W., *Birth of a Nation*, 56
Griswold v. Connecticut, 104
Groves, Ernest, 113

Hale, Elizabeth Grace, 21
Hall, G. Stanley, 105
Hanson, Ole, 42–44
Harding, Warren G., 10, 48, 79
Harlem, New York, 7, 25, 27–32, 85
Harlem Renaissance, 29–32
Harms, T. B., 7
Harper's Bazaar, 19
Harrington, Helen, 85
Harrington, John Walker, 118
Harrison Narcotics Act (1914), 91
Hartman, Andrew, 153–54
Harvard University, 96, 121
Hayes, Patrick, 97
Health insurance, 158
Hemingway, Ernest, 127–28
Heroin, 91
Hierarchies, social, 57, 163
High schools, 105
Hillbillies, 13, 146
Hobson, Richmond, 91
Hoover, Herbert, 3, 88–91
Hoover, J. Edgar, 45–46, 89
House Un-American Activities Committee, 157
Houston, Texas, 169n104
Hughes, Langston, 31
Hungarian immigrants, 38
Hunter, James Davison, 154
Hurston, Zora Neale, 7

Identity politics, 154, 161
Illinois, 21. *See also* Chicago
Immigration Act (1918), 43

Immigration/immigrants, xi–xv; alcohol and Prohibition, 69, 71–74, 92; assimilation and, 12, 38, 47, 74; citizenship and, 50; college education and, 176n47; crime and, 51–55; deportation, 43, 46; employment competition and, 49; Klan and, xiii, 64; mass culture and, 11–12; "new" immigrants, 36–40; parenting classes, 111; poverty and, 38; radicalism and, 35–36; rural communities and, 2; undocumented immigrants, 157; urbanization and, 3, 6, 8; whiteness and, 25, 38. *See also* Nativism
Immigration restriction, 23, 42, 47–51
Immorality, xii, 57, 74, 81, 100, 135
Income tax, 76
Indiana, Klan activity in, xiii, 57–59, 65–66
Individuality, 127
Individual liberty, xi, 158
Industrial capitalism, 42, 66, 71, 124
Industrialization, 2, 5, 24, 66; alcohol consumption and, 72; nativism and, 36; temperance movement and, 70; urbanization and, 8
Industrial Revolution, 40
Industrial Workers of the World (IWW), 42, 44
Inherit the Wind (1955), 147
Inherit the Wind (1960), 149
Internal Revenue Service, 82
Internationalism, xi–xii, 64
International Narcotics Education Association, 91
Intimidation, 62. *See also* Violence
Intoxicating liquors, definition of, 77–78
Irish immigrants, 37–38, 48–49, 60, 81, 157
Isolationism, 58

It (1927), 107
Italian immigrants, xii, 38, 51–54, 60

Japanese immigrants, 50
Jazz music, xii, 7, 16–17, 30, 83, 85, 107, 127
Jefferson, Thomas, 2
Jefferson State Bank (Illinois), 87
Jellies (birth control), 99
Jews, 46, 122; anti-Semitism and, 49, 60; immigrants, 38, 49; as Klan targets, xiii, 66; Orthodox, 160; urbanization and, 3
Jim Crow laws, 4, 22, 25, 62. *See also* Racial segregation
Johnson, Albert, 50–51
Johnson, James Weldon, 20, 27; "To America," 29
Johnson, Lyndon, 156–57
Johnson Reed Act, 51, 67
Jones Act (1929), 90

Kallen, Horace, 126
Kansas, 57
KDKA (radio station), 10
Kelley, Florence, 117–18
Kentucky, 134–35
Kerensky, Alexander, 41
Kerner Commission, 156
Key, Ellen, 108
Knights of Columbus, 60
Know-Nothing movement, 37
Koreans, 50
Krutch, Joseph Wood, *The Modern Temper*, 125
Ku Klux Klan (KKK), xiii, 55–67, 134, 162; decline of, 65–67; nativism, 55, 58, 60–63, 66–67; opposition to, 64–65, 67; post–Civil War origins, 56; racial violence, 26, 58, 61–62; resurgence of, 36, 57–64; in rural areas, 57–58, 65–66; in urban areas, 8, 58; women in (WKKK), 63–64

Laats, Adam, 148
Labor legislation, protective, 115–18, 178n105
Labor organizing. *See* Unions
Labor unrest, 71, 74, 87; strikes, 24, 40–44
Ladies Home Journal, 19, 104, 111
La Guardia, Fiorello, 50
Lakewood Park (Atlanta), 13
Larson, Edward, 122, 147
Law and order, 56–57
Law enforcement, 82–83; expansion of, 88–93, 158. *See also* Criminal justice system
League of Nations, 41–42
League of Women Voters, 101–2, 117
Lear, Norman, 154
Le Corbusier, 7
Lee, Martha, 16
Lee, Robert E., 157
Leisure activities: alcohol and, 84, 92; commercialization of, 10, 19; secularism and, 125; sports, 128. *See also* Amusements, public; Dance halls; Jazz music; Mass culture; Nightlife
Lenin, Vladimir, 41
Lewis, Sinclair, *Babbit*, 31
Liberal religious theologians, 124, 130
Liberals, 154–55
Lindbergh, Charles, 11, 128
Lindsey, Ben, 64, 103; *Companionate Marriage*, 108–9
Lippmann, Walter, 5–6
Lithuanian immigrants, 38
Locke, Alain, 28–30
Los Angeles, 5, 7–9, 58, 169n104
Lost Generation writers, 127
Louisiana, 150
Loyalty, 39–40. *See also* Americanism; Patriotism
Luker, Kristin, 175n21
Luna Park, 12
Lutherans, 122

Lynching, 22. *See also* Violence
Lynd, Robert and Helen, *Middletown*, xi, xv, 2–3, 17–18, 58, 81, 109, 112, 122, 129

Macartney, Clarence, 130
Machen, J. Gresham, 130
Macy, John, 96
Madison Square Garden, 16
Magazines, mass-market, 10, 100, 107, 112
Malone, Dudley Field, 122, 136, 140–41, 149–50
Marchand, Roland, 10
Marijuana, 85, 91
Marriage, 15, 18, 102, 105–10, 119; companionate, 108–10, 114; equality in, 114. *See also* Family
Martin, Trayvon, 156
Marx, Karl, 40
Massachusetts Public Interest League, 118
Mass consumer culture, 32–33, 153; dating and, 20; sex and, 100
Mass culture, 3, 5, 9–13, 62; Prohibition and, 92; racial and ethnic identities and, 11–13; sex and, 14, 106–7. *See also* Consumer culture
Massey, Douglas S., 168n80
Materialism, 127. *See also* Consumer culture
May Day parades, 43–44
McCarthy era, 147, 157
McGirr, Lisa, 83
McKinley, William, 132
McVey, Frank L., 135
Men: as breadwinners, 113; courtship etiquette, 18–19; working-class, alcohol and, 73–74. *See also* Gender norms; Sex norms
Mencken, H. L., 139, 148, 150–51
Messenger, 31
Methodists, 122

Mexican immigrants, 8, 91
Middle-class women, birth control and, 102
Middle-class youth: alcohol and, 74, 80–82, 92; dating and, 106; nightlife and, 84–85
Middletown (Lynd and Lynd), xi, xv, 2–3, 17–18, 58, 81, 109, 112, 122, 129
Militancy, 31
Millay, Edna St. Vincent, 54
Miracles, 143
"Missing link" (in evolution), 126
Mitchell, Langdon, 36–37, 46
Modernity, xi–xv, 64, 126–28; city life and, 5; mass culture and, 9–13; Scopes Trial and, 141, 145–47, 151
"Mongrelization," 50, 60
Monogamy, 102, 109, 122
Montana, 57
Moonshine, 79–80
Moore, Colleen, 105
Moral ambiguity, 32
Moral ambivalence, 98
Moral authority, female, 102
Moral depravity, 74
Morality: antievolutionism and, 121–22; fundamentalist, 124; public schools and, 148
Moral Majority, 134, 154, 161
Moral policing, alcohol and, xiii, 71, 93
Moral purity, xii–xiii, 56, 63–64
Moral superiority, 57, 72
Moran, Bugs, 87
Morgan, J. P., 43, 46
Mormons, 123, 153
Morone, James, 97–98
Mortgage loans, 155
Mothering, 110–12, 117
Movie industry, 7–9, 83; Klan opposition to, 62; portrayal of "G-men," 89; secularism and, 125; sex and, 100

Movie theaters, 2, 11–12, 18
Multiculturalism, 154, 157
Mumford, Kevin, 14
Mumford, Lewis, 5
Muncie, Indiana, 2–3, 17–18, 58. See also *Middletown* (Lynd and Lynd)
Murder. *See* Violence
Murnau, F. W., *Sunrise*, 1–4

NAACP, 8, 22, 27, 61
Narcotics, 91, 158
Nash, Roderick, 128
Nashville Tennessean, 121
The Nation, 118
National American Woman Suffrage Association (NAWSA), 115; Congressional Union, 116
National Birth Control League, 101
National Broadcasting Company (NBC), 11
National Commission on Law Observance and Enforcement, 88–89
National Consumer's League, 117
National Federation of Business and Professional Women, 112
National Guard, 44
National Security League, 46
National Women's Party (NWP), 102, 114–16, 118, 178n105
Nativism, xii–xiii, 35–67, 134, 156–57, 162; birth control and, 102; immigration restriction and, 42, 47–51; Klan and, 55, 58, 60–63, 66–67; Prohibition and, 69, 71–72, 81–82, 92; Sacco and Vanzetti trial and, 51–55; urbanization and, 8
Neal, John, 137
Negri, Pola, 62
Neighborhood associations, 25–26
Neoconservatism, 154
Newark, New Jersey, 156
New Deal, 88, 158

"New negro," 28–33, 64
New Republic, 5
New Right, 134, 150, 159–60
"New woman," 107. *See also* Women
New York, 5; birth control agitation, 97–98, 100–101; educational policy, 133; flapper style, 107; immigrants in, 38, 81; immorality and, 17; mass culture and, 9; nightlife, 15, 83–84; population, 6, 169n104; Prohibition and, 79, 83–84; race riots, 21; as vice-filled, 122. *See also* Brooklyn, New York; Coney Island; Harlem, New York
New York Society for the Suppression of Vice, 100
New York State, mandatory sentencing, 90
New York State Federation of Labor, 80
New York Times, 78, 87, 118, 126, 138
New York Tribune (newspaper), 35
New York World, 58, 137
Nightlife, xii, 15–16; blacks and, 30–31; perils of, 16–17; Prohibition and, 83–84; white tourists in Harlem, 30
Nineteenth Amendment, xiv, 95, 114
Nixon, Richard, 36, 113
Norris, Frank, 124
Norvell, Stanley, 28
Nostalgia, 2, 36, 128, 141, 145, 147

Oakland, California, 61
Obama, Barack, 155
Obamacare, 158
Obscenity, 100
O'Hare, Kate Richards, 45
Oklahoma, 57, 135
Olmstead v. U.S., 90
Opium, 85, 91
Oregon, 57
Organized crime, 16, 86. *See also* Gangsters

Organized labor. *See* Strikes; Unions
Osborn, Henry Fairfield, 137, 142
Our Dancing Daughters (1928), 107
Outfit (crime syndicate), 86
Outlook, 50

Palmer, A. Mitchell, 43, 45–47, 52
Parenting, 96, 110–12
Parents League (Brooklyn), 107
Park, Maude Wood, 117
Park Avenue Baptist Church, 130
Parker, Bonnie, 89
Parmenter, Frederick, 52
Parsons, Alice Beale, 113
Partisan politics, 32, 154
Patriarchy, xii, xiv
Patriotic societies, 39, 46–48
Patriotism, xii, 39–40, 157; Klan and, 55, 58, 60; Prohibition and, 76
Paul, Alice, 115–19, 178n105
Paul VI (pope), 104
Pennsylvania, 21; Eastern Penitentiary, 90
People for the American Way, 154
People's Party, 132
Pessaries, 99
Pessimism, 127
Petting, 18, 63, 163
Philadelphia, 6, 38, 79, 169n104
Philippines, 132
Physical Culture, 103
Piltdown, England, 126
Pittsburgh, 7, 10
Police: technology and, 89–90. *See also* Law enforcement
Police brutality: against blacks, 27; against immigrants and radicals, 44, 46
Polish immigrants, xii, 38, 48
Population data: 1890 census, 50–51; urban, 6. *See also* Racial demographics
Portuguese immigrants, 38
Pound, Ezra, 127

Poverty, 23; birth control and, 102; fundamentalism and, 124; immigrants and, 38; rates, 74; urban, 70, 85, 102, 130, 156; women and, 115
Powerlessness, 58, 65. *See also* Status anxiety
Premarital sex, 107
Presbyterians, 122, 130
Presidential elections: in 1928, 3, 80–81; radio coverage of, 10
Prison system, growth of, 90, 92, 158
Producer-oriented culture, 14
Products, 9. *See also* Consumer culture
Progress, 2, 141
Progressive Era, 2, 88, 117, 158
Progressive movement, 70–71
Progressives, 41–42, 45
Progressivism, 69, 115, 131, 154
Prohibition, xi–xv, 69–93, 134, 162; city vs. town and, 69, 72, 81, 92–93; intoxicating liquors, definition of, 77–78; Klan and, 60; legacy of, 158; nightlife and, 16; official beginning of, 78–82; organizations, 73–78; roots of, 70–73; state laws, 75–76; town culture and, 5–6
Prohibition Bureau, 89
Prohibition enforcement, 67, 82–93; arrests, 79, 87; criminal justice system and, 88–93; gangsters and, 85–88
Property values, 27
Prostitution, 69, 74, 86–87
Protestants: African American, 123; evangelical, xii, 150, 154, 161; Klan and, 61; Prohibition and, 71. *See also* Fundamentalism, Protestant
Psychology, xiv, 107, 111, 125
Public education. *See* Educational policy
Public Ledger, 35

Public sphere, 14; women in, 18–20, 64, 96–97
Publishing industry, 7. *See also* Magazines, mass-market
Puerto Rico, 132
Pullman strike, 40

Quickening, 98

"Race" records, 13
Racial conflict, xiii, xv, 87; in 1960s, 156; race riots, "Red Summer" of 1919, 20–21; in the South, 22–23; in urban areas, 20–21, 29, 33
Racial covenants, 25–27, 155
Racial demographics, 155, 157
Racial discrimination, 4, 23, 25–27, 32
Racial equality, 134
"Racial integrity," 61
Racial segregation, 4, 72; in churches, 123; in education, 106; in public amusements, 13, 21, 32; urban, 21–28, 32–33, 62, 155–56, 168n83
Racism, 4, 65, 162; black resistance to, 26–33; evolution and, 123; scientific, 60–61, 71–72, 133; stereotypes, 33; in suffrage movement, 116
Rader, Paul, 123
Radicalism, xv, 35–36, 41–47, 52, 54, 87, 137. *See also* Antiradicalism
Radio, 7, 10–11, 83; crime fighting and, 89; fundamentalism and, 123; local audiences, 13; Scopes Trial broadcast, 138, 144
Radio Corporation of America (RCA), 11
Ralston (judge at Scopes Trial), 140
Randolph, A. Philip, 31
Rappleyea, George, 135–36
Reagan, Ronald, 149, 154, 160–61
Recession (1920–1921), 48
Reconstruction, 56

Redlining, 155
Red scare: in 1919, xii, 36, 40–47, 54, 67, 69, 103, 118, 134; post–World War II, 157
"Red" states, 14, 32, 155, 162, 169n104
Reed, David A., 51
Reed, James, 76
Reedy, William Marion, 13
Reitman, Ben, 101
Relativity, theory of, 125–26
Religion, 13, 153–54; state and, 160–61
Religious freedom, 144
Religious fundamentalism, xi. *See also* Fundamentalism, Protestant
Religious revivals, 129
Religious right, xv, 150, 154, 160
Rent parties, 13, 30–31
Repression, xiii, 6, 28, 46–47, 55, 127
Reproductive rights, 97–104, 108–9, 119, 154, 160, 175n21. *See also* Abortion; Birth control
Republican Party, 32, 56, 153–54, 161
Respectability: blacks and, 73; fundamentalism and, 146; the Klan and, 58–59; Prohibition and, 84; queer nightlife and, 16; upper-class dating and, 19–20
Rhode Island, 77
Right-wing ideology. *See* Christian Right; New Right; Religious right
Riley, William Bell, 123–24
Ritz-Carlton (Boston), 84
Riverside Church, 130
Rockefeller, John D., 43, 46, 129–30
Rodman, Henrietta, 113
Roe v. Wade, 160
Rogers, Will, 69
Roosevelt, Franklin Delano, 155
Roosevelt, Theodore, 39, 71, 132
Ross, Nellie, 110
Rural areas: alcohol and, 81; culture and values, xii, 1–4; Klan and,

Index

57–58. *See also* City *versus* town narrative; Towns
Russell, Howard Hyde, 79
Russian immigrants, xii, 38, 46
Russian Revolution, xii, 41, 45, 113
Ruth, Babe, 128

Sacco, Nicola, 51–55, 171n39
Sacco-Vanzetti Defense Committee, 53
Saloons, 69, 72, 74, 80
Sanger, Margaret, 97–98, 100–104
Sanger, William, 101
Saturday Evening Post, 41
Scapegoating, xiii, 36, 47, 54, 58, 65, 67
Schlafly, Phyllis, 119, 159
Science, xv, 4, 121, 125–26, 146, 149; parenting advice, 110–12; religion and, 125, 131, 133, 135, 137, 141–51; social science, 88. *See also* Evolution; Scientific racism
Science Education Act (Louisiana), 150
Science League of America, 146
Scientific racism, 60–61, 71–72, 133
Scopes, John Thomas, xv, 131, 135–36, 145
"Scopes II," 150
Scopes Trial, xv, 121–22, 126, 128–29, 131, 160; background, 134–40; events of, 140–44; legacy of, 144–51
Search warrants, 90
Sears Roebuck Company, 11
Seattle, Washington, 42–44
Secularism, 125–29, 154, 162
Segregation, class-based, 24. *See also* Racial segregation
Senate Committee on Bolshevism, 45–46
Senate Judiciary Committee, 118
Seneca Falls convention, 114

Sensationalism, 2, 83; crime reporting, 87; evolution and, 144, 146
Sentencing, mandatory, 90
Sentinels of the Republic, 118
Settlement houses, 39, 107, 111
Sex education, 13
Sex norms, xi–xv, 160; in 1970s, 119; cities and, 4, 13–14; colleges and, 104; Klan and, 63; modern, xv, 17–18, 67, 102, 105–10, 155, 162; premarital, 107; Prohibition era nightlife and, 84–85; secularism and, 125; Victorian, xiv, 14, 63, 107–8; women and, 96–110. *See also* Gender norms
Sexologists, 107
Sex radicals, 14
Sexual freedom, 134
Sexuality, 1, 63; consumer culture and, 4; laws restricting information on; 99–100; petting, 18, 63, 163
Sexual liberalism, 108
Sexual pleasure, 103, 107
Sexual revolution, 14–17, 32
Sharecropping, 23
Shields, Art, 53
Shipley, Maynard, 146
Showalter, Elaine, 96, 112
"Silent Majority," 36
Simmons, Christina, 113
Simmons, William, 57
Sinclair, Upton, 54
Sixteenth Amendment, 76
Skyscrapers, 6–7
Slater and Merrill Shoe Company, 52
Slavs, 38, 46
Slee, James Noah H., 103
Smith, Al, 3, 64, 80–81
Smith, Bessie, 13
Smith, Charles J., 106
Smith College Weekly, 95
smoking, 16, 83
Social Darwinism, 132

Social gospel, 124
Social hierarchy, 57, 163
Social hygiene, 13, 100
Socialism, 40–47
Socialist Party of America, 41, 45
Socialized housework, 113
Social reformers, 117
Social welfare agencies, 111
Sociology, 125–26
South Carolina, 21
Southern culture, 5; racism in, 72; towns, 139; urban, 23
Southern European immigrants, 38, 71–72
Southern whites, 13, 22–23; antievolutionism, 123
Soviet Union, 113; divorce rates, 109
Spanish-American War, 132
Speakeasies, 30, 82, 84
Sports heroes, 128
Stanton, Elizabeth Cady, 114
Status anxiety, 36, 56–57, 65–67, 161–62
Status quo, 42, 64, 66, 106, 151; challenges to, 36; town culture and, 5–6
Steffens, Lincoln, 45
Stein, Gertrude, 127–28
Stereotypes, 33, 148, 150
St. Louis, Missouri, 156
Stoddard, Lothrop, 60; *The Rising Tide of Color against White World-Supremacy*, 49
STOP-ERA, 159
Storer, Horatio, 99
St. Paul Pioneer Press, 3
Straton, John Roach, 107, 121–22, 135; *The Dance of Death*, 17
Stratton-Porter, Gene, 128
Strikes, 24, 40–44. *See also* Labor unrest
Strong, Anna Louise, 42
Suffragists, 101–2, 107, 114–15

Sunday, Billy, 17, 69, 78–79, 107, 123–24, 129–30, 134–35
Sunrise (Murnau, 1927), 1–4, 32
Supreme Court, U.S., 90, 145, 149; on privacy, 104; on racial covenants, 25–27
Survey, 113
Survey Graphic, 28
Sweet, Ossian, 26–27

Taft, William Howard, 75, 132
Taxes, 76, 83
Technological developments, 89
Temperance movement, 70–74, 83. *See also* Prohibition
"Ten Most Wanted" list, 89
Tennessee, 21, 135, 138, 140–41, 145
Tennessee Supreme Court, 145
Terrorism, 43, 157. *See also* Bombings
Texas, 21, 57
Thayer, Webster, 53
Tolerance, 32, 147
Torrance, Mary Fisher, xi
Towns, xi–xv, 1–6. *See also* City *versus* town narrative; Rural areas
Traditional values, 128, 141, 145; agrarian, 2, 4–5 (*see also* Rural areas); community life, 2–3; courtship, 18–19; gender norms, 102, 159; Scopes Trial and, 151. *See also* Culture wars; Victorian era
Trocadero (nightclub), 15
Trump, Donald, 155, 161–62

Union of Russian Workers, 46
Union Record, 42
Unions, 13, 40–45; immigration restriction and, 49; race relations, 24; Scopes Trial and, 138
Union Theological Seminary, 130
United Mine Workers, 44
Universal Negro Improvement Association, 31
University of Georgia, 63

Index

University of Kentucky, 134–35
Upper-class youth: dating, 18–20; nightlife and drinking, 84–85, 92
Urban areas: alcohol and, 81–82; black migrants in, 3–4, 7–8, 20–33; ethnic neighborhoods, 38; northern, 24–25, 27; northern cities, 27; poverty, 70, 85, 102, 130, 156; southern, 23. *See also* City *versus* town narrative
Urbanization, xi–xii, xv, 4–9, 155, 162; Klan protests against, 58; nativism and, 36; Prohibition and, 92
Urban planning, 156
Utopianism, 69

Valentine's Day massacre, 87
Values. *See* City *versus* town narrative
Vanderbilt family, 16
Vanity Fair, xv
Vanzetti, Bartolomeo, 51–55, 171n39
Venereal disease, 14, 74
Versailles Treaty, 42
Vice, 74, 82, 85, 122, 124
Victorian era, 127; gender and sex norms, xiv, 14, 63, 107–8; sex and gender norms, xiv
Violence: anti-Klan, 65; bombings by radicals, 43, 45, 47, 52; domestic, 73–74; by gangsters, 85–88; lynching, 22; police brutality, 27; race riots, "Red Summer" of 1919, 20–21; racial, 26–27, 32, 56, 58, 61–62, 72, 156; against striking workers, 40–44. *See also* Crime
Volstead, Andrew J., 77, 79
Volstead Act, 77–78, 81–82, 87, 90, 92
Voluntary Parenthood League, 104

Walcott, Victoria, 13
Walker, Stanley, 84–85
War Information Board, 40

War on drugs, 90–92, 158
War Prohibition Act (1918), 76
Washington, D.C., 21; educational policy, 133; race riots, 26
Washington Post, 107
Watts riot, 156
Wealth, 125, 127, 132
Webb-Kenyon bill, 75
Webster Hall, 16
Wells, H. G., 136
Wells, Ida B., 72
"Wets," 75–76, 78, 80
WGN radio, 138, 144
Wheeler, Wayne B., 77, 79
White, middle-class, native-born, Anglo-Saxon, Protestant Americans, 8, 42, 70; Prohibition and, 72; status anxiety, 36, 56–57, 65–67, 161–62
White flight, 27–28, 155–56
White jurors, 140–41
White middle-class women, 158–59; "having it all," 95, 110, 112, 114, 119; in the Klan, 63–64; work and family roles, 104–14
White slavery, 17
White supremacy, xii–xiii, 21–22, 56, 61–62, 64, 66–67, 72, 157, 162
White tourists in Harlem, 30
White women, birth rates of, 100
Wickersham, George, 88
Wickersham Commission, 88–89
Wiebe, Robert, 2
Willard, Frances, 73–74
Williams, Eugene, 21
Wilson, Woodrow, 22, 41, 44, 48, 77, 129, 132
Wine, 77–78
Wiretapping, 90
Wolcott, Victoria, 21
Women, xii, 95–119; bobbed hair, 85, 105, 107; calling system and, 18–19; as different from men, 115–19, 159; equality for, 115–19,

Women (*cont.*)
158–60; nightlife and, 84–85; political rights, 95–97, 119, 162; reproductive rights, 97–104; sex and marriage, 95–97, 104–10; smoking and drinking, 16, 84–85, 106; voting rights, xiv, 67, 95, 101–2, 114–16; work and family, 104–5, 110–14. *See also* Gender norms; Sex norms; White middle-class women

Women of the Ku Klux Klan (WKKK), 63–64

Women's Bureau, 117

Women's Christian Temperance Union (WCTU), 73–75, 79, 81

Women's Trade Union League, 117

Working-class communities, 8, 155

Working-class men, alcohol and, 73–74

Working-class women: birth control and, 102; family and, 114; nightlife and, 16, 19

Working-class youth: nightlife and drinking, 84–85, 92; sex and dating, 13, 15, 19, 109

World's Christian Fundamentals Association, 123, 136

World War I, 41–42, 127, 131–32; black soldiers in, 23, 61; Prohibition and, 76

Wright, Richard, 24

Writers, 31, 126–27

Xenophobia, 36, 65, 157

Yale Club, 79

YMCA, 15, 18

Youth culture, 108

YWCA, 18, 112

About the Author

Erica J. Ryan, PhD, is associate professor of history and director of the Gender and Sexuality Studies program at Rider University in New Jersey, where she teaches courses on modern American history and the history of sexuality and gender. She holds a PhD from Brown University. Ryan published *Red War on the Family: Sex, Gender, and Americanism in the First Red Scare* in 2014, contributed essays to the *Encyclopedia of the Jazz Age* and *Notches: (Re)marks on the History of Sexuality*, and published numerous book reviews. Her research interests include the significance of the family as a social and political construction, the development of modern American conservatism, the cultural history of the 1920s, and masculinity in late 20th-century America. She lives in New Jersey with her partner, daughter, and two cats.